PRAISE FO]

MW01611503

'How to do hypnosis is a big title. Graham Old absolutely nails it and with style.

'This is a book that all hypnotists will find of immense value. It is jam-packed full of how to do hypnosis, but much more importantly, it invites the reader to consider why they might use a particular method, and what their client or Hypnotee might experience as a result.

'To be a really successful hypnosis practitioner, one must know that we create an experience for our clients using their imagination and skills. We do not do hypnosis; we facilitate it and to do that we must be hypnotic.

'As a hypnosis educator, I find the questions students struggle with are "why am I doing, what I am doing?" and "how do I explain that to my subject in a meaningful way to them?" In this book, you are guided through many hypnotic techniques, but with real-life transcripts rather than scripts that breathe life and insight into each technique. You will gain understanding of the how and an essential grounding of the why, and how to do that with confidence, presence and a magical flourish that with resonate with your subjects.

'Are you are a thinking hypnotist who cares deeply about the outcome of your work and places your client at the centre of a hypnotic experience? Do you desire to be not just a great hypnotist but to be hypnotic? If your answer is yes, then this book is essential reading as part of your journey toward achieving hypnotic excellence.'

– Kaz Riley, Award-winning hypnotist, Sex Educator, and author of *Woman*.

'This is a fantastic and long needed book for practitioners of all skill levels. In a truly readable style, Old offers a genuinely comprehensive and practical exploration of hypnosis. While the field of hypnosis is full of strongly held opinions and disagreements, the author goes beyond such limitations and simply shows us what works in an open-minded approach as he shares the broadest range of processes and techniques that I've ever seen under one cover. He does this with a depth of understanding and a breadth of experience that makes this a real contribution. Simply put, you need this book in your library.'

– Michael Watson, Principal Trainer, International Association of Counselors and Therapists

'Packed with common sense and clearly written, this is an ideal book for anyone wishing to start learning how to hypnotise others or prepare for a career in hypnotherapy.'

– Stephen Brooks, Founder of The British Hypnosis Research and Training Institute

How to do Hypnosis

Graham Old

The Practical Introduction to

Therapeutic Hypnosis

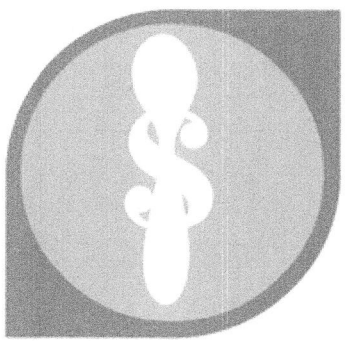

How To Do Hypnosis: The Practical Introduction to Therapeutic Hypnosis

Published 2021 by Plastic Spoon

ISBN 978-1-8384000-1-9

www.plasticspoonbooks.com

Acknowledgements

Hypnotists often know better than most that, whilst words can change lives, in and of themselves they are not enough to truly express what is in our hearts and minds.

So, I will keep this short and sweet. This book is dedicated, with sincere thanks:

To Stephen Brooks, for making me a better hypnotist.

To Jon Old, for making me a better therapist.

To my children, for making me a better person.

Disclaimer

This book is not meant as a replacement for proper training in hypnosis or psychotherapy. Please be aware that any experimentation with the ideas presented in this book is undertaken at your own risk and responsibility.

At all times when practising hypnosis, it is your responsibility to ensure that you comply with the laws, regulations and codes of your home country, region, state or territory.

Also by Graham Old

Fiction

Of Madness and Folly

Non-fiction

Mastering the Leisure Induction

Revisiting Hypnosis

The Elman Induction

The Hypnotic Handshakes

My Friend John

Hypnosis with the Hard to Hypnotise

Therapeutic Inductions

The Anxiety Guide

Use Hypnosis to Stop Smoking

Use Hypnosis to Overcome Blushing

Memory Tools

Let it Be

Contents

INTRODUCTION

One of the underlying currents weaved throughout this book is the idea that a hypnotic encounter is an experiential journey.

In much the same way, my hope for the reader is that this book will itself be experienced as something of a journey. Although I intend to share any and all wisdom I might have on the topic of hypnosis, I do not claim to answer every question the reader - or I myself - might have.

Instead, I sincerely hope that you might finish this book with more questions than you had when you began. Different questions, certainly, but questions nonetheless.

To facilitate this generation of new and unanswered questions, the current book is peppered throughout with invitations to pause and reflect. If your goal is to zip through the book, mining it for data in as short a time as possible, such interruptions may be perceived as a slight annoyance. However, if you aim to learn, think and grow, I would encourage you to embrace these invitations.

Keen readers will note that I may be thought of as an Ericksonian, to some degree or another. I believe my clients are their best resource and I see my role as largely eliciting their inner resources. You can think of this book as similarly Ericksonian, drawing out from you your own wisdom, insights and revelations.

It is my sincere wish that readers will reach the end of this book with more questions than answers. The most disappointing reaction I can envisage is someone reading the whole book and agreeing with everything I have written. I'm not sure that *I* even agree with everything I've written!

Practical Introduction

In the pages to come, I will offer some fairly basic techniques, in my own particular way (always preferring to use transcripts where possible, rather than mere descriptions or 'scripts'). At times, I will provide commentary and/or tips on the transcripts seen. This will vary, however, depending on how much explanation is needed, as well as any future discussion in the book.

I will share some ideas, tools and techniques you will likely already be familiar with. However, I hope that the way I group them, link them, describe them and explain them, may provide a few fresh perspectives. Hopefully, before you reach the end of this book, you will have a strong sense of the direction we are heading in and an appreciation for the foundations we are laying.

Finally, I will ask questions. Lots of questions. (To be honest, you might end up doing more work here than me!) My goal is that as you consider these questions – in light of the various transcripts and perspectives – that you will find yourself discovering a fairly solid yet fresh foundation for moving on to volume 2 in this series and practising hypnosis therapeutically and effectively with a wide variety of clients.

As the subtitle asserts, you can think of this book as a *Practical Introduction to Therapeutic Hypnosis*. This involves a particular way of viewing and doing hypnosis, for particular reasons. This book and the next will unpack this approach, without in any way aiming to suggest that this is the way to proceed.

The notion of this book as an introduction is significant. You will not learn everything you need to learn about hypnosis and therapeutic hypnosis from this book. (Hopefully, any hypnosis trainer worth their weight would say the same about their books!) You can not learn how to be or work effectively with anyone through a book. You have to get out into the real world.

However, the sense in which this book is an 'introduction' perhaps goes further than that. I will reference and recommend a number of ideas, practices, perspectives and techniques that you and your clients may find helpful. Yet, I may not always have the space or opportunity to fully unpack everything I discuss. They are the times when I hope the reader will be intrigued, even excited. Think of them as clues or invitations to begin researching for yourself, exploring and diving into a whole new world.

Experiential Hypnosis

More than anything, this book and its successor aims to unpack a simple statement that I strongly believe and have verified in over two decades of private practice:

> 'Change in therapy is best elicited by the experiences people live, not the information they receive. Hypnosis is fundamentally an experiential method.'
>
> (Jeffrey K. Zeig)

I do not personally believe I have read anything more significant regarding the value of therapeutic hypnosis. I have, however, experienced the truth of this statement time and time again.

It is my hope to share with you what such an approach might look like in practice.

In Rob McNeilly's book, *Learning Solutions in Hypnosis*, the forward by Stephen Gilligan states:

> Simplicity is the highest intellectual achievement. When I was in graduate school in the Stanford Psychology Department, we had a Friday afternoon department-wide

> seminar where some luminary would present recent ground-breaking research. Amidst all the heady talk, it was just a matter of time before Gordon Bower, the department head (and my mentor), would clear his throat, and say kindly but loudly: *I grew up in the (poor) Appalachian mountains, and my grandmother only had a third grade education. I figure that if psychology has anything interesting to say, they should be able to say it in a way that my grandmother understands. So how would you tell my grandmother what you're saying?*
>
> ...When I studied with Dr. Erickson, he was an enfeebled old man, and I was a very young university student, committed to intensive exercise regimes. I would stay in the small bedroom in the office complex adjoining his main house, and one evening around dinner I walked through the backyard and knocked on the screen door of the kitchen, looking to give Mrs. Erickson something. I heard Erickson's voice inviting me in, and I walked into the kitchen to see him in a purple athletic workout suit, completely focused on cutting vegetables for the kitchen dinner. He looked at me with sparkling eyes, saying, *I'm getting my workout!* To a young student committed to martial arts, what he was doing did not fit any definition I had of a "workout"! He smiled and added, *Most people focus on what they can't do. I focus on what I CAN do and take great pleasure from that!*

It is truly my wish that some readers will work through this book and be surprised at its simplicity, perhaps scoffing the lack of novelty or complexity. At the same time, I hope that some will find the seeds of an approach and a journey that will grip them and never let them go.

Terminology Used

As you will soon discover, my work aims to avoid aligning itself with any particular school of hypnosis or hypnotherapy. I prefer to focus on the experience of the client, rather than supporting or promoting any specific theories of the practitioner.

One result of this is the inconsistent terminology you will find in the pages to follow. Throughout this book, you will find me referring to 'trance' and at times using terminology such as 'subconscious,' deepening, somnambulism, being 'under' hypnosis and so on. Please bear in mind that these are phenomenological descriptions, merely meant to convey what the hypnotee (i.e. the person being hypnotised) may be experiencing.

What Do We Mean By Hypnosis?

I may as well start with the big question that almost all books on this subject begin with – what is hypnosis?

I feel like I could answer that question in a number of ways. However, they all essentially mean the same thing – we really do not know!

We simply don't know what hypnosis is. The fact is, one of the few things you can be fairly certain of, when it comes to the nature of hypnosis, is that anyone who suggests they *do* know what hypnosis is (with any degree of certainty) is most likely trying to sell you something!

This is not to say that there has not been decent research on the subject. There has actually been a great deal of research on questions like: what is hypnosis? how does it work? what is happening in the brain of hypnotised subjects? and so on. However, such research is not without its difficultics.

For one thing, despite objections to the contrary, most researchers are setting out to prove a point. It is rare that an Academic has the freedom, time or funding to explore a subject with no agenda whatsoever. Instead, they are more often than not seeking to prove or disprove a hypothesis.

As a result, it sometimes seems as if all of the research on the subject of hypnosis has simply served to continue dividing theorists and practitioners into a number of competing camps. Then, unsurprisingly, the ongoing research produced by such camps ultimately does little more than solidify their own position, fails to take competing positions seriously and confuses the general public.

This should not be taken to mean that all of the research has been in vain. There have, now and again, been some interesting conclusions that most sides can agree upon. To give but one example, using a hypnotic induction increases suggestibility. However, it may only increase suggestibility by approximately 10%. Additionally, other factors – such as motivation, or simply labelling an experiment 'hypnosis' – have also been shown to increase suggestibility.

Similarly, it does appear that some specific brain activity is taking place during hypnosis. However, similar brain activity may also occur during relaxation, meditation, dreaming, or simply being engrossed in an activity or experience. It is then a daunting task for researchers to determine if the brain activity took place because the client was in hypnosis, or because of a number of elements that usually accompany hypnosis (e.g. relaxation, absorption and so on).

Some of us find such research fascinating and I have no desire to dismiss it all out of hand. The issue is that for us practitioners, academics are not particularly close to conclusively demonstrating what their findings set out to prove. Therefore, the research may well be significant in a number of areas. However, interpreting the significance of that research may still be some way off.

Metaphors and Models

This is not to suggest that all of the research that has been carried out on the nature of hypnosis has taught us nothing of any real value. It may be that we can look at the more reliable findings as descriptive, rather than explanatory.

Instead of definitively proving what hypnosis is, perhaps we can think of the various models on offer as descriptions of how hypnosis is commonly experienced. So, for example, I could say with some confidence, that many people do seem to experience something akin to 'dissociation' during hypnosis.[1] Yet, this need not be taken as an absolute statement of brain activity, or cognitive processes. It is simply an acknowledgement that an experience of something like dissociation is, for many people, a regular aspect of hypnosis.

In reality, I would argue that discussions regarding the nature of hypnosis have been metaphorical or figurative, at best, for as long as there has been this phenomenon that is called hypnosis. For example, Elman famously wrote of 'bypassing the critical faculty.' Yet, I do not need to literally believe in something called a 'critical faculty' to appreciate the type of experience Elman is referring to.

I personally think of such descriptions as a simple short–hand way of saying something like, 'if we imagined that there was a critical faculty, we can think of hypnosis as bypassing that barrier.' (Other more colloquial descriptions, speak of sleeping guard-dogs and suchlike.)

Therefore, is it possible that if we consider the various models of hypnosis as metaphorical and descriptive, rather than explanatory or definitive, we may find some real value in a number of contemporary models?

Let's have a look and see for ourselves! Below are two models that might merit further consideration. I do not offer these models as answers to the question, 'what is hypnosis?' Instead, I provide them as interesting ways to frame the discussion around how hypnosis is experienced. That is, I am moving away from debates around the essence of hypnosis, to focus on descriptions of the experience of hypnosis.

Cold Control Theory

The Cold Control theory of hypnosis builds on the Higher Order

1 In this setting, dissociation refers to a perceived distancing between a person's sensory experience, thoughts and sense of self. Some people who experience such dissociation, report a sense of unreality and/or lose their connection to time, place, and even aspects of their identity.

Thought (HOT) theory of Rosenthal (2002). Developed by Dienes and Perner (2007), it is essentially based upon a distinction between a) being in a certain mental state and b) being aware of being in that mental state.

The Cold Control Theory of hypnosis argues for the theoretical possibility of 'unconscious executive control.' Thus, according to this theory, hypnotic responses may involve executive control without conscious awareness. In short, someone intentionally responds to a hypnotic suggestion, whilst being unaware of that intention.

The experience of doing something you do not feel like you chose to do is fairly common-place. In actual fact, this is a frequent reason why some people seek out the services of a hypnotist. People may feel like they smoke, drink or overeat, even though they do not want to. Some people will go so far as to say that they were sat in front of the television, engrossed in a film, when they looked down to find an empty family-sized bag of crisps in their hands. Not only did they not recall consciously eating the crisps, some of them were not even aware of having gone to the cupboard to acquire the crisps in the first place!

An experience commonly referenced by hypnotists is the phenomenon known as 'highway hypnosis.' This involves driving a familiar route and reaching a point in the journey when you suddenly realise you had not been 'consciously' driving. You may have no recollection whatsoever of turning at junctions, going round roundabouts and (hopefully!) stopping at Traffic Lights. Yet, somehow, your brain appears to switch into auto–pilot and safely guides you home.

This well–known experience is often presented as an example of one of the ways that people might slip into 'trance'[2] on a daily basis. However, it equally serves to demonstrate a possible occasion when we have willingly done something, we are simply not conscious of that fact.

2 I will provide a simple working definition of 'trance' later in the book.

When I turn to consider therapeutic approaches later in this series, I will spend some time considering meta–cognition. This refers to 'thinking about thinking,' and we will see that it is a useful skill to be able to step aside from (or above) our thought processes to consider them. It may be that Cold Control Theory offers us an accessible framework to begin exploring meta–cognition and sub-cognition – and the ability to traverse between the two – as a core component of hypnosis.

At the very least, it would seem that Cold Control Theory provides us with an alternative way to speak of 'subconscious behaviour.'

Activation of the REM State

The Human Givens model of hypnosis describes it as 'the artificial activation of the REM state.'

An interesting observation from that theory is the realisation that the REM state can be routinely activated outside of the dream state. The Human Givens camp argue that 'trance' is a focused state of attention. Dreams, they go on to posit, are an example of the deepest trance state that humans enter. And the common denominator between dreaming and hypnotic phenomena would appear to be the REM state.

Some might note that many of the popular methods for inducing hypnosis are paralleled by aspects of how the REM state is normally induced and maintained. Shock inductions, when hypnosis is apparently instantaneously induced through an unexpected occurrence, fire an orientation response into action, just as happens at the start of REM sleep. And inducing deep relaxation creates the same electrical patterns in the brain as occurs in REM sleep. The same might be said of rhythmic behaviour, guided imagery or following a swinging watch as it moves to and fro in front of our eyes.

If there is merit to the REM model, it could mean that hypnosis mirrors – perhaps even utilises – the dreaming brain. This may provide a comprehensive framework for understanding how hypnosis so often leads to creative thinking, psychological flexibility and eureka–type discoveries.

Of course, this may also go some way to legitimise the centuries long connection between hypnosis and sleep. In our enlightened times, we might reasonably argue that it is possible for hypnosis to exist in a 'waking' state. Thus, it is often argued these days, that the eyes–closed, head–dropped–forward experience of hypnosis is a culturally determined phenomenon. Yet, if we consider the entirety of human experience and history, is it really that easy to dismiss at least some kind of relationship between hypnosis, trance–states and sleep?

Interestingly, Griffin and Tyrell write that the 'REM state is like a theatre where the dream takes place.' When a hypnotist leads someone into that theatre, we might see them as scripting their client's dreams. This has delightful echoes of Dave Elman, who described hypnotists as 'Dream pilots,' directing their client's thinking.

The Experiential Model

The usual responses to the question "What is hypnosis?" span the gamut from a special altered state of consciousness all the way through to social role–playing. Rather than rehearsing all of the arguments for each position, I have argued that there is currently no conclusive way to answer the question in this manner.

Instead, with the Experiential Model I attempt to change the question completely. It is simply a matter of perspective and intention. Do I aim to demonstrate conclusively what is happening in the brain of a hypnotised person? Or – and I would suggest this is a far more relevant line of enquiry – do I seek to describe the experience of hypnosis?

As a practitioner, ask yourself which angle is likely to be more important to your clients: a possible neurobiological or socio–cognitive explanation as to the nature of hypnosis, or a practical description of how hypnosis is commonly experienced?

After all, what is it that our clients are actually asking when they ask us, "What is hypnosis?" I argue in *Therapeutic Inductions*, that when it is clients – rather than academics – asking such a question, they are seeking clarity as to what they are about to go through. They are not, as a rule, enquiring which portion of their brain will be most active, or which cognitive processes will be employed. The question then becomes, "What is hypnosis like?"

So, my understanding of hypnosis unashamedly speaks about what it is that will be experienced by the hypnotee. As I present it, hypnosis is not something you do to another person, or even a thing that they go into. Hypnosis is an experience you share with someone.

To use my full definition, hypnosis is:

> An imagination–fuelled, creatively engaged, shift in a person's perception of themselves, the world & their relationship to it.

In other words, it is helping someone imagine (and engage with) a new reality. Essentially, what we are dealing with is a 'reframe.' However, it is reframing things so effectively that the client engages with it thoroughly and creates an altered perception and experience of reality.

Mesmerising Movies

When clients ask me what hypnosis is, I usually begin talking about films and speak about watching a Thriller or Horror movie. Most of us have had the experience of watching a film and – before you've even noticed the creepy music in the background – the hairs on the back of your neck have started to stand up. Your heart has begun to beat more quickly and your breathing pattern has changed.

And even though you know that this is a just a film, your body begins to prepare its 'fight or flight' response. Even though you know all about CGI and make–up and Camera trickery, you still manage to respond to events in these films as if they are really happening there and then – and as if you are somehow caught up in it! I often say to clients that it's a bit like part of our brain is trying to comfort us by saying, "It's not real. It's not real..." whilst another part is saying, "But what if it is?!"

In fact, as I am explaining this to people, I am on the look–out for the exact same physiological responses. If I talk about the first time they ever felt scared whilst watching a film, it is not uncommon to see them shiver slightly, or for the hairs on the back of their arm to stand up. And that is merely through speaking about being afraid!

I then say, "Actually, it's a bit like this..." and go on to demonstrate *Magnetic Hands.* If you don't know or use Magnetic Hands, I would strongly encourage that you become acquainted with it. I have found it to be a powerful and simple tool to practically demonstrate the point of the horror movie explanation above. You can find a description of magnetic hands, both as a response routine and a full induction later in this book.

Once the client has experienced the routine, I say to them, "That is what hypnosis is like. It is as if you imagine something so effectively – and engage with that so thoroughly – that it actually becomes part of your new reality."

At this point, it may be useful to clarify that regardless of my client's experience of magnetic hands, I tell them that their experience of hypnosis may well be the same. Some people feel slightly "spaced-out," even if their hands freeze and all they feel is a ball of energy in the middle; others feel nothing at all, yet they still see their hands moving. A very common response is that people report feeling "slightly different." This appears to be an experience of dissociation, as they report both feeling in the room and as normal as ever, whilst also being somehow not there, or not their usual self. Either way, if they had any kind of experience at all, I take that and suggest that their experience of hypnosis will likely be very similar.

In fact, if someone feels completely "normal," but their hands still move, as a hypnotist I find it very useful. I can explain to them that they do not need to feel in a "trance-state," or controlled like a puppet or zombie, in order for their subconscious mind to respond to my suggestions. I state that their response demonstrates that their subconscious is clearly ready and willing to respond to my words and that is all that counts.

If the horror movie explanation seemed to work for them, I return again to the subject of movies. How is it, I ask them, that we can feel sorry for a millionaire pretending to cry over the death of his millionaire colleague whilst they play-acted being husband and wife? How is such a ridiculous scenario able to evoke genuine emotion in us, sometimes as strong as if we were actually there and it was really happening to people we knew well? The obvious answer is that we have chosen that for the next two hours, this is our reality. And it is a choice that we accept so wholeheartedly, that we forget that we are pretending the actors are not pretending and our perception of the world – our current window on reality – changes.

Describing the Experience

I have never had a client seek a more thorough explanation of hypnosis before a session begins, after having gone through this process of describing – and then demonstrating – various experiences. So, I commend to you the idea that we should stop answering the question "What is hypnosis?" and begin answering the far more pertinent question, "What will I experience?"

As stated above, the answer to that question will differ from person to person. However, it is useful to have metaphors or exercises that you can call on to answer the question in a rather content–free way, allowing your client to fill in the gaps. The movie explanation and magnetic hands are offered as two excellent examples.

The thing to focus on is that you are not seeking to explain every possible nuance of all of the various models of hypnosis out there. All you are seeking to do is explain things in such a way that you can move seamlessly into hypnosis. You are looking for a model that will enable you to help someone experience hypnosis. Nothing more and nothing less.

The important thing is that we provide an experiential answer to the question, "What is hypnosis?"

Is it not more effective to reframe the question – getting to the core of what is being asked – and answer in the only way we really can?

"Hypnosis is an experience. Shall we have one?"

EXERCISE

Is the Experiential Model a useful addition to current discussions regarding the nature of hypnosis?

Or is it simply a means of avoiding debates and refusing to come up with any solid conclusions?

Why are the cinema and 'highway hypnosis' descriptions of hypnosis considered so useful by many practitioners of hypnosis?

Unpacking the Experience of Hypnosis

This chapter provides a description of what I might describe as the 'journey' of therapeutic hypnosis. Obviously, this will vary from person to person. However, the process that follows is a reliable representation of how hypnosis is progressively experienced for a good number of people.

It will take you from the very earliest stage of consent to be hypnotised, all the way through to seeing hypnosis make measurable changes in someone's life.

Importantly, this chapter lays the foundation for everything that follows, establishing how and why I proceed as I do – and how that relates to any later therapeutic work.

The Active Ingredients of Therapeutic Hypnosis (A4+2)

I refer to this journey of (therapeutic) hypnosis as "A4 + 2." In reality, it could probably just be called "A4" or "A6," but where's the mystery in that?

Here are the steps that – all other things being equal – I would generally expect to see in all genuine experiences of therapeutic hypnosis:

- Agree Expectations
- Attract Attention

- Absorb Awareness
    - Activate Imagination
    - Arouse Emotions
- Alter Experience

I don't know how you first encountered hypnosis. Perhaps it was a stage show, or a therapy session, or simply a video clip online. However, if it was anything like my first encounter with hypnosis, it may have left you with the impression that hypnosis – and the induction in particular – is some sort of wizardry.

Many of the videos you will find online – that demonstrate someone hypnotising someone else – almost give the impression that something magical is taking place. Now, of course, those of us who have dedicated our lives to hypnosis would likely say that it *is* magical, but that is not quite what I mean. I am talking about presentations of hypnosis that imply it involves some secret knowledge and that the induction (in particular) is like a special spell that needs to be recited with the exact right words, in exactly the right way, for the hypnosis to take effect.

One thing this 'magical' approach does not do is encourage much experimentation or innovation. After all, if you do not know the secret words, how can you be expected to perform the magic?

However, an experiential understanding of hypnosis – such as I have been recommending – challenges all of that. After all, if an induction is nothing more (or less!) than a way to imaginatively begin to reframe reality, then not only can we teach the skills to do that, but we can actually break down the DNA of inductions and show exactly how they create hypnosis and provide the opportunities for reframing to take place.

And that is precisely what A4+2 seeks to do.[3]

---

3 These points do not always follow this exact sequence. However, this is an order

Agree Expectations

Aside from being ethical, gaining consent and establishing a "hypnotic contract" provides your context and intent. This provides the What? and Why? of everything that will be taking place.

Similarly, it may be necessary to establish (overtly or covertly) the roles to be played by each participant in the hypnotic encounter. In the past, the emphasis may have been upon the 'prestige' that the hypnotist had. Nowadays, people are more likely to speak of 'rapport' between both parties. I would suggest that there is no need to choose between these two options.

I will return to this theme later, but I think it is a mistake to think of rapport as merely being liked by one's client. Instead, the best definition I have come across is, being on the same page as your client. And being on the same page can mean agreeing that I am being a bit of a jerk (if working in a 'provocative' way). That is why I speak of E.C.O. – *Explicit Collaborative Outcomes* with most clients that I see nowadays.

My sessions begin, naturally enough, with us speaking about what my client hopes to get out of it. I then surprise them by telling them what *I* would like to get out of it! This almost always elicits an amused curiosity and – as I explain what I mean – almost universal agreement. I speak about the unique responsibilities placed upon my client: to be honest, not to share anything they want to keep to themselves, not to fake anything or try to force anything to happen in an attempt to help me, etc. I might then say something about hoping to try out one or two techniques I picked–up at a recent conference, or that I am hoping to engage in a thoughtful and open conversation and so on. Together, we make a plan of action – a contract – and the induction is the beginning of that plan being put into effect.

Of course, if we are thinking of a less therapeutic context, it is

in which they often naturally occur. My advice is to not think of the following steps as a formula to be followed, but as the best ingredients available for making effective hypnotic inductions.

possible to come across people who appear to go into hypnosis without any introduction or initial agreement at all. However, experience has lead me to conclude two things about the majority of such cases. Firstly, consent is almost given instantly in situations like this, normally in the split second between the induction and the 'deepener.' Secondly, if agreement is not given then the old saying, "easy come, easy go" applies. You will find that they will be likely to pop out of hypnosis, just as easily and quickly as they slipped into it. After all, what reason do they have to be invested in what happens?

In some cases, a sense of expectancy is achieved in the pre–talk, or through the curiosity generated from a good Response routine. In others, it comes from the mystery and reputation that surrounds hypnosis in popular culture. It can also be achieved simply through the demeanour of the hypnotist and the prestige spoken of above. Look at someone like Jonathan Chase, with his commitment to "Be The Hypnotist" and it's not difficult to believe that you will do whatever he tells you to do!

Alternatively, as Irving Kirsch suggests, the induction itself may be the mechanism that creates expectancy. It is here that one of the purposes of hypnotic phenomena comes into play. The Elman induction is a good example of this, building on the expectation that is created in the client as they find themselves increasingly responding to your suggestions. Likewise, a good relaxation–based induction often surprises a client with how quickly they can relax. When they associate this with your words, their expectation level is thereby raised. However, even an arm–pull achieves this, albeit very rapidly. The sudden shock sends an instant message that something of significance is happening. In that split–second, the client can choose to go with the experience (the consent spoken of previously), or pull–back. The key with moments of decision like that is...

Attract Attention

Attracting your client's attention is, in one sense, merely the initial step to absorbing their awareness.

"Put your feet flat on the floor, and look at me..."

"Listen..."

All you are aiming to do at this stage is catch your client's attention. You want to re-direct their gaze (literal or metaphorical) from the world around them and focus it on the words you are saying. In reality, you are actually simply teaching them to focus on the here and now, but I can come back to that.

Once you have their attention, the next stage is to get all of it!

Absorb awareness

"Pick a spot on the wall... look at the back of your hand... notice your breathing..." and so on. These are frequently used directions intended to narrow the client's focus, resulting in what Michael Heap describes as an experience of 'inner absorption.'

This absorption allows the hypnotist to more easily redirect the client's attention/awareness inwardly – with the hypnotist included. This creates a frame whereby the hypnotist is part of the new reality-making process. And this is essential.

Many inductions create this condition almost instantly, through shock or surprise. One theory is that an inability to process the external stimuli seems to cause the hypnotee to 'go inside' to search for something to make sense of the experience. Some people believe that we see something similar take place with confusion inductions, where the hypnotee apparently gets caught in a loop of analysis, thereby narrowing their focus and becoming absorbed in their own inner world.

I'm not sure I would say that trance is *necessary* for hypnosis, but personally I would say that trance is almost always present when we have hypnosis. As you will have sussed by now, I do my best to avoid debates around the terms we use to describe an experience. I would much rather just describe that experience. So, for me, I would use the word 'trance' very loosely and vaguely to mean something like: 'Absorption in a particular experience...'

If I have used my words as cleverly as I intended to, hopefully that means nothing at all and has just allowed me to deftly dodge another of the persistent debates in hypnosis!

The point here is simply that your client perceives their attention and/or awareness becoming absorbed either in what you are saying, or what they are experiencing. It is very common that hypnotees report a kind of tunnel–vision, even as they have their eyes open, as their visual field appears to follow what is happening to their mental focus. And, of course, once you have absorbed their attention, it is far easier to direct it.

Once you have absorbed your client's awareness, you have created an environment where you can activate their imagination and arouse their emotions. And when you can do that, you can begin to truly alter their experience in profound and lasting ways.

Activate Imagination

The ability to spark another person's imagination is one of the most powerful tools that a hypnotist possesses. It is the imagination that enables us to access previously untapped inner resources and envisage our best hopes for the future.

Engaging the imagination can be as simple as having someone remember a time when they felt so relaxed it was as if they were sinking into the chair. Alternatively, it might involve stories and metaphors, intended to fuel expectancy or invite reframes. Or it may be helping someone imagine and then experience a new version of their preferred future, along with the steps to getting there. Or thinking about spending future years with their loved ones.

To use a therapeutic example, it is the imagination that sustains a phobia. Therefore, this element may include teaching someone how powerful and flexible their imagination is, with the intention of then guiding them to consider and experience other possible reactions.

You may already have encountered a number of clients who insist that they "cannot imagine anything." In my own personal experience, these people are often like those who say they "cannot relax" – they very often turn out to be absolute virtuosos. I remember with some fondness a young man who told me that he could not really imagine anything. I asked him what it would be like if he could and he went off on the most vivid descriptions of the world of imagination![4]

It may be necessary to inform some people that "imagination" does not necessarily mean the same thing as "visualise." So, I like to inform people that if I say something like "picture yourself at the top of a staircase," it can mean a whole range of things from see, imagine, realise, pretend, or become aware of being there. Part of that is about active versus passive imagination (because poor visualisers often over–estimate what good visualises see and how they see it), and part of it is providing a broader meaning to the word 'imagine' than merely visualising something.

Arouse Emotions

As you guide someone into their reframe, whether that's experiencing hypnotic phenomena or discovering inner resources, you will need to provide them with a reason and powerful motivation for doing so.

It is not enough to enable someone to imagine a different reality – they have to want it and engage with it. Emotions both fuel and feed–off of the imagination and cause the client to buy into the reframe you are helping them experience. If nothing else, they are what empower us to move towards our goals or move away from our

4 It is true that some people appear to lack the ability to voluntarily create images in their mind (though it is rare). However, aphantasia is not quite the same as the inability to imagine something.

fears.

What I am saying is that, from a Therapeutic Inductions perspective, all effective inductions naturally involve an element of emotion. It may not be explicit and it may not be for long, but it will be there.

Bear in mind that with a Therapeutic Inductions approach, there is little if any boundary between the induction and the therapy. And, for any therapeutic change to be effective, it has to appeal to the emotions. It has to be meaningful, in more than an intellectual sense.

At all times, both you and your client need to know why you are doing what you are doing. If you have sufficiently aroused their emotions, this will never be in question.

Alter Experience

It was the apparent 'magic' of inductions that first attracted me to hypnosis. Many experienced hypnosis practitioners eventually move beyond that initial fascination. Yet, if anything, my interest in inductions has only increased over the years.

As I see it, an induction is a microcosm of the entire hypnotic encounter. The induction teaches a client *how to be hypnotised, what to expect* and *how to alter their experience* as a result. The induction establishes A4 + 2, in preparation for a larger or deeper experience.

In this way, I think of an induction as a transformative experience of absorption. Rather than a simple series of steps I take someone through, presumably to make them more suggestible, an induction provides a window into a world of alternate realities.

If the induction does not leave my client thinking, "Woh! The rules have changed. It's like anything is possible here..." then what am I really achieving?

Just think for a moment, of the fluidity of what I have tentatively called 'trance.' Someone could be completely fixated on the phobia that they perceive as ruining their life, or unable to think of anything except the poor opinion that their colleagues have of them, then often in a matter of minutes their mind has somehow found some sort of lubrication that allows their thoughts and realities to shift, morph and transform. All of a sudden, that rigid and morbid reality they were fixated on seems pliable and no longer inevitable – and all sorts of possibilities present themselves.

That unbelievable shift can be achieved with a simple induction.

Yet, more than an occasional trip to wonderland, such fluidity can be taught and developed through the effective use of hypnosis. Some people call such a skill, Psychological Flexibility. Others call it Emotional Agility. I am confident that by the time you have read this book, you will view it as an integral aspect of the approach I am presenting.

Such is the magic of therapeutic hypnosis.

EXERCISE

What do you think of the A4 + 2 description of hypnosis?

Was the role of emotion a previous component of your understanding of hypnosis?

Does this understanding of hypnosis seem too basic, or too simple to you? Or both? Or neither?

SETTING THE SCENE

Sometimes, doing the ground-work is doing half the work.

Sometimes, it is doing so much more.

Preparation

If you go for surgery, the medical staff will usually prepare the area to be worked on before putting you 'under' and reaching for the scalpel. You may also be asked to prepare yourself by e.g. not having eaten since the night before. You may even have had to make more long-term preparations, such as losing weight, or other lifestyle changes.

Similarly, if you were attending a counselling session, the therapist would likely have prepared by acquainting themselves with your case. They will hopefully have checked that their room is welcoming, accessible and not too intimidating. In the same way, you might have prepared by ensuring a good night's sleep the night before, making sure that you were wearing appropriate clothing, reviewing any topics you wished to discuss, not being intoxicated and so on.

When you look at it, there are very few social interactions that do not involve at least some form of preparation. This is especially true for those interactions which require participation from both parties for an agreed upon positive outcome.

Given the role of expectation in hypnosis, it will come as no surprise that preparing yourself, your client and your environment can play a significant part in achieving successful outcomes. In this section, I will consider a number of steps that can be taken to effectively set the scene.

This includes the general approach you take, your "pre-talk," and also any possible informal hypnotic phenomena (otherwise known as suggestibility tests, 'set pieces,' mind games, or imagination exercises,) that you wish to employ.

Your Approach

It makes sense for us to begin at the beginning, with your – and your client's – whole approach to the hypnotic encounter. For ease of recall, I call this the P3 Approach.

This is not so much about techniques to use, or scripts to follow. Instead, it is how I recommend hypnotists *be* with their clients. This is actually about how you are and what atmosphere you are contributing towards.

I will explore this further in a later chapter.

The Pre-talk

The pre-talk can be thought of as anything you say between meeting/approaching your client and formally beginning hypnosis.

The purpose of such a talk is generally thought of as refuting any believed myths surrounding hypnosis, or addressing any fears that the client may have. However, there are other ways to make use of a pre-talk and I will provide 3 versions to consider in this section.

Routines

Traditionally referred to as Suggestibility Tests, or more recently known as Set Pieces, the routines in this section offer a gentle introduction to hypnotic phenomena.

Previously, I have referred to these phenomena as 'Imagination Exercises,' because I believed that such a label more accurately reflected what was actually taking place, regardless of whether or not it leads on to further experiences with hypnosis. However, for reasons that I will unpack later, I now enthusiastically embrace the label,

"Response routines."[5]

(It should be noted that I am presenting a fairly artificial division between your approach, the pre-talk and the exercises. In reality, all 3 elements will flow naturally together. I am simply breaking things down in this way to allow a closer examination of each aspect of your pre-induction activities.)

Anthony Jacquin has referred to exercises like this as 'the first rung on the hypnotic ladder.' That is a great description, but they can also be so much more besides. I would see the advantages of Response routines as including:

1. Helping get a subject into the state/belief that they can/will be hypnotised
2. Helping the Hypnotist practice and develop skills and confidence
3. In some cases, demonstrating the suggestibility of a subject
4. Inspiring and utilising the imagination, focussing attention and building expectation (in both the hypnotist and the client)
5. Introducing the experience of hypnosis
6. Familiarising all parties with hypnotic phenomena

Though often undervalued, I highly recommend becoming acquainted with the routines in the coming chapters. In my experience, they are less threatening for those who are more nervous about being hypnotised, but they normally produce a desire to go on and experience more.

So, without further ado, now would be a good time for us to set the scene.

5 Strictly speaking, I view these informal phenomena as "Responsivity routines." However, "response routines" seems to roll off the tongue more naturally.

The P3 Approach

If I had to choose, during a hypnosis encounter, I would much rather have the air itself sizzle with electricity, than have someone be impressed with my persona or academic expositions.

So I want to share with you a simple approach I use in every single session I am involved with. Whether it is a little demonstration in the middle of a training, or an impromptu setting, or a hypnotherapy client, I always use what I am about to describe.

The P3 Approach

In essence, this is how I train my students to BE with clients. This is about far more than what techniques you use with clients. It is actually about HOW you use those techniques. In fact, it's more than that – it is about how you are.

What atmosphere and environment are you creating? What expectations are you provoking? What future are you laying the foundations for?

When I teach this in a training course, it is usually off-the-cuff and probably takes about 5 minutes, but I suspect that it is probably the most important thing I teach.

By adopting a P3 approach, when you are starting with a client, you aim to contribute towards the following kind of environment:

– Positive

– Powerful
– Presence

In such a setting, there is often a tangible sense that anything could happen.

POSITIVE

The first step of P3 is conveying an atmosphere of positive change. I would actually suggest that this is essential for all effective hypnotic encounters.

You can project – through your tone of voice, eye contact, and more – that you are not there primarily to impress your client, or test them. You are not predominantly seeking to make a name for yourself, or to make a fool of them.

You are there, before all else, to generate good changes for them. Everything that takes place is for their good. Every single thing that occurs does so in that context, for that purpose.

POWERFUL

Hypnosis is most effective when it is powerful. However, we should bear in mind that how you convey "power" is totally dependent on your personality, your style and the impression you want to give.

For example, if you look at some of the old school hypnotists like Gil Boyne, or modern-day folks like Bob Burns, they exude a sense of authority. That works for them, it is completely congruent and matches their personality and style of hypnosis.

Yet, it really does not work for me. I am simply not like that… and I don't want to be like that either. Equally as important is my conviction that I do not want to present hypnosis like that either.[6]

Therefore, my preference is to make liberal use of response routines and phenomena. I also aim to employ phenomenal inductions. That is, every induction – in fact, every single thing – I go through with clients involves an actual experience of some kind. Phenomena is not a secondary stage with such a model, or an optional extra. It is inherent in the most effective inductions.

From the moment I begin talking about hypnosis, I want to be giving my clients the sense that, "Okay... something unusual is happening here!"

PRESENCE

All of these points are of course related. These are not 3 separate items. Instead it is one thing: a positive powerful presence. And that positive power is often seen most clearly in how PRESENT we are with our clients.

One of my slight misgivings with some of the ways that some people practice *Street Hypnosis* is that they can appear to pay more attention to their audience, than their client (or 'subject'). Of course, from a safety perspective, that could be precisely the right thing to do. The hypnotist may be checking that they still have an audience, that no one too drunk is approaching them and so on. Additionally, to be fair, it *is* a performance.

However, such performances often risk losing that positive focus I have been speaking of. They can treat the client like a tool, a prop, like a deck of cards, intended to make the hypnotist look good.

I'm fond of the story I heard of someone watching Stephen Brooks give a hypnosis demonstration to a room of students. Now, I heard this a few years ago, so I may not have it all exact. But the story

6 I prefer the metaphor from ACT. The therapist is not a more experienced 'climber' on the mountain(s) of life – they are simply standing on a different mountain and from that perspective can see where you could safely step next.

goes that whilst Brooks was working with his client, he turned to them at one point and said something like, "in this moment, I would like you to know that you are the most important person in the world to me..." and then he carried on to demonstrate some technique or other.

Afterwards, the audience asked various questions about different techniques they had seen, or aspects of Brooks work they had picked–up on. Then, at the end, one person asked, "I noticed you tell the client that they were the most important person in the world to you. What was the reasoning behind that?" Brooks replied, "It was simply the truth. They were the most important person in the world."

I love that! Regardless of whether or not you think it's helpful to say something like that to a client, I'm sure you can imagine the impact it has on a client to know that they have 100% of your focus and intention, that you are there powerfully for their positive good.

All of this is about more than simply having a warm charismatic character, though that is no doubt a part of it. It is about being there completely, powerfully, for their good.

When I first did my initial hypnosis training, it was suggested to me that the goal was to be able to hypnotise someone simply by being in the same room as them. It's a worthy goal and something that P3 aims to facilitate.

I am convinced – and my clients and students and I have seen this time and time again – that when you approach people with a positive powerful presence the air itself crackles with possibilities.

When you set things up in that way, before apparently, even beginning the hypnosis, you will find that there is magic in the air. You will see their understanding of reality becoming just a little more pliable and their window on what's possible becoming wider as they open up to – and even expect – something new and powerfully positive.

In such an environment, there is an almost tangible sense that something enchanting is about to happen. And it usually does!

The Pre-Talk

Introduction

A pre-talk is simply a brief talk about what hypnosis is, often addressing any fears or concerns the client may have. There is no need for a 30 minute-lecture on the nature and history of hypnosis. In fact, 3 minutes can be plenty of time on some occasions!

Given some of the popular myths and misconceptions surrounding hypnosis, you may choose to address some of these. Of course, doing this is a great way to drop in suggestions and increase expectancy. For example, "when you feel that wave of relaxation as you begin to go into trance..."

It is common for hypnotists to explain that their clients would not be asleep during hypnosis, they will still be able to hear you speaking to them, they will remain in control, etc. I might also let them know that they will not be made to do anything against their moral or ethical code, or that makes them feel uncomfortable, because the whole idea is that they are going to relax and enjoy it.[7]

Transcript

> Is there anywhere in your memory, or your imagination, that's a special place to you? Somewhere that just thinking about produces feelings of relaxation, calm, peace, safety,

7 This is one of the ideas that hypnotists are keen to dissect and debate in online groups and forums. However, the philosophical nuances are not usually of interest to our clients.

serenity...

— "Definitely."

Excellent. What I'd like you to do is take four deep breaths and on any of those four breaths you can let your eyes close and imagine yourself in that special place, seeing those sights that calm you, hearing those tranquil sounds and feeling that sensation of deep relaxation. Okay?

[Wait for Client to close their eyes]

...That's it. Down into that place of deep peace and serenity. Down deeper into relaxation... And we all have times like this, where we feel so relaxed and at peace that our brain kinda just zones out a bit. And that is something that we hypnotists call 'trance' – and this is what hypnosis often feels like.

Some people think that you become a zombie, or just zonk-out completely, but it's not like that. What you'll experience is more like the first few minutes when you wake up in the morning and you're just floating in that hazy space between being not quite awake but not really asleep. Or, like when you day-dream and your mind just drifts off to some other place.

You're still safe and in control and could snap yourself out of it any time you chose to. (But the truth is that you're normally so relaxed that you just don't want to!) Or, those times you have when you're driving on a familiar route and your conscious mind kinda takes a back seat. And when you get home, you're left thinking, "how did I get here?!"

You know exactly what I mean. Trance feels just like what you're feeling now, as you enjoy that special place. And any time you hear me talk about 'trance' you'll know that it's really just a hypnotic code word for relaxing down into your special place and enjoying those feelings of peace and tranquillity and deep, deep relaxation, as your conscious mind takes a nap and your subconscious opens up to suggestions and your imagination is given free rein.

So, when you're ready, you can open your eyes, feeling fresh and alert and raring to go...

The Positive Pre-talk

Introduction

As we have seen, it is common for hypnotists to use the pre-talk primarily as a means of addressing misconceptions and allaying fears.

However, one valid criticism of such a practice is that it could potentially suggest concerns to the client that they had not even considered. For example, some hypnotists will tell their clients that they can not get "stuck" in hypnosis. Yet, I am not personally aware of ever having worked with a client who held this belief. Therefore, addressing such a fear with these clients might do little more than imply this is something that may warrant some anxiety!

I am grateful to Jason Linnet for taking the lead in enthusiastically and consistently promoting the idea of a completely positive pre-talk. I have provided an example below.

Transcript

> In a moment, when you are in hypnosis, you will remain alert throughout the entire experience. You will be able to hear what I say, and any other sounds you hear – the traffic, the air conditioning, the clock – will simply remind you what an everyday process this really is.
>
> In movies, they give the impression that the person in hypnosis is under someone else's control. Yet, in actual fact, this whole experience is about *you* regaining control of

those various parts of your life that have, until now, felt a little out of control.

Do you remember what it was like at school, when the teacher is talking and your mind is just miles away? And they are calling out your name, but you are away off in your own world? Well, some people become so engrossed in what they are experiencing here, that they might wander off and momentarily focus more on their own internal experience than the words I am saying. And that is absolutely fine!

And if you ever find that happening, you can simply allow your focus to easily flow back to the words I am saying and enjoy the experience you are having.

Just notice whatever you notice, think about anything I ask you to think about and allow yourself to experience whatever takes place.

Don't fight it. Don't fake it. Don't force it. Simply flow with it.

And if, at any point, you feel the need to itch, or shift in the chair, you can do whatever it takes to help you relax even further.

So, do you have any questions before you experience hypnotize?

The Pre Conversation

The following outline is not a script to follow, or an exact replica of how I work. After all, as I have said many times, no one wants to see lots of little clones of Graham Old running around! However, this is fairly close to the sort of model I personally use and serves of a useful example of things you may want to include, or at least consider.

This is explicitly not offered as the way to deliver a pre–talk. (That is precisely why I have included two pre-talks before this one.) As with the majority of the content in this book, this is provided as an example to provoke discussion and inspire practical experimentation.

We have seen how hypnotherapists often use the pre–talk to address any fears or misconceptions that their clients may have. We have also considered how important it is to ensure that in the process they are not installing any concerns that did not previously exist.

An area that may deserve fresh consideration is the over–reliance on pre–scripted information to be shared during the pre–talk. It is understandable that hypnotherapists will want to ensure that all relevant or important information is recalled. However, reliance on a formal script can inhibit freedom and flexibility.

It seems to me that rather than having a pre–scripted pre–talk it may be preferable to simply have a conversation with your clients. Rather than listing all of the potential fears that someone may have, to then address these one–by–one, why not ask a natural question like, "So, how are you feeling about experiencing hypnosis?"

Paying attention to what your client says, as well as their body language when doing so, will provide plenty of information with which to proceed. Similarly, asking, "Is there anything you're not sure about?" gives your client the option to raise any fears they may have without necessarily implying that they should have some.

This is not to say that you should definitely never have any notes or pointers with you. However, I would encourage using this time to have a dialogue, rather than delivering a one–way lecture.

This is a simple framework of the sort of conversation I tend to adopt, in preference to a scripted pre-talk:

1) Have you experienced Hypnosis before?

– If their experience was negative, discuss this. Explain how your approach is different

– If their experience was positive, congratulate them on their hypnotic ability. Build expectations.

– If they have not experienced Hypnosis before:

2) So, how are you feeling about experiencing hypnosis today?

– Discuss any concerns / misconceptions that arise

- Highlight any positives with a sense of excited curiosity

2b) Is there anything you're not sure about? Any questions?

– Discuss any concerns / misconceptions that arise

3) Experiential explanation

– Compare hypnosis to a day–dream (including the common experience of varieties of depth in dreams).

Describe this as a natural capacity of the human brain

– Cinema comparison – we focus and choose to lose ourselves in an alternate reality

– Include phenomena to aid the explanation and preview what is to come.

4) Shall we do this?

I almost always jump straight into hypnotic phenomena.

***

Regarding this last point, I may already have used something like magnetic hands as part of the experiential explanation. I might then enthusiastically say something along the lines of, "Well, let's see what else your mind is eager to achieve, shall we?" I would then either opt for another Response Routine, or move on to a phenomenal induction.

In the latter case, I generally use an induction that feels like a natural progression from the phenomena they have already experienced. I do not want to jump too far ahead and lose the rapport we have gained. So, if I had already used magnetic fingers as a routine, I would likely move on to Magnetic Hands. If the balloon and book routine had just taken place, I would tend to use something like the Modified Wicks induction, an arm levitation of some kind, or the Bandler handshake.

EXERCISE

What do you think of the arguments in favour of a positive pre-talk?

Could a pre-talk that addresses concerns a client may have result in suggesting concerns to the client that they had not even considered?

If so, could it also work the other way round?

Could a pre-talk be used to make indirect positive suggestions to a client?

Response Routines

As I have already mentioned, I now refer to the type of phenomena I will look at next as 'Response routines.' You may be surprised how much debate takes place over what to call these (apparently) pre-hypnotic phenomena![8]

Traditionally, they have been referred to as 'suggestibility tests.' However, over time this description has been used less often. On the one hand, the person being hypnotised may not like the notion of a test, with the implication of pass or fail. Additionally, these 'tests' were often used purely to inform the hypnotist if the person they were working with was suggestible enough to proceed. However, not only has a fixed level of suggestibility not been conclusively proven, but some people felt that such one-sided information-gathering does a disservice to the client (apart from potentially informing them that they have 'failed'!). Surely it would be better to approach these early phenomena as of interest and benefit to both the hypnotist and their client?

Some of those influenced by the Street Hypnosis community refer to these experiences as being "set pieces."[9] This is certainly a good way to frame things for the hypnotist. It allows them to have any number of routines in mind that they know they can walk through in a progressive order, before moving on to the next stage, which could

8 Some readers may believe that I would suggest terminology is irrelevant; it is the experience that counts. Whilst this is a commendable expression of priorities, it is also possibly somewhat naive. Hypnotists – more than anyone – are aware of the power of words and the impact of framing on any following experiences.

9 This is largely due to the influence of Anthony Jacquin and his exceptionally useful book, *Reality is Plastic.*

be the induction.

Despite this improvement on the label of "suggestibility tests," the idea of a set piece has never particularly appealed to me personally. It reveals the performance roots of the term, which is not necessarily a negative. However, I prefer my clients to not feel like I am putting on a show for them, or anyone else. I also feel as though the idea of a set piece is potentially a little rigid and not as explicitly and intentionally flexible as I personally prefer to be.

Unhappy with any of the other terms in popular usage, I began to use the description, "Imagination Exercises." I especially liked the non-threatening nature of this description, as did many of my clients. I was also particularly keen on the use of the word "exercise," as it can carry the implication of practising, or a drill that we go through to improve at something.

So, depending on who I was working with, I might at times present the exercises as a way of priming their imagination, seeing how active their imagination currently is, or – as I sometimes express it – "greasing the wheels."

Nevertheless, although I used this description for a number of years, it began to feel at odds with my developing views on hypnosis, inductions and informal or formal phenomena. If I was honest with myself – and my clients – all I could say with any degree of certainty was that these little exercises demonstrated that the client was responding to my words *at that point in time*. There was – in that moment – a responsiveness being expressed, without conclusively proving that they were naturally or ordinarily "responsive," or "suggestible."

Now, when I refer to "response routines," I almost always inform my clients that there is no right or wrong way to respond. In fact, I usually tell them that even doing nothing is responding. So, what we are going to do is see how they respond to me and to the ideas and suggestions offered.

Clients often inject their own meaning into this phrase. Some see a response routine as revealing that their subconscious is in-tune with me and ready to respond to anything I say. Others see the routines as helping them respond, showing them *how* to respond, or even conditioning them to respond.

Either way, the meaning that you or your client attach to these routines is more significant than how you label them. So, aside from strongly encouraging you to avoid using the term "test" – unless you have your own specific and intentional reason(s) for doing so – you are obviously welcome to choose your own descriptions. My suggestion would simply be to remember that the words you use often carry meaning in themselves (at least, in the mind of your clients) and can therefore frame your client's responses.

EXERCISE

Does it really matter what we call any pre-hypnotic phenomena?

How do you typically refer to such exercises?

Would it be beneficial to adjust your terminology, depending on your audience?

Magnetic Fingers

Introduction

Here is a very popular routine that many hypnotists use as their first example of informal hypnotic phenomena.

Transcript

> Okay, let's try a simple exercise to help you enjoy the power of your imagination…
>
> In a moment, I would like you to clasp your hands together like this, as if you are praying.
>
> [Demonstrate by holding your hands out in front of you, palms touching, with the elbows bent and fingers interlocked.]
>
> And, when I say, "Go!" you can just extend your fingers and point towards the ceiling, with the fingers about an inch or so apart, like this..."
>
> [Continue to demonstrate by sticking your forefingers up, about an inch apart.]
>
> And – here's the fun bit – as you part those fingers, I will click my fingers and that will magnetise those finger-tips. And then… well, just watch and see what happens!
>
> So, go ahead and clasp your hands together, that's it, palms

touching, nice and tight.

And now stick your fingers up and part them… and watch.

[Click your fingers]

Look at your magnetised fingers… that's it, already twitching… pulling them… closer and closer. Just like they're magnets.

Now, as they touch you can allow your eyes to close and relax. And let your hands drop down into your lap.

Good! You can open your eyes now. You've got a great imagination.

Thank you.

Commentary

This is an incredibly simply routine that usually takes longer to describe than it does to go through!

Magnetic fingers relies almost exclusively on a purely physiological element. When the hands are placed in the correct position at the beginning of the routine, the tendons in the index fingers will tighten.

This does not mean that the routine is merely a trick though. It is certainly possible for someone to intentionally keep their index fingers apart, if they so desire. Therefore, I could argue that there is at least an element of suggestion with the routine. However, the suggestion is easier to follow and – because all that is needed is the relaxation of muscles, not excitation of muscles – the client will therefore feel the effects of the suggestion effortlessly and almost immediately.

So, whilst Magnetic fingers may be seen by some as something of a parlour trick, I tend to think of it as a routine that is strongly weighted in your favour. It is then a good lead-in to something like Magnetic hands.

On some occasions, you may use Magnetic fingers with someone who knows about the role of tendons in the routine and dismisses the experience. At times like that, you can utilise their belief and objection:

> "Yes, that predominantly works due to the tightening of the tendons. And you *could* have resisted that but you didn't. So, the fact that you were willing to have the experience – and go with it – shows that you are ready to experience something new."

At that point, I might proceed straight-away with *Magnetic hands*, perhaps like this:

> "I think you are ready for the next step. Put your hands out like this [demonstrate the placement of the hands for Magnetic hands] and see what new experiences your mind can create for you, with or without the help of tendons..."

I think of Magnetic fingers as a good demonstration of rapport. Aside from the physiological element involved, the key is to have your client focus their attention on imagining magnets, not on fighting the suggestions. If they do so, their fingers will almost certainly come together.

If someone's fingers do not come together, this is often a sure sign that they are fighting to keep them apart. That does not necessarily mean that they are 'resisting' the experience, or trying to give you a hard time. It may simply mean that they are not aware of their role in the routine.

Remember that we are seeking to create experiences here, not simply impress someone or achieve specific results. So, if someone's fingers do not come together, take that as a good time to receive some feedback.

Ask the client what happened as they focused on the space between their fingers. Or ask what was going on as they imagined the magnets on the ends of their fingers.

They are likely to reply that nothing happened. Or to admit that they were not focusing on the space between their fingers, or the imagined magnets. They may say, almost apologetically:

> "Oh, I wasn't doing that. I was trying to keep the fingers up."

This does not mean they were resisting. Instead, they just were not clear on what they were meant to be doing. So, this is *good* feedback and shows that you are not yet both on the same page.

If I have a client say that they were trying to keep their fingers up, I might proceed by saying something like:

> "Well, you clearly have a strong mind and can not be made to do something you do not want to. So, let's use that and see what happens when you do want something to happen. This time, want the fingers to come together. Don't force or fight it. Don't fake it, either. Simply imagine those magnets and let yourself experience what your mind can achieve when you use it for your good..."

I would then do the routine again, with almost guaranteed success.

As Magnetic fingers is so simple and weighted so strongly in favour of success, many hypnotists like to use it as a starter routine. They see it as almost priming their client for the next routine.

Magnetic Hands

Introduction

Many hypnotists treat Magnetic Hands as something of a step-up from Magnetic fingers. They may start with magnetic fingers and when the client responds well to that, they then say something like, "That's great. That shows us that you can *focus* really well and you can use that to your hypnotic advantage. Now let's see how ready your *imagination* is to engage..."

You may choose to not say anything about what the routine 'teaches' you, until after you have seen how your client responds. So, you could say something as open as, "That was excellent. So, let's see how your subconscious likes this one..."

Alternatively, as mentioned previously, I might use Magnetic Hands as a routine when I am initially discussing what hypnosis is like. After having used the movie explanation, I might then say, "Actually, it's a bit like this: Just place your hands out in front of you, like so..."

In the transcript that follows, there has not been a previous routine and the hypnotist jumps straight in with magnetic hands.

Transcript

Can I borrow you for a moment, to demonstrate the power of your mind? You'll enjoy it, trust me. All it really is, is a simple, fun, exercise that will show just what happens when you concentrate and focus, allowing your imagination to run free.

Okay, *in a moment* I'm going to ask you to close your eyes and place your hands out in front of you, like this.

[Demonstrate by placing your hands about 6 inches to a shoulder width apart, palms facing each other]

Then I want you to imagine that you have two powerful magnets strapped to the palms of your hands, pulling them together. When they touch, your head can simply fall forward as you relax.

So, now, place your hands out... and focus on the space between them... Now, close your eyes and imagine two powerful magnets strapped to the palms of your hands, pulling them together.

You can feel the force of that magnetic field between your hands, as you *concentrate on that space between the palms* [Wait for movement in the hands] ...that's right. Feel the pull. You don't have to force it. You don't have to fight it. Feel it now getting stronger and stronger. And the stronger it gets, the closer the hands come together... that's right... and the closer they get the stronger it becomes.

Just enjoy the power of your imagination, as you feel those magnets pulling the hands together, until they touch... Now... you can let your hands drop into your lap, as your head drops forward and you... relax.

Commentary

There are a number of things we can focus on, even with this brief example. You start with 'compliance.' This does not need to be as blatant as commanding the client to do exactly as they are told. Such a bold move so early on can run the risk of ruining any rapport you were developing. In reality, the compliance at this point is more often than not simply a case of asking them to place their hands out in front of them, in the way that you demonstrate.

To reinforce the compliance, it can be helpful to adjust their hands just a little, moving them in or out slightly, up or down, simply to reinforce the idea that you are setting the parameters (or explaining the rules of the game, as it were).

If you are uncomfortable with the idea of compliance – and that's nothing to be embarrassed about, as many of us intuitively are in this day and age – you might think of it as simply guidance and cooperation. When someone is working with e.g. a yoga instructor and the instructor tells them to adopt a certain position, they may not think of their result as compliance or obedience to an authority.

More likely than not, they might consider themselves as willingly going along with their instructor's wishes. Either way, the result is the same: the instructor sets the frame for the coming experience and the client respects, accepts and anticipates this.

Hip Twist

Introduction

This remarkably simply response routine can be a matter of some controversy. That is because it heavily relies upon physiological effects, like a number of routines in this section. I will discuss the pros and cons of this feature in the commentary following the transcript.

It is essential to begin by asking your client if they have any issues with mobility ("or anything else")[10] in their arms, hips, shoulders, back or neck. To begin, have your client stand upright, with their feet together.

Transcript

> Let's start by having you stick your arm out in front of you like this, thumb-up, in case you're hitch-hiking or something...
>
> [Demonstrate by standing next to, or in front of, your client and sticking your arm straight out in front of you. Have you fist closed, but your thumb pointing upward.]
>
> Now, on the count of 3, go ahead and move your arm round in a clockwise direction, as far as you comfortably

10 Personally, I say, "You don't have any issues with mobility or anything else in your..." I do *not* say "any issues with mobility or pain..." as there is no need to give any cause for concern or pre-emptive anxiety if it does not apply.

can, without moving your feet from the position they are currently in. And when you do, keep staring at your thumb, like this...

[Demonstrate by focusing on your thumb as you twist your hip and move your arm round.]

Then, when you reach the point where you can not comfortably move any further, kinda make a mark on the wall like this, to record where you reached.

[Show your client what you mean by flicking your thumb up and down as if you are marking the wall beyond it. Then twist back round to your starting position.]

Okay, got that?

- "Yep."

So, go ahead and focus on your thumb and now move your arm round as far as you comfortably can...

[Wait till client stops twisting round]

Now, look past your thumb and imagine making a mark on the wall so you know how far you got.

Okay, now gently spin back round to the beginning and put your arm down. That's great.

Now, I would like you to close your eyes and imagine that your arm is still up in front of you. And now imagine that you are once again rotating your body in a clockwise direction, whilst staring at your thumb just as before.

And just imagine being able to move much further than before, without discomfort and with the greatest of ease and speed. As if it was possible, you can even see yourself turning all of the way round. Move even more than that.

Then, imagine spinning back to the beginning, drop your imaginary arm and open your eyes.

All good?

- [Smiles] "Yeah."

Great.

Now lift your arm up as it was at the beginning and repeat the exercise. This time, notice how much further you can turn, with much greater ease.

And when you've reached as far as you can without causing any pain, mark it on the wall. And see how much further you have got.

- [Laughs] "Oh my goodness!"

Look at that. Good for you! You can go ahead and turn round gently and put your arm down. Good job.

Commentary

I might tell my clients that this demonstrates that their imagination knew they were capable of more than they thought they were. I then congratulate them on having a powerful subconscious mind and say that I look forward to seeing what more they can do with it.

However, that is not the whole truth. This exercise may be well-known to physiotherapists of other body-workers. Even without the extra imagined twist round, most people will find that they can twist further on the second attempt. This may simply be down to warming-up the muscles and knowing what to expect.

Having said that, I have experimented with this routine. I have observed the difference between simply using two twists and then also adding the imagined/hypnotic elements.

There are a number of explanations I might give for routines like Magnetic Fingers and the Hip Twist, if I was caught out:

- You were subtly checking that they were willing to follow your instructions
- You were gauging how co-operative they were feeling today [In my opinion, it is better to phrase it this way than to say you were checking how "resistant" they were]
- You were starting with baby-steps to engage their imagination. However, they are clearly ready to just jump straight-in.

It's even possible to justify the first 'lie' with a second one!

> It was never actually about the hips (or fingers). Through all of that, I was actually watching your eyes and assessing how easily you can focus all of your attention on one spot. Not everyone does it as effortlessly as you do.

That then provides an easy way to move things up a notch.

> I think you are ready for the next step. Put your hands out like this [demonstrate the placement of the hands for Magnetic hands] and see what new experiences your mind can create for you, with or without the help of tendons (or muscle memory).

So, what do you think? Is there ever a justification for lying to our clients?

Balloon and Book

Introduction

This routine is sometimes known as the heavy/light hands test. It involves experiencing a levitation in one arm, which is contrasted with an experience of weight or fatigue in the other.

Transcript

> What I would like you to do is extend your arms out in front of you, like so… and you can place your left–hand palm–up, with your right hand facing palm–down.
>
> Perfect. And now just go ahead and close your eyes.
>
> And you can now imagine a huge helium–filled balloon tied to this wrist [taps slightly under right wrist], tugging at the arm. Maybe you can already feel the gentle pull of that.. That's it.
>
> And here on your left hand [tap the palm], you can imagine a heavy hard–back dusty library book... feel that weight on your hand.
>
> And as you feel the weight on your left hand, your right hand can feel like it wants to float-up with that balloon, up in the air.

Maybe go ahead and imagine 5, 10, 15 bright red helium balloons, rising up into the air, taking that arm with it...

As I place another heavy book on that left hand, getting heavier and heavier now, the right hand is floating higher and higher, floating upwards with those balloons. Now 20, 25 bright red helium balloons, swaying to and fro in the wind, floating higher and higher.

And as that right hand continues to rise, we can place another book on the left hand, heavier and heavier...

It might even seem as if one hand gets heavier as the other gets lighter. And as you become aware of one hand rising, the other lowers... and lower..."

[When there is a clear gap between the hands, you can proceed as follows:]

Now, you can open your eyes and see just how powerful your imagination is...

Commentary

The Balloon and Book routine is a wonderful example of utilisation. Like magnetic hands, this can be used as a natural advancement from magnetic fingers. This is because it partly relies on physiological elements, with added results achieved via suggestion and imagination.

The key is to observe how your client is responding and proceed accordingly. As one hand lowers – partly due to the natural fatigue of holding it in place – this is offered as evidence that the client is responding effectively and suggestions for the other arm to raise higher are offered.

Speaking of fatigue, this would be a good place to offer a tiny piece of practical advice, that you might find useful. (And if you don't, the alternative advice is priceless!)

As the majority of people are right-handed, they will tend to find it easier to keep their right hand elevated than their left. Therefore, their left hand is more likely to be the one that lowers. So, you just need to remember the incredibly simple phrase, "Left lowers, right rises." That reminds us to place the book on their left hand (so it lowers) and attach the balloons to their right wrist (which will rise).

Of course, it is not necessary to remember this phrase, or work on the assumption of right-handedness! You can begin instead by openly asking if they are right or left-handed. Then invite them to place their hands out in front of them.

They will usually extend their hands out, with them both palm-up, or palm-down. This gives you the opportunity to engage in what I call 're-posturing.'[11]

> You said you're right-handed?
>
> - "Yeah."
>
> Okay, then just turn your right hand over for me...
>
> [Demonstrate by showing your right palm facing upward and your left palm downward.]
>
> Actually, no, you know what? ...Let's try something a bit different...
>
> [If you have already established consent to touch, take hold of their hands and turn the right hand palm-down as you turn the left hand palm-up. If not, you could say something like...]
>
> Let's mix this up and do it this way...
>
> [Demonstrate by changing your hands, so that your right hand faces downward and your hand faces up.]

11 Others have described this as 'compliance testing,' or 'witch-doctoring.' However, I enjoy the ambiguity of 're-posturing,' with its various implications.

You then proceed with the routine as you usually would. This re-posturing does a few things.

1) It establishes compliance or co-operation, setting a pattern of successfully following instructions

2) It allows clients with an instinct to take charge to adopt a more flexible mind-set

3) It introduces an air of mystery, as you ask your client to switch hands, with no explanation as to the reason

4) Following from the above point, it suggests that something unusual is happening, as why else would you need the hands to be placed in a specific way?

5) It allows you to place your client's dominant hand in the position where it will be the one to rise and the weaker hand will be the one to experience fatigue and lower.

If this is the first time you have heard of the idea of re-posturing (or however it is termed), I commend it to you. It is a very beneficial little preparation tool.

EXERCISE

What do you think of the concept of re-posturing?

Can you come up with any extra benefits to be gained from it, besides the 5 mentioned in this chapter?

Begin practising re-posturing in your daily life, with everything from buying a coffee, to washing the dishes. Notice how often/rarely your re-posturing is questioned or challenged.

Stiff Arm

Introduction

This delightful phenomenon goes by a number of names: Stiff arm, steel arm, unbendable arm, arm catalepsy and arm bar. However, they all refer to the same basic occurrence. The hypnotist has the client place their arm out straight in front of them and tells them to imagine that their arm is so stiff that they cannot bend it.

Transcript

Hold your arm straight out, like this …

[Demonstrate by holding your own arm straight out in front of you, palm facing to the side (i.e. little finger is at the bottom, thumb is at the top.) Continue to demonstrate as you say:]

Good… now make a fist…

[At this point, tap or push against their first with each word you say]

Make it tight… really tight… tighter…

[Tap, push or grip the fist each time you say the word tight, to emphasise the word and the feeling.]

Good… now just imagine that that arm is made of stone…

with a solid iron rod right through the middle of it... and steel cabling all around it, encasing that stone solid arm. Imagine it is solid with an iron rod right through the middle.

Now imagine that this arm is so solid, that it is completely unbendable.

[Grip their fist as you say this, emphasising its solidity.]

Make it so solid that even if I really tried, I could not bend that arm.

[When they are demonstrating white knuckles, or their arm is shaking a little, attempt to bend their arm towards their chest. Do not try so hard as to cause injury, but it must be hard enough to feel genuine to them. No doubt they will use all of their strength to stop you bending their arm.]

That's it... and now I want you to imagine... make that arm so solid that even you could not bend it. When you know that you've made that arm solid enough that even you cannot bend it, go ahead and try... You'll see that the harder you try to bend it, the more solid it becomes...

[Wait and let them try for a few seconds. Then take hold of their arm by the wrist.]

Perfect! Now stop trying...

[Begin to shake their arm gently from side to side...]

And just let it go... let all the tension in the arm go... take a deep breath and let it all go... As your arm releases it all and you feel that wonderful surge of relaxation, you can open your eyes and tell me what that was like for you.

Commentary

One of the first things to comment on in the transcript above is that the hypnotist has the client hold their fist up, with the palm facing out (not downward) and their thumb on top.

Secondly, they tap, push, or squeeze the fist as they say the words "tighter." If this seems insignificant to you, I would invite you to ask someone to take you through the routine. I suspect you will find that this simple physical action gives an extra sense of meaning to the word and reinforces the suggestion.

Thirdly, just before you tried to bend their arm, you gripped their fist.

These three points may seem completely unnecessary and unrelated. Indeed, some hypnotists will not use any of them. However, you have strongly primed your client for success with these related subtle physical details.

When your client's palm is facing to the side (instead of facing down), it can be difficult for them to bend their arm without twisting their wrist, or elbow. Your final grip or push on their fist emphasises that they should keep the arm at the angle it is currently at. This makes a simple arm bend towards their chest feel slightly unnatural.

Eye-Lock

Introduction

The simple routine that I have come to refer to as "McGill's Eye-Lock" goes by a number of names. In many ways, it may be thought of as the first part of the Elman induction, without any of the additional steps.
However, it also includes a unique element, which whilst not completely necessary, does give it an increased degree of success.

Transcript

In a moment I am going to ask you to imagine a spot a couple of centimetres back from the top of your forehead, almost like you've got a window on the top of your head from which you're going to stare up at the ceiling.

[As you describe where the spot will be, you might gently touch the top of your client's head, to demonstrate where they should be focusing.]

So your eyes are going to roll up a little bit – don't allow them to get too uncomfortable – and while you have your eyes closed I need you to imagine looking up at that spot, through that, and then we'll begin this little thing.

[If you have been demonstrating where to look with you finger, remove it now.]

And take a comfortable deep breath… then as you breathe out let your eyes gently close and just imagine you've got that spot there on the top of your head and then simply allow your eyes to roll up as if you are looking up through spot, up at the ceiling.

Imagine your eyes rolling up, looking up through that spot, through the ceiling, up into the open sky.

Now as you continue to look up through that window in the top of your head. Start to imagine that your eyelids are becoming locked into position, as you focus so intently with all of your interest and imagination on that scene you can see through the top of your head. Keep your eyes engaged on looking through that spot, your eyelids locking into place to enable you to do that.

Imagine it so that as long as your eyes are fixed and looking up through that window in the top of your head then your eyelids are comfortably locked into position to the point where even if you tried to open them you couldn't... because you are so focused on looking up, looking through...

As soon as you sense that your eyelids are locked because your eyes are fixed looking through that window, focus on that scene above you and find that your eyelids are locked and sealed into position... try to open them and realise you can't at the moment, because you are enjoying the experience of looking through the top of your head and focused on that…

And the harder you try to open your eyelids – whilst looking through that window – the more locked your eyelids become...

Commentary

This transcript is far more involved than it needs to be. More on that later.

As you will no doubt have noticed, the unique extra element with this routine is the act of imagining your client is looking through the top of their heads. This obviously causes the client to roll their eyes back into their head. Such positioning makes it all but impossible for them to open their eyelids very far without bringing the eyeballs back down.

There are just a few things to note about this.

Firstly, if you wait too long, your client is likely to try extra hard and either strain their eyes, bring their eyeball down, or find some other way of forcing their eyes open.

Secondly, if you wanted to use this routine therapeutically, you could have your client look through the top of their head and 'up' into a uniquely special or relaxing place for them (e.g. sitting in a garden, resting on the beach, swaying in a hammock, etc.). This can then be utilised later in your work together.

Thirdly, the version of the eye-lock presented here relies upon a process that I will describe later in the book: *the Chain of Command.* As you will see when you read up on that principle – and you really should – this whole routine could have been achieved as easily as:

> Imagine there is a window in the top of your head. Now, close your eyes and look through that window. See what you see. Really focus on that scene. And don't stop doing that until I say, "release."
>
> And, now, whilst still looking through that window, try and open your eyes and find that you can't...
>
> Now, "release..."

I have also seen another hypnotist achieve the same result more quickly by having someone imagine they are flying through the top of their head into their perfect place. Then, whilst they are flying, they can try in vain to open their eyes.[12]

Finally, the key with the eye-lock as a Response routine is to provide you leverage you can build upon. If the routine does not work as expected, that is almost always simply because your client did not understand your instructions, or chose to disregard them (for some reason you can have fun unpacking later on!).

If the eyes do appear locked, you can then proceed from there. You might say,

> Great. That demonstrates how skilled you are with following instructions that are good for you...

Or:

> Perfect. That shows us that your imagination is powerful enough to effect your experience...

And then you might naturally flow into a more involved routine, or something that feels like a natural step-up, such as the Stiff Arm. Alternatively, unless it nullifies anything you have previously told them, you can expand the routine into an induction.

This would then just proceed as if had been intending to do the e.g. Elman induction all along:

> Perfect! Now, you can simply stop trying, let yourself relax and let those eye-lids rest and stay comfortably shut.
>
> Of course, the secret – just between you and I – is that your eye-lids have been relaxed this whole time. The rest of your face (and maybe your conscious mind) was trying to get them to open, but they were so engaged with imagining looking through the top of your head, that they were like,

12 With such an approach, it is important to be aware of how long your client has been looking 'up,' with their eyes rolled-back. If you leave it too long, you risk uncomfortable eye fatigue or strain.

> "Nope, I'm good. I'm just gonna stay here like this."
>
> It was as if they were comfortably chilling on a hammock, while the rest of you was trying to force them to open!
>
> [This is said with a smile on your face, which the client will be able to hear, even if they are unaware of doing so.]
>
> So, now, that quality of relaxation you are allowing in your eyes is the quality of relaxation I'd like you to let yourself enjoy throughout your entire body. So take that same quality, bring it up to the top of your head... And send it down through your body from the top of your head to the tip of your toes. Let go of every muscle. Let go of every nerve. Let go of every fibre... And let yourself drift much, deeper, relaxed. You got it.

Additionally, you could treat the eye-lock as an induction in itself. Ormond McGill was a famous Magician and Stage Hypnotist from the last century. He had a very authoritative style. If he saw a subject failing to open their eyes, he might there and then tell them to "forget about your eyes now. They are closed so you can go to sleep. Go right ahead and go to sleep."

I will confess that such an approach does not come naturally to me. However, you are welcome to learn from that, if it appeals to you.

Teapot Test

Introduction

The 'Teapot Test' was first devised by Patrick McCarthy. When he shared his protocol with the professional community – to analyse and improve it – he wrote:

> Expectancy has often been declared to be the single most important factor in the success or failure of any hypnotic intervention. Given this truism that expectancy is so crucial, this article shows how a potential patient's expectancy can be influenced and lowered or raised by the words and actions of the therapist. The essence of this innovative, simple, and quick method is that it is an expectancy-enhancement procedure that masquerades as a hypnotisability assessment. What makes this method powerful is the author's emphasis on the theatrical components of therapist performance (it even includes acting instructions). No one fails this test.[13]

To begin the 'test,' ask your client to sit back in the chair, make themselves comfortable, and close their eyes. Then ask them to imagine they are in their own kitchen.

---

13 *International Journal of Clinical and Experimental Hypnosis*, Volume 66, 2018 - Issue 3.

Transcript

I want you to imagine that you are picking up the kettle or jug … and taking it to the tap. Turn on the tap. SEE the water pouring from the tap, into the kettle.

As the water pours into the kettle, LISTEN to two distinct sounds. The sound the water makes as it leaves the tap, and also the sound the water makes as it fills the kettle. Then notice the kettle getting heavier with the weight of the water as you FEEL the weight of the kettle filling.

When there's enough water in the kettle, turn off the tap. Notice if the tap makes a noise or a squeak as you turn it off, or if it is silent.

Then put the kettle on to boil.

Now CHOOSE a cup. Any cup. It can be any size of cup, any shape, any weight and texture. It might be your favourite cup. Or your least favourite cup. NOTICE the shape of the handle. It might be semicircular shaped or shaped like the letter D, or it might be more like a question mark. HEAR the sound the cup makes as you put it down on the bench-top.

Then open the fridge and take out the milk container. NOTICE the kind of milk container—it might be cardboard or plastic—and how full it is. It might be full, half-full, or almost empty.

HEAR the sound of the warming noises coming from the kettle. Then get out a teapot, and into the teapot put tea leaves or tea bags, whichever you prefer.

HEAR the sound of the kettle boiling now, and SEE the steam coming out of the spout. Then, carefully, pick up the kettle and pour the hot water into the teapot.

FEEL the way the wrist moves as you tip the water in.

SEE the steam rising from the teapot. Then put the kettle back down and put the lid on the teapot and wait for it to infuse and become ready.

Then off to the RIGHT ... SEE a bowl of fruit. At the front of the bowl there are two oranges and a banana. And at the back there is a lemon.

Pick up the lemon and NOTICE if the lemon is completely yellow or still has some green colour. FEEL the lemon and notice if it is a smooth, shiny-skinned lemon or whether the variety you have chosen is more crinkly in texture. NOTICE the shape of the end of the lemon. Some lemons are rounded at the end, others have a little pointed bit at the end.

Now SMELL the lemon. Notice the tangy, citrusy, lemony smell. Then take the lemon over to a chopping board and CUT the lemon in half.

SEE the spray of juice in the air.

And SMELL the lemon more clearly now.

Pick up half of the lemon and SEE the cut, wet, glistening surface of this juicy, juicy lemon.

Bring the lemon up to your nose and SMELL that lemon smell more clearly. Then BITE into the lemon and TASTE the lemon juice.

Now pour some tea into the cup. You can add milk or sugar to taste, if you want. Take a sip of the tea and wash away the TASTE of the lemon.

Notice the TASTE of the tea and FEEL the WARMTH of the tea. Take another sip of the tea. Then OPEN your eyes, and let's talk about your experiences.

Commentary

The bulk of this commentary will be devoted to the questions that the hypnotist asks after the 'test' – and how they respond to the answers given.

The enthusiasm and excitement of the hypnotist is a crucial aspect of this exercise. There needs to be plenty of smiling, affirmative encouragement and non-verbal communication of pleasure. Every reply should generate excitement, no matter what the client says.

Post-test Questions

Following the test, the first question the hypnotist asks is:

> Could you SEE the things that I described?

If the client says, "yes," then smile and say something along the lines of, "Visualization - excellent. Well done."

If they say they could *not* visualize the household scene (which is rare, though not unheard of) do not presume that this is resistance or proof that hypnosis will not work. McCarthy responds to this 'failure' to visualise, by stating:

> Wow. That's impressive! What some would consider to be a very simple and basic memory and imagination assessment, yet your subconscious and conscious mind chose not to see those common items.
>
> Obviously, your conscious mind knows what a cup and a lemon look like, of course, but for some powerful reason your subconscious mind chose today to not visualize them.
>
> This is actually *really* interesting. That often means that your subconscious for some reason has a powerful and strong need to be in control – at the moment – and not to be told by someone what to think. I'm so glad I found that

> out today. It protected you, even though I'm sure that you wanted to see the cup and the lemon.
>
> That's a really impressive defence. Your subconscious now knows that I understand and appreciate and respect that. When I teach you the type of non-controlling hypnosis that I now know will help you, just raise your right hand if for any reason you ever feel that you are starting to not feel or be in control. We'll stop and change tack at that point.

According to McCarthy, no hand has ever risen during the ensuing session.

> Could you HEAR the sounds? The sound of the running water or the kettle boiling, for instance. Did you imagine in your mind those very familiar sounds?

If they say, "yes," you smile and say, "Auditory awareness – excellent. Well done."

> Could you get a sense of the FEEL of the cup or the lemon, it's texture or perhaps the weight of the kettle?

If they say, "yes," smile and say, "Kinaesthetic awareness – excellent. Well done."

> Could you SMELL the lemon?

If they say "yes," then smile and say, "Olfactory awareness – excellent. Well done."

Some people may struggle to recreate smells. Your first response may be to ask if they have any nasal allergies or smell problems. If they say, "yes," then smile and tell them that explains why they did not get the smell easily.

If they say, "no," then I smile and say something like, "Between you and me, this is the least important skill to employ - and not one that we will need to help you today."

> Did you get the TASTE of the lemon or the tea?

If they say, "yes," I smile and say, "Gustatory awareness – excellent. Well done."

Some people will not get the taste of the lemon but *will* get the tea. In that case, I smile and say, "Wonderful! You were able to choose to experience the pleasant suggestion of tea and to discard the unpleasant one of lemon. Fabulous control!"

No matter what response they give to the modalities of visualization, auditory, kinaesthetic, olfactory, and gustatory, I smile and explain that their answer makes them very suitable for hypnosis.

Dissociation Proneness

The next part deals with what McCarthy labels, 'dissociation proneness.' He asks his client if they experienced the scene in the first person or third person.

> Did you see your hands holding the kettle and cup, or were you detached and watching your whole body carrying out the instructions?

If they indicate first person, smile and say, "Good, you were associated. Fully engaged." I then explain how some other people give a different answer, but the response that they have given is usually the best one for hypnosis.

If they say, third person or detached, then I smile and say, "Good, dissociated, highly skilled. You automatically and cautiously used this as a defence mechanism. You saw yourself carrying out these tasks while you observed from a distance. *She* picked up the kettle and the cup and the lemon and did the pouring, smelling, and biting. So only she could feel these things. It's good to know that you can choose to do that, because when we do the hypnosis I don't want to teach just *her* the really helpful skills and end up not treating *you*."

Compliance and Concordance

The next series of questions is about compliance and concordance. The hypnotist smiles and asks, using a presupposition:

> "How did you handle the mistakes I hope that I made?"

(Note the assumption of "handle" and the implication that mistakes were deliberate.)

Examples of mistakes might be that they normally put a teabag in a cup and may not even own a teapot. (In fact, as I'm writing for an international audience, I have to reluctantly accept that some people may even choose coffee over tea!) The position of the fruit bowl may be different from that suggested. There may not be the exact fruit in it that I suggested.

They can show concordance by, for instance, inventing a teapot, or having the teapot hover over their stove, or having a lemon in the bowl when they normally have lemons in the fridge.

I smile and explain that even when I get it wrong, they can instantly use their own creativity to cope with my story being different from their actual kitchen.

If they insist on using just a teabag or resolutely have the fruit bowl in the other direction, then I point out that this is non-concordance and shows that they have control and autonomy. If they don't like my suggestion for whatever reason, they are free to choose their own. I then point out that if this happens in therapy, they may even find it helpful to point it out to me, as I would not want there to be too much difference of shared imagery.

Conclusion

If all has gone according to plan, after this series of "assessment questions," you can then state something along the lines of:

> So YOU are great at visual, auditory, kinaesthetic, olfactory, and gustatory imagination. YOU are associated, which is good, and you are partially non-concordant for the taste of lemon. This gives me a great insight into how to deliver the best type of hypnosis that will work for YOU.

Thus, as McCarthy states, the Teapot Test really is an expectancy-enhancement procedure masquerading as a hypnotisability test!

I would re-read that last sentence, if I was you. This really is a uniquely beneficial tool that has a positive impact on the success of the subsequent hypnosis sessions.

With practice, it only takes approximately 5 minutes to go through, and – if carried out with theatrical gusto and enthusiasm – can significantly add to rapport and co-operation between hypnotist and hypnotee.

EXERCISE

Experiment with the tea-pot test, informing your practice-partners that you are not going to go all of the way into hypnosis on this occasion.

Re-read the test and consider the creative ways you will respond if your clients 'fail' at various points.

Is the tea-pot test a helpful tool for accurately assessing a client's current capacity to respond?

Styles and Approaches

Some hypnosis trainers will place significant emphasis on discovering the style of induction that is appropriate to your client. I will discuss the selection of inductions later in this book.

At this point, it might be helpful to consider the more general approach you will take, as a hypnotist, to the whole endeavour.

Authoritarian or Permissive?

For example, will you be adopting an authoritarian or permissive approach? We see the former with hypnotists like Gil Boyne. Erickson is, rightly or wrongly, often celebrated as an example of the latter.

Are you planning to give instructions, which your clients will be expected to follow? Or offer suggestions that they may or may not want to consider? Or a mixture of the two, or something altogether different (e.g. possibilities to ponder)?

Direct or Indirect?

These two options are related to the two I have just discussed, but not identical. For example, an authoritarian hypnotist could still give indirect suggestions, to support their more direct approach.

Below is an example of a direct suggestion, delivered in an authoritarian manner:

"Take a deep breath and close your eyes."

Whilst a permissive approach might sound more like:

"If you happen to notice your breathing, it is fine for your eyes to stay open or closed, as you continue to relax..."

However, in reality, things are rarely that segregated. It would not be unusual to hear an otherwise direct hypnotist saying:

"Take a deep breath now and when they are ready, you can let those eyes close."

Or you might hear a generally permissive hypnotist say something like:

"And as you allow your attention to shift to or fro, you may find it resting on your breathing from time to time. And I don't know if you will relax more deeply as you breath more deeply, or breath more deeply, as you continue to relax. But you can take some time to pay attention to that now..."

The point is that the most important idea may be to remain flexible, especially as you are starting out. You will see later in the book that I take a unique approach to deciding which style of induction to use. However, choosing which *approach* to take with your client is an earlier decision you will encounter.

My advice, for what it is worth, is to go with what feels right. I know how vague and unhelpful that may sound, yet it is advice I stand by. It does not take an over-abundance of intuition or empathy to know what approach *not* to use. (For example, a bullied client may not be able to ensure an authoritative approach.)

Beside that, it is important to be true to yourself. Personally, I could never act as authoritative as someone like Dave Elman, or Jon Chase. That does not mean I cannot learn from them, or incorporate elements of what they do. However, on the whole, unless the situation (or client) argues otherwise, I would suggest adopting an approach that most suits you, your personality, strengths. ethos, beliefs and so on.

As Richard Nongard writes:

> Your style is just that - your style. The more you practice, the more you learn, and the more you practice some more, the more your style will be refined and defined until eventually you don't really even have a 'style' any more to talk about; you just do what you do as necessary, knowing that it works best for you and your individual clients.[14]

14 Richard Nongard, *Inductions and Deepeners*, p. 21.

EXERCISE

In the previous chapter, I wrote:

'However, on the whole, unless the situation (or client) argues otherwise, I would suggest adopting an approach that most suits you, your personality, strengths. ethos, beliefs and so on.'

How do you feel about that?

Is such an attitude compatible with a client-centred approach?

Re-read the quote above from Richard Nongard.

How do you feel about it? Would you re-word it, or add a different emphasis?

THE INDUCTION OF HYPNOSIS

In this section, we will consider the purpose of hypnotic inductions?

Do we even need them?

And, if so, how do we choose which inductions to use?

I will introduce the solution-focused approach to the selection and purpose of inductions.

What does an Induction Do?

I have talked briefly about the nature of hypnosis, and I am going to move on now to look at the elements involved in effective inductions. However, it might be useful first to ask, what is the induction for? What do inductions actually do?

"They Increase Suggestibility?"

This is a very popular answer. And, if we are going to stick with an experiential approach, it's easy to see why. An objective observer may look at someone experiencing hypnosis and it may be as clear as day that after the induction they now follow suggestions that they would not have done beforehand. Therefore, it's a natural assumption that something about the induction increases the levels of suggestibility in those being hypnotised.

Yet, interestingly – given that this is one of the more common answers to the question I'm asking – the research does not particularly support it as a conclusion. It appears that formal inductions may increase suggestibility, but that even when they do, the increase is minimal. Irving Kirsch concludes that it is roughly 10%.[15]

Academics continue to debate the question of hypnotisability and suggestibility, with a number of studies suggesting that inductions are not needed to increase either. Other mechanisms such as 'task-motivating instructions,' role-playing or even simple relaxation have

15 Kirsch, *Essentials*, pp.33, 41.

been shown to sometimes demonstrate as much of an effect on suggestibility as a traditional induction. So, even when an induction does achieve that 10% increase, it may not necessarily be down to the induction itself.

So, what other reasons do people give for using inductions?

"To Get Someone Into Hypnosis!"

I don't have the statistics to hand, but I'm guessing that this is the most common reason given in answer to my question. It seems obvious that an induction is something that is done to get someone into hypnosis or trance. I've said elsewhere that my hunch is that this view is the reason why we see so many new hypnotists acting as if the induction is an end in itself, not sure what to do once they've "zapped" someone.

Yet, once again, there may be a further problem with this commonly held view. For, after decades and decades of scientific research, there remains no firm evidence of a distinct state that we can call hypnosis.

As we've seen, hypnosis itself is not a straightforward thing to define. So, we may well think that an induction is something used to get someone into hypnosis, but if we don't actually know what we mean by that, then what good does it do us? And if, as I've suggested, hypnosis is not something you go in to, as much as a transformative experience you go through, we need a more thorough explanation of the purpose of inductions.

Inductions Build Expectancy

Irvine Kirsch, whom we have seen is a firm believer in the role of expectancy, states that expectancy increases after an induction, before any further hypnotic actions.[16]

However, this is questioned by Margaret de Groh, who finds that 'subject's experiences during a hypnotic induction either support or fail to support preconceived notions of what a hypnotic experience "should" be like.'[17]

Therefore, it may be more accurate to say that inductions affirm or negate any expectancy previously present. There's no denying that an effective induction can confirm and increase the anticipation generated by a good pre-talk. So, an induction can perhaps be seen as an extended 'suggestibility test.' It serves to further convince the client that hypnosis is powerful and can work for them. Yet, can inductions create expectancy if there was none present? The jury seems to be out on that one.

I'd like to offer one of my favourite answers at this point, because it is related to expectancy, but not as commonly known. The British hypnotist Anthony Jacquin has been known to say:

"An Induction Technique is a Vehicle for Your Confidence, Your Persona, Your Intent to Hypnotize."

Jacquin is saying that an induction is a tool used to convey your intention to hypnotise. An induction is not just clever mechanics, because hypnosis is less about techniques and more about the client believing that you are *The Hypnotist.*

This makes perfect sense. As with the confirmation of their expectation mentioned above, an induction can be seen as giving the client reasons to make those shifts in their perception of reality. In

---

16 Essential, P. 40

17 Quoted in Spanos, p. 40. De Groh further states that, 'postinduction expectancies [alone] fail to even account for half of the variance in susceptibility scores, which is much less than one would expect from a cause-and-effect relationship.' (P.41)

this view, that reason is YOU.

That's a useful understanding, but I would suggest that it does not go far enough. As well as conveying your intention to hypnotise, a good induction can also convey *how* you want to hypnotise, how you view your client, what part *they will play* in this, what it all means and even more.

"Inductions Teach Compliance"

If you think about it, a number of inductions begin with actions like instructing the client to put their feet flat on the floor, inviting them to shake hands or telling them to stare at a spot on the wall. These behaviours, coupled with the expectancy-building spoken of above, teach the hypnotee to associate what they are experiencing with their obedient following of instructions.

However, I think I would still want to argue that we need more. As with suggestibility, it is possible to achieve compliance without an induction. Additionally, my assumption would be that if compliance is not there before the induction, it will not be there in any massive quantities afterwards.

And that's all before we even ask if conscious compliance is actually something that we desire. Getting caught up in playing a role, such that we have what Sarbin described as 'believed-in imaginings' is one thing. Just acting is something else altogether.

Do We Need Inductions?

Induction-less hypnosis is gaining popularity pretty much to the same degree that interest in *Street Hypnosis* is growing. When the focus is on quickly and reliably achieving phenomena – and we know (and the research confirms) that phenomena can be achieved without an induction – why waste precious time on something that may not even be necessary?

No doubt, many of my readers will be familiar with the idea of 'Street Hypnosis.' I would add suggest that an interest in Street Hypnosis – specifically the speed with which it achieves hypnotic phenomena – is one of the main reasons that we are seeing more and more people suggest that we do not need inductions at all.

The late Jeff Stephens – who had an approach to hypnosis that was nowhere near my own – once wrote:

> 'There is no such thing as hypnosis without an induction. The moment I engage another person's reality, to make it be what I want it to be, I have induced hypnosis.'

Simply put, however you begin the hypnotic process, that is your induction. So, in a sense, the most accurate answer to the question, what is an induction for, may have be: to start things off. And my feeling is that you may as well start well.

The moment you begin to engage another person's reality, to make it be what you want it to be, you have induced – or you have begun to induce – hypnosis. So, let's give that moment some credit. Let's not rush it, dismiss it, or discredit it.

It seems to me that engaging another person's reality fits quite nicely with the reality reframe understanding of hypnosis argued for earlier in this book. So, it would appear that Jeff Stephens and I may have shared a similar understanding as to the nature of hypnosis after all. Or it may be that we would have both stubbornly refused to give a definitive answer! Either way, the question of induction-less hypnosis seems to only come up in settings where the aim is to hypnotise someone to perform some phenomena or other. Yet, what if the induction was about more than something we did to simply get someone into hypnosis?

Some people say you need an induction to get someone into hypnosis, to follow your commands. Other people say you do not. I would say, that's all irrelevant. What if an induction was about more than something we did to simply get someone to follow your commands?

If you took an experiential approach to inductions, you would see that there are a number of things that inductions appear to achieve. Some of these I have alluded to already; some I will turn to in a moment.

Building Rapport and Expectation

An induction can be used to ensure you are both on the same page, to increase motivation, to get their imagination running a bit, to amplify expectations, thinking outside of the box together... How you begin can achieve all of that, so you may as well do it well.

Assigning roles

This would fit well with Sarbin's model of hypnosis, but it also includes Anthony Jacquin's quote on the role of inductions. You establish yourself as the hypnotist, but what kind? Through an induction, you can convey that you are the commanding hypnotist, to whom they will comply. Or you might demonstrate that you are a co-traveller with them, planning to explore new destinations together. How you view yourself as the hypnotist, and them as the hypnotee – and, in fact, hypnosis itself – can all be expressed through how you begin.

Frame-setting

I will turn to this in a moment. At this point, suffice it to say that however you begin with someone sets the frame for what is to follow. You set the boundaries, the parameters for what is to come. You express your intent and share through words and actions the kind of things that you will be doing together.

A Learning Experience

I will also look at this in more detail when I explore the concept of *Therapeutic Inductions.* Yet, this goes back to that essential question that I would like to tattoo on the inside of all my reader's minds - what if the induction was about more than something we did to simply get someone into hypnosis? The kind of things that can be taught through an induction can be as simple as, "I have the ability to relax," or, "I can do more than I thought I could." Or they can be as profound as realising that you can dissociate from pain and achieve analgesia.

To support the Jeff Stephens quote that I wrote above, I would add the following observation: the early stages of any conversation sets the character of the interaction that follows. And if that is true, to put it crudely, induction-less hypnosis may be the equivalent of trying to take someone to bed without even buying them a drink. In your eagerness to get to the action, you are skipping the stuff that actually counts. And that can be disrespectful, it can be a sure-fire way of guaranteeing that the action is anti-climatic, and it doesn't get you a second date!

So, do we need inductions? We have no choice. We have to begin somewhere. So, let's begin well and let's begin with bigger goals than merely getting someone into hypnosis.

EXERCISE

What is your view on the purpose of inductions?

Do you subscribe to any of the opinions on the purpose of inductions discussed in this chapter?

Has your opinion changed at all, or would you consider more experimentation as a result of this chapter?

Choosing your Induction

A Person-Centred Approach

A very common means of deciding which induction to use is to match it to your client's personality or place in the world.

The main problem with this approach is that it relies heavily on assumptions. For example, some people would suggest that you cannot be authoritative with someone in authority. However, it is equally true that many people in authority have a hard time respecting someone who is not. Similarly, if someone takes a generally passive role in life and their personality is quite placid, then it may seem obvious that they will respond well to an induction where the hypnotist is essentially telling them what to do. However, equally, they may react with disappointment at encountering yet another person who presumes they have the right to push them around.

The key with this kind of approach is to be flexible and respectful. Even in cases where you are taking control and performing what Charles Tebbetts refers to as a 'paternal' induction, you can do so with respect. (In fact, I might argue that it is especially necessary in such circumstances.)

The following suggestions relate to the style of the hypnotist, as much as the category of induction. However, do not get tied to such lists. Remain flexible and if it turns out that you've chosen the wrong induction or approach for the person in front of you, learn from it and move on. After all, that's exactly what you would want your client to do.

Passive, Relaxed or Easy-Going People

Obviously, a progressive muscle relaxation will be well-received by such people. However, be aware that they may be expecting more, particularly if they feel like all you've done to them is what their Yoga instructor does every Thursday evening! Yet, on the whole, almost any induction will work here. Gerald Kein is certainly correct when he suggests sticking to a 'maternal' or permissive style and to keep things flowing. That is key. Anything else may appear too abrupt.

Powerful or Successful People

There are two mutually exclusive approaches to take with people who are used to being in charge. They are simply: i) take charge or ii) give permission. If you are taking charge then you need to make it very clear that they must recognise your authority. Not all hypnotists will be comfortable with this, but if you are then use rapid authoritarian inductions.

If you do not feel that such an "I'm the boss now!" approach will work for you, then take the opposite approach and use permissive or indirect language. You can still do this fairly quickly, by tweaking something like the Thain wrist-lift[18] or using a confusion induction.

Analytical Types

Contrary to popular opinion, people who tend towards analytical thinking are no more difficult to hypnotise, but they may require a more creative approach. There is no need to be put off by their ever active minds. Instead, take comfort from the fact that they are regularly absorbed in their own analysis.

As above, either use an authoritarian induction - to give them less time to overly critique - or, if you have to use a slower induction, use

18 http://howtodoinductions.com/inductions/wristlift

permissive language or confusion. A useful approach is to teach them the skill of going into hypnosis, perhaps utilizing fractionation. The two most important points to make are a) it is wrong to presume 'resistance' from such people and b) they often need convincers.

'Subordinates,' e.g. Police

People who are comfortable taking orders are usually straightforward to lead into hypnosis. Common wisdom recommends using rapid authoritarian inductions with them, but my earlier caveat applies. My suggestion, especially in a therapeutic setting, would be to go for an induction that crosses a number of the categories and is quick, but not abruptly so. The Elman induction, Bandler Handshake, PHRIT or Rehearsal Induction are prime examples.

This is another group who may respond well to experiencing the induction as a learning opportunity.

Metaphysical / Spiritual

People in this category will often have excellent imaginations. A good pre-talk is useful for such types as they may hold certain fears or misconceptions regarding hypnosis. Be aware, that they often also seem to suffer from the need to try to help the hypnotist.

I tend to employ themes like "the power of your subconscious" and so on. Any kind of physical phenomenon is useful, from arm drops, to relaxation, to ideomotor responses. Once again, Elman works well, as it includes so much, though I have also found that a good My Friend John tale tends to draw them in effectively.

Types, Styles and Approaches

In his book, *Hypnosis: A Comprehensive Guide*, Tad James offers a chart to distinguish between your approach to your client (discussed previously) and your style of induction. I may not agree with all of his conclusions, or his terminology, but it is not an unhelpful chart to share at this point.[19]

Type of Hypnosis	Approach to Client	Induction Style	Type of Trance
Traditional	Authoritarian	Direct	Sleeping
Ericksonian	Permissive	Indirect	Waking
NLP	Authoritarian	Indirect	Waking
Elman	Authoritarian or Permissive	Direct or Indirect	Waking or Sleeping

EXERCISE

How to do you choose which induction to use?

If you were exceptionally skilled at one particular induction, would it be sensible to mould the client to that induction?

Or should the personality or role of the client be the deciding factor in which induction is used?

Or are both approaches lacking?

19 See p. 152.

A Solution-Focused Approach

In contrast to the person-centred approach, much of my hypnosis career has been spent on practising a solution-focused means to selecting an induction.

The following pages provide a number of questions or discussions that can be used to gently nudge things in a solution-focused direction.

This approach to selecting an induction is different to the person-centred one above and relies on a thorough commitment to the therapeutic purpose of inductions. Essentially, you want to ask yourself the following three questions:

1. What skills or resources does the client have that they need to access in order to reach their goal?
2. What frame of mind does the client need to be in to utilise those resources?
3. What kind of experience is needed to bring about 1-2?

These may or may not seem like incredibly simple questions to be asking. Yet, in my experience, answering these questions will provide the information you need to generate a solution-focused induction, specific to your client's situation.

The first step in becoming more solution-focused is simple. Focus less on what the client wants to get rid of or change and more on where they want to get to. So, when working with a client who has arachnophobia, you may want to adopt an induction that helps them establish the state of mind they want to experience when faced with a spider. This could be dis-interest, curiosity, relaxation or amusement.

"If Not That, Then What?"

It takes some practice to develop the habit of being solution-focused. The question, "if not that, then what?" can be a useful means to accessing the kind of answers you will find useful.

For example:

Client: "I don't want to freak out in an elevator."

Hypnotist: "If not that, then what?"

Client: "I'd like to be kind of, almost enjoying it."

Or:

Client: "I don't want to climax so early in bed"

Hypnotist: "If not that, then what?"

Client: "I want to finish at the same time as my wife."

Or:

Client: "I don't want to procrastinate so much"

Hypnotist: "If not that, then what?"

Client: "I want to make plans to do something and then do it."

Think about the types of resources and skills that someone would have who had overcome the issue your client is facing.

Now consider if your client has such resources – which you could tap into – or if they could begin to discover them during the induction. View your induction as a learning exercise, where someone experiences their preferred future now. After all, there's no better way to tackle a problem than from the stand-point of someone who has already conquered it!

"What Was The Key?"

I sometimes tell clients that usually the thing that resolves a problem for us is not an astounding revelation, or enormous change. More often than not, it is something quite small.

Now, that 'quite small' could have big consequences. We could be talking about the corner card in a house of cards here, but the point is that we do not need to figure out how to resolve everything all at once. Sometimes all we are looking for is that one thing, that first small difference that can have a knock-on effect.

One way to explore this is by asking your client to give you hints – "but only hints" – as to a possible solution. Alternatively, I may quite blatantly ask my clients to do my job for me. I might say to them:

> Now, if I came to you and I said [describe their problem in their terminology], and if you only had 5 or 10 minutes to help me – no time to get to the bottom of everything, you just want to pull on that thread, to get things moving – what do you think might be the key to seeing some difference here today?

You'll notice that although I am asking them to comment on me, my terminology at the end relocates us in the therapy room with the issue before us.

Quite often, you will get the response, "I have no idea."

Very often, that response is given because they do not have an immediate answer to mind and they feel like they are being rushed to answer. Or, they are in your office in a complete problem-focused state of mind and cannot even begin to imagine the key.[20]

There are some standard phrases that I use when faced with an "I don't know." I might use one or more of these, whilst I wait for an answer:

> "It's okay, there's no rush."
>
> "But what if you did know?"
>
> "Humour me. Pretend you know. What might it be?"
>
> "What might part of the answer be?"
>
> "If there was one thing, just one small change that could begin a larger series of changes, what might that be?"
>
> "If you had to guess?"

It's amazing how many people will be able to answer, given more time.

"Let's Talk About YOU!"

There is no reason that you cannot change direction during a conversation with a client and say something like:

> "Okay, we've talked about your problem, but I'd like to ask a few more questions about you. How would you like to be different when you leave this office?"

Or:

> "So, after that problem is resolved, I want you to imagine that you bump into someone who knows you well. But they don't know yet that the problem has gone, even

20 Alternatively, they may think that I'm asking them to solve the problem in one easy swoop. Not at all. Sometimes, the key can seem to be something completed unrelated to the problem.

> though they can tell something is different. What are they going to notice about you that tells them that problem is no longer a problem?

Making the Problem Impossible

A useful way to get more information on the kind of mindset your client needs to access can be ascertained by asking what would make the problem impossible.

Learning From Our Heroes

A similar approach for getting some idea of the mindset we are after is to ask your client to pick a role model. This is someone who responds the way that they want to respond in the situation.

Effectively, this is the exact same technique as the previous one. However, I have found it useful to switch backwards and forwards between the role model and the client. If you get lucky, you will even have occasions where they forget which person we are talking about and confuse their own reactions with their role models. And all kinds of fun can be had then!

One of the things that is useful about this technique is that because you are looking at the problem – and their response – in such minor detail, you can have minor revelations about changes that could already take place. This can include breathing differently, getting up and moving around, facing the problem, keeping focused and so on.

> So you say they do something called 7-11 breathing. Is that something you could learn?
>
> – "I already know it. I just forget to do it."
>
> Well, not any more, eh?

EXERCISE

Is a solution-focused approach to choosing an induction a new idea to you?

If so, does it seem helpful? Intriguing? Worthy of further consideration?

How easily could you incorporate this notion into the way you currently practice hypnosis?

Therapeutic Inductions

> 'The induction is both the vehicle and the route to the therapeutic end... Without a good induction there can be no good hypnotherapy.'[21]

I have already given some answers to the question, what does an induction do? However, I would invite you to consider the following less recognised answers, which provide the basis for a therapeutic approach to inductions.

I would assert in the strongest terms, that I am not stating that these are the correct answers. I don't believe that these are the definitive and unquestionable reasons why we use inductions. That's not really how I tend to think. However, these are the reasons why *I* use inductions as I do and they are the basis for the therapeutic inductions approach that I practice and teach.

So, I would invite you to consider them, with an open mind and look for those places where you can apply them to whatever it is that you already do.

Inductions are 'Therapeutic Frame-setters'

This approach views the induction as a frame-setter and an essential part of the therapy, not merely the gateway into hypnosis. This is so significant that I am going to do the thing that speakers do which I know can annoy a lot of people: I am going to repeat myself,

21 *Handbook of Hypnotic Inductions*, George Gafner & Sonja Benson, p.ix.

a little slower, to give the impression of great profundity!

The Therapeutic Inductions approach views the induction as a frame-setter and an essential part of the therapy, not merely the gateway into hypnosis.

As you will be aware, many schools of hypnosis have a working model that goes through something like the following steps:

- Induction [to achieve hypnosis]
- Deepener [to access a deeper state of hypnosis]
- Phenomena and/or Therapy
- Awakening

A Therapeutic Inductions approach proceeds on the basis that the induction is not something you do merely to get someone into hypnosis, where the real magic takes place. Instead, very often, the induction is all that you do!

Previously, I have defined hypnosis as 'an imagination-fuelled, creatively engaged, shift in a person's perception of the world & their relationship to it.' However, this process of enabling someone to engage with a reframed reality begins with the induction, if not before. At the very least, the induction sets the theme and frame of the therapy.

If this is true, then it naturally follows that the induction can not be separated from your therapeutic goals. You might say that the induction sets the ground rules – or even that it does the groundwork – for the therapeutic reframe.

So, if you have someone dealing with stress-related issues, it might make perfect sense to proceed with a Progressive Muscle Relaxation. Yet you might not use same induction for an athlete seeking increased motivation.

I should clarify here that when I speak of something being 'therapeutic,' I am not only thinking of clinical hypnosis. In fact, all hypnosis can be therapeutic. Even sticking someone's hand to their pint of Beer can teach them about the power of their mind and how to use that power to undergo shifts in their perception and experience of reality.

An Induction is a 'Reframe Ritual'

Reframing is the key to hypnosis, hypnotherapy and in fact, I would argue, all therapeutic work. It is essentially seeing and experiencing yourself, your issue or problems and your relationship with the world from a different perspective. It is considering a new reality and then evaluating everything in the light of that reality. As the beginning of that process, an effective induction allows the client to see a new world of possibilities opening up before them and within them.

For example, in most people's model of the world, their arm does not rise into the air on its own, unless they choose to lift it. Yet an arm levitation induction teaches them that the hypnotist can be trusted to guide their reality – and/or has the authority to direct it. It teaches them that they have untapped skills and resources of which they were not yet aware. It also demonstrates to them how quickly and effortlessly they can shift their focus of attention. It can then seamlessly move on to catalepsy, glove anaesthesia or other physical phenomena, making it perfect, for example, for someone learning pain control.

Jeffrey Zeig has stated that – and I love this quote and don't know why it is not more well known – 'Psychotherapy is at its best when it is weird.' The novel and unexpected can function as a cue to anticipate something unusual. In this sense, an induction acts as a 'weird' ritual to open up a whole world of previously unconsidered possibilities.

We are all capable of far more than we realise. The trouble is that we don't always know how to tap into that ability. It's all well and good telling women stories about mums who lifted up cars to rescue their babies. But unless you are going to go and stick babies under cars, how do they take those stories and act upon their untapped capabilities? A good induction enables us to access reasons and resources to transform our experience of reality. It can provide a trigger which allows our minds to make those seemingly instant switches (that often seem so spontaneous) when the right motivation, resources and opportunity converge.

I have worked with more than one ex-smoker who spent decades trying to kick the habit. Then they had one heart attack, faced a brutally honest doctor who told them the risk they were in, and they never smoked another cigarette. They always possessed this ability to quit smoking with the click of a finger. They simply did not know how to access that resource.

Seen in this way, the induction itself can function as a reframe ritual. It becomes a reason for things to be different, a resource to draw upon and a reframe for considering and experiencing new realities (as well as laying the groundwork for further reframes during therapy!).

I'm almost embarrassed that I used to use inductions just to get people 'under'! Yet, more than that, I am excited about the possibilities now before us.

A Learning Experience

When we look at solution-focused inductions below, we will see that the induction can be viewed as a means to learning what the client needs to know to move forward.

At times, this will be something that the client needs to be doing, that they currently struggle to do. At other times, it will be something that they do, but need to stop.

The induction, as a reframe ritual, becomes a moment of revelation, a means to access the resources needed to resolve the issue in question. In a sense, the induction becomes the click of the fingers, or the heart attack, that the smoker appears to need for them to make that switch in their head and stop smoking.

In fact, the induction can be a spontaneous learning event. Yet, it can also be a progressive means for your client to learn or access skills or resources that are needed for them to resolve their issue. This may be learning how to do something they do not yet know how to do, or learning what is needed to enable them to stop something that they currently do.

EXERCISE

What do you think of the 3 solution-focused questions for eliciting which induction – or type of induction – to use?

Can you think of other questions that might achieve the same outcome?

Does the therapeutic inductions approach seem beneficial or workable, in your opinion?

Do you feel curious, nervous, or excited about beginning to learn more?

INDUCTIONS

We turn now to look at 30 inductions that might be used to induce hypnosis.

These are transcripts of the inductions 'in action,' not scripts to be followed verbatim.

The benefit of approaching these inductions as transcripts is that they will each teach a variety of skills, rather than merely a series of steps to be followed.

Despite how rigid some of the following transcripts may seem, think of them as more like records of a conversation, more than a formula to copy.

The inductions are intentionally jumbled-up a little, rather than being categorised into groups, e.g. rapid, relaxation-based and so on.

The Elman Induction

Introduction

Dave Elman was born David Kopelman, on May 6th, 1900. He died December 5, 1967. As a hypnotist, Elman taught groups of doctors and dentists how to use hypnosis to relieve pain. His book, *Hypnotherapy*, originally titled '*Findings in Hypnosis*,' evolved from these teaching sessions with medical professionals. It is still widely regarded as a classic – and rightly so. Elman developed his induction to take people into trance in the shortest possible time. For this reason, it was considered ideal for medical professionals. The transcript below is Elman's, taken directly from *Hypnotherapy*.

Transcript

> Take a long deep breath, fill up your lungs real good and hold it for a second. Now when you exhale, close your eyes down... And let yourself relax. Get rid of that surface tension in your body, let your shoulders relax. It's ok to relax today.
>
> Now put your awareness on your eyelids. You know that you can relax those eyes beautifully. You know that you can relax those eyes so deeply, that as long as you choose not to remove that relaxation, those eyelids just won't work... And when you know that you've done that, hold on to that relaxation, give them a good test, make sure they

won't work... And notice how good it feels. Test them hard, it's ok. [pause] That's good. Stop testing, let yourself relax much more.

That quality of relaxation you are allowing in your eyes is the quality of relaxation I'd like you to let yourself have throughout your entire body. So take that same quality, bring it up to the top of your head... And send it down through your body from the top of your head to the tip of your toes. Let go of every muscle. Let go of every nerve. Let go of every fibre... And let yourself drift much, deeper, relaxed. You got it.

Now let's really deepen this state. In a moment I'll ask you to open and close your eyes. When you close your eyes, send a wave of relaxation through your body, so very quickly, you'll allow this physical part of you to relax... Ten times deeper. Just want it and you can have it. Let your eyes become open... Close your eyes... And really... Let go. Feel your body relax, much more. You're doing fine.

In a moment I'll ask you to open and close your eyes again. This time when you close your eyes, double this physical relaxation... Really let it grow twice as deep. Let your eyes become open... Way down... Deeper... Deeper... Relaxed.

In a moment we'll do it one more time... And notice how well it comes in this time as you learn how simple it is... At least double it. All right let your eyes become open... Way down... really let go. That's good. That's good.

In a moment I'm going to lift your right arm and drop it. Don't help me lift that arm... And when it drops down, just notice how much more, your body can relax very easily. [arm drop] perfect. Way down. Great...

Now the body's relaxed... so let's get the mind relaxed, that's really what we want to do. When your mind's relaxed you really can achieve anything you can think of, within certain restrictions of course. In a moment I'll ask you to slowly begin counting out loud, backwards, starting with the number 100. After each number, simply say the words, "deeper relaxed." After each number double your mental relaxation, let your mind grow twice as calm and still and serene. Now if you do this, you'll discover by the time you just say a couple numbers, doesn't take long, you've relaxed your mind so beautifully and so completely, you've actually relaxed all the rest of the numbers out. Want that... And you can have it quickly.

Slowly begin counting out loud, backwards, starting with the number 100. Saying the words, deeper relaxed... And relax those numbers right out of your mind.

– "100 deeper relaxed"

That's good.

– "99 deeper relaxed"

That's fine.

– "98 deeper relaxed."

Now you can let those numbers grow dim and distant, they're not important.

– "97 deeper relaxed."

And when you're ready just push them out.

– "96 deeper relaxed."

Now push them on out, just tell them to leave and they will go. Just let them go... And let them be gone.

...Numbers all gone ?

– "yes."

[Or, continue until yes is the reply]

Commentary

The Elman induction perfectly captures Dave Elman's understanding of hypnosis:

> 'Hypnosis is a state of mind in which the critical faculty of the human mind is bypassed, and selective thinking established.'[22]

It is rather unfortunate that, over time, the Elman Induction has been presented more often than not as a script to be followed, precisely and in an exact order.

Larry Elman (Dave's son) wrote a booklet in 2010 which challenges this approach. I thought that Larry's ideas were so helpful, that I later devoted a whole book to the topic of the Elman induction, promoting Larry's perspective.

Elman Jr. suggests that a script approach to the Elman Induction should be avoided for the following reasons:

1. Scripts do not show how or why something works
2. You lose credibility, as clients can tell you are reading
3. You can come across as insincere
4. Scripts do not prepare for the unexpected
5. You lose flexibility.

All of this is perhaps secondary to the fact that Dave Elman himself explicitly taught a *process*, based on a number of principles, with a specific goal in mind. He did not produce a script.

22 ibid., p. 26.

Tips

The role of eye closure and the consequent eye-lock plays a vital role in the Elman Induction. Eye closure, followed by catalepsy of the eye-lids is, according to Elman, 'the entering wedge' of hypnosis. This is because Elman understood that when you have catalepsy of a group of small muscles – in this case, the eyelids – you have a bypass of the critical faculty.

Having said that, the earliest difficulty you may encounter with the Elman induction is that you client opens their eyes following your suggestion that they stay shut. There are a number of reasons why this may happen.

Firstly, they may simply not have understood your suggestion properly. It is reasonable that they believed you expected them to try as hard as they could to open their eyes, so they did. They went right ahead and opened their eyes! This situation is easily rectified by saying something like, "Well done. You've demonstrated that you can open your eyes. As I said, you remain in control at all times. Now, I want you to demonstrate that you *can't* open your eyes. So, go ahead and close your eyes again and relax them so well that they are just too relaxed to open. And then demonstrate to yourself that you've relaxed them that well by keeping hold of that relaxation whilst you try in vain to open them."

A second reason that someone may open their eyes is fear. Despite a positive pre-talk, they may still equate not being able to open their eyes with being controlled by you. In that case, you can proceed with a more permissive version of the eye-lock, or use something other than their eyes.

Another issue that may occur involves the 'amnesia by suggestion.' Elman's preferred means of achieving this amnesia was by having patients count backwards from 100, relaxing more with each number, until amnesia for the next number is experienced.

Cal Banyan recommends counting up, instead of down.[23] Part of

23 See http://www.hypnosiscenter.com/free-article-elman-banyan-hypnotic-

his reasoning is that if you are counting down from 100 then people have a target – namely, the number 1 – to aim for. This may encourage them to keep counting, instead of reaching amnesia. However, if you count up then counting any further than a few numbers (as suggested by the hypnotist) becomes a futile endeavour, because the counting can keep going forever.

Despite Banyan's argument, I side with Elman in suggesting counting down. The main reason for my choice matches the argument of Larry Elman.[24] Counting up is an easy reflexive practice that it can be more difficult to stumble over. Similarly, counting down from, for example, 300 in groups of three may be too taxing a practice and encourage an over-focus on the numbers coming up next. Counting down from 100 is a good compromise that is neither too reflexive nor too taxing.

Having said that, anything can be used to demonstrate the blank mind expressed in amnesia. On rare occasions, some clients will struggle with forgetting the numbers, perhaps due to working with accounts, for example. In reality, this does not happen as often as is presumed, but it is not unheard of.

This is perhaps the most feared problem that comes up for people using the Elman induction, especially if they have been trained to approach it like a script. Thankfully, it is by no means insurmountable and there are a number of things that you can do if your client struggles to 'lose the numbers.'

Firstly, you may want to explore your terminology. 'Losing the numbers' is not a desirable description and perhaps provokes the concern that you will not be able to find them again. Preferable language might speak of 'letting the numbers go' or 'relaxing them away.'

Another approach is to use something as an alternative to forgetting numbers. You can have someone forget letters from their name, or how to spell a word, for example. (In my book, *The Elman*

---

induction.htm

24 Elman, H.L, (2011), *Blueprint of the Dave Elman Induction*, pp. 33-35.

Induction, I share a transcript of someone forgetting the letters of their name and also another of someone forgetting a word they often thought as part of their negative self-talk.)

More often than not, the issue with failure to achieve amnesia is due more to the congruity and delivery of the hypnotist, than the engagement of the patient (e.g. because they work in accounts).

Nevertheless, I have found that the approach used by Elman is a reliable and effective way to address the issue of stubborn numbers:

> Elman: [to doctors] Let me show you again the technique I use when the numbers don't disappear. I lift his hand and say, "When I drop your hand the lights will go out and you won't see any more numbers... There you are... The lights are out and all the numbers are gone...[25]

In effect, this is a slight pattern-interrupt, followed by alternative visualisation. It is fairly common that the reason someone struggles to achieve amnesia is not so much because of a resistance to losing the numbers, but because of a failure to fully understand your directions. In such instances, a different approach to the same goal is recommended.

As well as the visualisation used by Elman, you might have them picture numbers floating away on clouds, or numbers on a TV screen getting smaller and smaller, or further and further away.

Related to the issue of not fully understanding your directions, some clients will need you to be more explicit. They may not fully appreciate how amnesia is to be reached, or what it would feel like. So, I may at times employ descriptions like, "...the way that someone's name can be on the tip of your tongue, but you just can't find it..." or "Like when you know that you know an actor's name and you stumble around in your mind but you just can't grasp it. You know you know it, but right now it is just out of your reach, just on the tip of your tongue, but you can't quite get it..."

---

25 ibid., p. 113.

Finally, another approach is to adopt a more abrupt pattern-interrupt. This is especially useful if you suspect that their conscious mind has become too pre-occupied with keeping the numbers and resists letting them go. In such a situation you might choose to switch to something like a hand-drop induction, before carrying on with the Super Suggestion seen in the next section.

The Fake Induction

Introduction

The 'Fake–it–till–you–Make–it' Induction might be seen as a combination of revivification (seen in, for example, *the Leisure Induction*) and fractionation (see *The Fractionation Conversation*). This induction involves taking the client along a 4 stage process of:

1. Pretending to be hypnotised
2. Imagining they are hypnotised
3. Experiencing what it feels like to be hypnotised
4. Being in a hypnotic trance

Of course, in reality, the difference between those stages is one of degree, not kind, but it helps the subject to frame it this way.

The inspiration for this induction came from Steven Heller's excellent *Monsters and Magical Sticks (There's No Such Thing As Hypnosis)*. Some ideas have also been borrowed from Igor Ledochowski's "Act as if" induction (in *The Deep Trance Training Manual*), though his lacks the elements of explicit revivification, fractionation and conversation.

Transcript

You've never been hypnotised. Is that right?

– "Yes"

Am I right in thinking you're fairly sceptical about hypnosis?

– "Yes"

But you're happy to go along with a few things here, aren't you?

– "Yeah"

That's good.

Okay, what I'd like you to do is simply take a deep breath, in and out. Again, take a deep breath... [wait for out–breath, or full in–take] and relax.

That's okay, isn't it?

– "Yes"

And, you know, in reality hypnosis is little more than breathing and relaxing. So, you're half way there!

[Said jokingly, and client smiles accordingly]

Well, it sometimes involves imagination as well, so let's start firing that up.

Can you think of an occasion in the past when your mind has been totally absorbed in one thing, or has even drifted off and been totally absorbed in absolutely nothing?

– "Yeah, everyday at work!" (Laughs)

That's good. What does that feel like?

– "It just feels incredibly boring. Like I want to bang my head against the wall."

Okay, so that's why your mind drifts off... to escape. And

believe it or not, the experience of your mind entering that kind of day–dream state, is what we in hypnotic circles call "trance."

– "Okay."

And we probably enter a trance state of some kind a number of times throughout the day. We can be sitting listening to a Seminar and our mind begins to drift off. Or, we can be watching a film and get so engrossed in the plot, that we're willing to suspend aspects of reality for a few minutes, as we enter the world of the film and lose ourselves in the story. You might have driven somewhere, on a route you know well, and after a while, you can find your conscious mind drifting off. You go into a daydream like state. You've had that, haven't you, when you get home, or you reach a certain landmark on the way and you think, "how did I get here?" And it's interesting, because it's as if your subconscious mind takes over, whilst your conscious mind floats off into it's own little world, and you go into trance.

[Client nods]

Good. I'm not surprised here to hear that you have that experience. And I'm sure you'll have it again, aren't you? [Said whilst nodding.]

Yes, because as I said, it's a very common and completely natural experience to go into trance.

I bet that as you sit there listening to me go on and on about hypnosis here, you're probably getting ready to go off into a trance now, aren't you?! [Said jokingly. Subject laughs and says, "Yeah, nearly."]

Good.

In that case, what I'd like you to do take another deep

breath, in and... [wait for out–breath] out. And just do that a few more times. In... and out. And as you keep doing that, what you'll find is that it's actually relaxing you more than last time you did it. And, you know, with every breath you take, you become more and more relaxed, for the simple reason that you are getting more oxygen to your brain.

Now, I wonder if you could pretend to be a good hypnotic subject, for me?

– "Okay."

Good. I'd like you to pretend to be in a trance for me right now?

It could be when you're drifting off at work, when you're absorbed in a film, maybe gazing almost hypnotically into a log–fire, or looking out to sea, or entranced by fish...

– "Okay."

So, what would your body posture be like if you're a good hypnotic subject, in hypnosis?

– "I guess, relaxed? Kinda slumped."

Good. Okay, so just sit how you would sit if you were to... [wait for out–breath] go into trance... [wait for out–breath] right now.

[Subject shifts around a bit and slides down the chair a little.]

That's good

The interesting thing... is that even pretending, you're becoming deeper and deeper relaxed, aren't you?

[Subject nods]

You've obviously got a great imagination. So, imagine that you were just sinking, drifting... [wait for out–breath] deeper into trance... That's it... [wait for out–breath] right now. What would your face look like? Imagine how you would feel and how relaxed that would look when you're deep in trance.

[Subject closes eyes and takes a long, deep sigh]

That's good. And your eyes are already closed, because you're a good hypnotic subject, so that's how ready your mind is to slip into trance whilst you relax. And you might want to take another deep breath... and out. That's it. And you can do that a few more times, in and...out, becoming more... *relax with each breath.*

You can actually do one better than pretending you're in trance, you can actually experience what it would feel like if you were to really go into trance. Now. Good actors use a technique called "method acting" which means that they pretend to become a character from the inside out, they begin to think and feel and act as if they were that person. It's almost as if they are absorbed in that experience. So let's try a little method acting now. Can you just ... [wait for out–breath] slow your thoughts ... [wait for out–breath] right down, until they just drift and float by calmly and serenely?

[Pause]

Now, feel the comfort that that brings. Allow that just to... [wait for out–breath] sink in, to the point where no one could tell that you're pretending... they wouldn't know you were using your imagination... they would simply see you feeling the deep relaxation and experiencing what it feels like to be in that place. Enjoy the experience of trance all the way deep inside yourself.

[Pause]

That's good. I wonder if you can experience imagining that you are experiencing an even deeper trance now... Deeper down with each breath... So relaxed... And as you continue to relax and enjoy that sensation, your mind can drift deeper and deeper into trance. And as you drift deeper and deeper into trance, you relax more and more as you sink down into the depths of calm, peace, serene tranquillity.

And if we were really doing hypnosis here and you were... [wait for exhalation] reeeeaally going… to... [wait for exhalation] go deep into trance, what you would do now is create in your mind a mental image of a grand staircase; a grand staircase that either curves to the left or curves to the right... It has a grand banister with ornate artwork.

[Proceed with Deepener]

Commentary

The Fake Induction works along the same lines as *My Friend John* and *The Fractionation Induction.* With My Friend John, you describe an induction and as the client indirectly takes on board the suggestions they find themselves slipping into trance. The Fake Induction is similar, but allows the client to imagine what they would experience if they were in trance. Unsurprisingly, they begin to experience the same sensations. After all, it's difficult to pretend to relax, without actually relaxing.

Tips

As with the Fractionation induction, you lead them gently to experience successive stages of a relaxing trance. It is completely up to you how you go about this. In the example transcript, I began with some revivification, which meant that the subject was fairly ready to enter trance as soon as they began 'pretending.' If they had not been so close, I might have split the stages up more, asking them how they thought their breathing would change, if their eyes would be open or closed and so on.

Beginning by having them think about an earlier occasion when they zoned-out gave them somewhere to head – and something to re-live – when they began pretending.

I knew this client, so had a good idea about how they relaxed in everyday life. I also knew that they spent hours unwinding by tending their fish-tanks, hence the mention of gazing at fish. As I spoke of how they would pretend, I put of lot of emphasis on visual and felt experiences. This matched their earlier description of how they relaxed.

Progressive Muscle Relaxation

Introduction

Progressive Muscle Relaxation (PMR) is a popular tool of hypnotists and therapists across the globe. Essentially, PMR is a simple, and influential, method of systematic and progressive deep muscle relaxation.

In more recent years, it has been criticised by some hypnotists who favour rapid or instant inductions. However, it seems to me that they may have simply underestimated the value and healing power of relaxation. It is the tendency of some contemporary hypnotists to dismiss the PMR – along with its unique value – that has compelled me to devote a chapter to it here.

In 1929 the Chicago physician Edmund Jacobson published the book *Progressive Relaxation.* In it he describes a method by which awareness of muscle tension can be heightened. Research conducted by modern neuro-psychologists shows that most people tend to underestimate the depth of muscle relaxation which they can attain. Jacobson's original method places emphasis on a slow, disciplined development of muscle tension awareness, providing a powerful weapon against stress symptoms. The transcript presented here is a more modern approach based upon his basic observations.

As well as deepening physical relaxation and heightening our awareness of areas and levels of tension, this technique reliably elicits the 'relaxation response' and effects a more general state of mental and emotional calm. The basic procedure may take a few attempts to get used to but once it is mastered the muscles can be relaxed more rapidly providing an ideal basis for other relaxation techniques, visualisation, or self-hypnosis.

Transcript[26]

What we are going to do today is go through a simple – and surprisingly effective – process of relaxation.

So, all you need to do to begin is simply make yourself as comfortable as you possibly can.

[Client shifts slightly in chair]

And, yep, it's okay to adjust your position at any time, to get even more comfortable.

This simple process we will be going through is often referred to as a Progressive Muscle Relaxation. And it is precisely that. We will gradually and increasingly relax the muscles in your body and – as a wonderful consequence of that – you will find your mind relaxing also.

Maybe you want to start by taking a nice deep breath in and out. As you breathe-in, just imagine that you are breathing-in peace and calm. And as you breathe out, you can let go of any stress and tension.

[Client breathes in] Peace and calm…

[Client breathes out] Letting go of stress and tension.

And you can do that a few more times. If you find it more comfortable to close your eyes as you do so, feel free to do that [that's it]… Letting go of stress and tension.

Now, as you continue to relax, maybe you can draw your attention to the muscles at the top of your head, the

26 The example seen in this transcript was inspired from a number of sources.

muscles in your brow, the muscles along your eyes, your temples, your cheeks… and simply notice, then let go of any tension in the muscles of your face or in the top of your head.

Notice especially any tension in your jaw, where we can carry so much of the stress of the day… and as soon as you notice any tension there, you can let it go.

As you relax even more… you may have already noticed how rhythmic and calm your breathing is becoming… And that's a good thing.

As you enjoy allowing your body to experience this state of relaxation, it is perfectly natural to let the mind wander and think of anything that brings you calm and relaxing thoughts.

Continuing to move down your body now, relaxing the muscles in your neck, along your shoulders, and in your upper back… Allowing the tension to simply fade and in time to disappear.

As you focus on your shoulders and back muscles, you may notice any tension there... or you may feel those muscles flex as you become aware of them. Now, let that tension just melt away.

Let your shoulders slouch as you relax those muscles… and notice how you sink deeper into that chair, as you relax even more deeply… noticing how easy and regular your breathing has become now.

It may even seem as if you can feel tension or stress from the muscles in your upper back and in your shoulders and in your arms begin to move down to your forearm and through the hands and out the fingertips.

In your mind, you can picture all of the stress of the day...

leaving your body... as you relax now.

Pay attention to the muscles in your chest and stomach... and in your lower back.

If any of these muscles are tense – or become tense as you focus on them – simply let go of that tension. Let it out and notice how good that feels.

Your muscles becoming limp and loose... as you experience the calm and peace spreading throughout your body.

As your body becomes more and more relaxed, your mind becomes increasingly relaxed, as well.

As you next breathe-in, gradually tighten all the muscles in your legs, from your feet to your buttocks. Do this in a way that feels natural and comfortable to you. Hold it… and as you breathe out release all those large strong muscles. Enjoy the sensation of release as you become even more deeply relaxed.

Sometimes the tension of the day can be stored in the muscles along the hip or buttocks or in your upper leg.

If you still notice any tension in those places, let that tension simply flow from the top of your leg though your calves and through the muscles of the feet and ankles and out through your toes.

And you can allow yourself to thoroughly enjoy this experience of deep relaxation. In this state, we can feel tranquillity and peace, feeling at ease with ourselves.

From the top of your head to the tip of your toes, you have allowed yourself to become completely and totally relaxed.

Your mind also has the capacity to relax. And I am sure you will already have begun to experience some of that.

This simple process is teaching you skills – at a deep, deep level – that you will be able to apply in a number of different areas in life.

Your body is now loose... and limp... and heavy... and relaxed... Notice how your body is sinking even deeper into relaxation.

And now, simply to reinforce what you have already achieved, you can imagine a wave of relaxation slowly spreading through your body beginning at your head and going all the way down to your feet.

Enjoy that feeling. Rest in that experience for a moment.

[Pause]

As you allow your entire body to be – and increasingly become – limp and loose and feel relaxed, you can recognise the gift that you have given yourself in this time.

You have gifted yourself a new skill and a valuable resource – the ability to positively influence your own body and emotions.

[Proceed to deepener...]

Commentary

The Progressive Muscle Relaxation is a classic hypnosis induction. It is also one of the first inductions many hypnotists learn. There are a couple of reasons for that:

- It's easy to understand the principles and deliver
- It works very well for a great deal of people

This is a non-threatening induction for beginners to learn. However, it is also non-threatening for the client. After all, who doesn't want to learn how to relax?[27]

Some people teach that the PMR works because it allows clients to relax their minds, as a consequence of relaxing their bodies. The client's mind is then more likely to let down its (metaphorical) guard and become open to suggestions.

This does not mean that relaxation and hypnosis are necessarily the same thing. Yet, it does seem the case that people who are relaxed find it easier to slip into hypnosis.

There's a sense in which this may be accurate. An example I sometimes use is that if one of my children came up to me and said, "Dad, can I have £10?" I might say, "What for?" However, if I was either deeply engrossed in a movie, or melting with bliss as someone massaged my shoulders, I might be more likely to simply say, "Yeah..." and even hand the money over without really thinking about it.

This might highlight an aspect of Progressive Relaxation that can be taken for granted. Deep relaxation – especially of the sort that one enters gradually, thus actually feeling ourselves relaxing – is an experience of intense focus and absorbed awareness. So, the movie and the massage may not be that far apart.

Typically, a PMR induction will not simply talk of relaxing, or of tension leaving your body. It will often include suggestions like, "the stress of the day leaving your body," or, "letting that tension that has built-up simply melt away." It may sound as if the focus is solely on the client's body, but these suggestions reference internal states as well. In that case, a well-delivered PMR provides an experience of physical and internal absorption. Is it then any surprise that many people find it an effortless way to enter hypnosis?

We shift the client's focus from their external world, or the issue that is bothering them, to their physical and inner world. Would it be

27 You may encounter some clients who insist that they cannot relax. In that case, I might opt for the *Tension Observation* variation of a PMR seen later in this book. I would also use synonyms for 'relaxation' and 'relax,' not the actual words themselves.

accurate to describe this as moving them from a problem trance to a more resourceful state? If so, then not only are we teaching them how to physically relax, we are also potentially passing on the gift of psychological fluidity, paving the way for further therapeutic work.

Tips

Despite a recent dip in popularity, in my opinion a PMR is still a great induction to use with clients, as it teaches them the process of relaxation that they can take away with them. It is pretty much the definition of a therapeutic induction.

I am sure this goes without saying, but the more relaxed you are as you deliver this induction, the more relaxing it will be for your client. It can help to almost feel yourself slipping into trance as you perform this. At the very least, your relaxed demeanour will be evident in your voice, inviting your client to follow you.

At first, it can be tempting to go through this too quickly. That's a common issue, but something that is easily overcome with practice. In the meantime, try timing your breathing to match your client. Try speaking – particularly if making any kind of command or suggestion – on their exhalation.

However, there are various ways to practice a PMR. Some hypnotists will have their client tense and release each individual muscle in turn, spending up to 45 minutes inducing hypnosis in this way. Others prefer a more streamlined approach, possibly focusing on groups of muscles. They may get through a PMR more quickly in that way, whilst still relaxing the body effectively.

If you do opt for a quicker approach, obviously you will need to remember that if your client feels rushed or pressurised in any way, this is likely to have an effect on how relaxed they feel. Nevertheless, it is certainly possible to hypnotise someone using a PMR in 5 to 10 minutes, particularly if the client has experienced it before.

Some hypnotists like to start the process at the top of the head and move down the body. Others start at the toes and move up. The benefits of the latter are that you are starting with muscles that are fairly easy to tense and then relax. And, of course, you finish up at the head, where you can speak of the mind relaxing. The transcript provided in this chapter moves from the head to the toes, which many people find to be a natural flow, perhaps reinforcing the feeling of going "deeper" into relaxation.

There are no hard and fast rules here. It would be beneficial for a hypnotist to be familiar with a variety of ways to utilise progressive relaxation. A version that can look quite different to this PMR can be seen in my later chapter on *Tension Observation.*

Incidentally, some practitioners may question how a hypnotist who spends 45 minutes relaxing someone has any time left for hypnotic therapy. My response is usually that a good hypnotist will have just spent 45 minutes doing precisely that. Like I said above, a good PMR is practically the definition of a therapeutic induction!

The Fractionation Conversation

Introduction

The following induction is my own version of Richard Nongard's *Fractionation with Discussion* induction. Richard's version appears in his excellent introductory text, *Inductions and Deepeners.*

My version of the Fractionation induction, is clearly inspired by Nongard's. I use his key elements, but have re–worded much of it and added a brief pre–talk that involves a number of embedded commands.[28] Having said that, as you'll see, the beauty of this induction is that it is virtually all pre–talk! (I've italicised some of these commands, but I'm sure you'll spot a few more, including spelling 'mistakes' and pronunciation 'errors'!)

Transcript

Before you experience hypnosis, I want you to experience what it feels like to be hypnotised before you actually *go into trance.* How is that?

– "Okay."

That's good. I'm sure you've had that experience when you're driving a Car and it's a familiar route that you know well. And after a while, you can *find your conscious mind drifting off.* You *go into a daydream like state.* You've had

28 We will have much more to say on this topic later in the book.

that, haven't you, when you get home, or you reach a certain landmark along the way and you think, "how did I get here?" And it's interesting, because what happens there is your subconscious mind takes over – but it's still you driving here.

In hypnosis, you're in a similar "day–dream" place. You know that feeling when you're mind is beginning to wake you up for work or school, but your body is still enjoying being fast asleep. And you sometimes hear people speaking in your dream, when it's actually the radio, or someone calling you to wake up. Once when I was younger – and lots of people have this experience – it was getting close to the time when I would be getting ready to go off to school and learn something new and in my dream out of the blue my Mum began calling me. And in the dream I was confused but I could hear my Mum's voice, even though I wasn't consciously aware of her being there. Of course, she was in the room trying to wake me up, whilst I was enjoying my deep relaxing sleep, but could still here her voice.

That's interesting, isn't it?

– "Yeah. It's like when..." [Client went on to give a brief account of a similar experience]

I'm going to make some suggestions to you as we go through this. The suggestions will be pleasant and peaceful and probably focus on helping you to *simply relax* and *enjoy this experience*. Sounds good?

– "Yep."

A friend of a friend told me about a colleague of hers who does hypnosis. They were at McDonald's when the waitress – who was a friend of their son – began talking to her about hypnosis. They hadn't *learn what you've learned* about the nature of hypnosis and wanted to know what it felt like. They said, "Close your eyes, for a second" and they did. And then they opened their eyes and she said, "That's what hypnosis feels like."

[Client laughs]

So, you're not going to turn into a zombie, or have some kind of mystical experience. You will always be in control. You will always be able to hear my voice even when you can't hear anything else. It really is the most natural thing in the world and we all *go into trance* and come out again and go into trance again, countless times throughout the day. So let's start, now.

Close your eyes. Close your eyes and keep them closed for 3 or 4 seconds.

1, 2, 3, 4. Open your eyes.

That's exactly what hypnosis feels like. Did that feel strange to you?

– "No."

No. It feels totally normal. It feels like you are sitting on a chair with your eyes closed, doesn't it?

"Yeah." [laughs]

Exactly. That's pretty much what hypnosis is going to feel like for you. Now I'm going to add some things to it here. I want you to close your eyes again and with your eyes closed, I want you to take a deep breath. So, go ahead and close your eyes... and take a deep breath.

Breathe in. Breathe out. And another deep breath... Breathe in. And breathe out. The amazing thing about taking a deep breath is that you are relaxing more and quickly increasing the flow of oxygen to the brain.

[Client nods.]

You can feel that already, can't you?

– "Yes."

It brings you to a state of physical relaxation. [Pause]

Now, open your eyes. How was that?

– "It was good. Relaxing."

Yes. *Relaxing.* Good. Now. I want you to close your eyes again. We're going to add a third part to it.

With your eyes closed... breathe in. Breathe out. And again... breathe in. And out. You can probably feel your heart rate slowing down, and your breath becoming more shallow.

– "Yes"

Yes. And as you *relax, with each breath* simply let your mind create a mental picture of somewhere you've been that was peaceful and relaxing to you.

Create a mental picture of... somewhere you've been and look at all the colours... and maybe the people if there are any others in your mental picture.

[pause]

Look at the scenery and the... world that surrounds you in that mental picture.

[pause]

If you are outside, you might be able to feel the cool wind or the warm air. Do you have a mental picture?

– "Yes."

Good. Open your eyes again. Tell me a little bit about the picture you created. What was the picture of?

– "A Beach, where we've been on holiday."

A relaxing beach. What did you become aware of in your picture as you pictured the beach?

– "It's quiet. Warm. Just the sound of a few children playing. Apart from that, it's completely peaceful."

It sounds safe and comfortable, as well.

– "Yes."

It's *relaxing just thinking about it,* isn't it?

– "Yes."

I bet that just... [wait for next time they blink] closing your eyes and taking a few deep breaths almost takes you straight back there, doesn't it?

– "Yeah, it's relaxing just thinking about it."

It's relaxing just thinking about it. It wouldn't be at all surprising to find that when you... [wait for next time they blink] close your eyes and take a deep breath you actually already being to float deep down into hypnosis. Would you?

– "No."

Creating a mental picture of somewhere we've been that is relaxing and quiet and warm and peaceful, can help us to *clear the mind of all of the stress and tension* that we are carrying around with us. ... [wait for next time they blink] That's good.

Another great way to relax is to let all of the muscles in our body go. In hypnotherapy we call this progressive muscle relaxation and people find that as they let go it really help them go into trance.

So you might want to just uncross your legs. Let your arms go. And just... [wait for next time they blink] *relax.*

Take another deep breath. Breathe in. Breathe out.

[Therapist has been blinking in time with the subject and now slows that down. As the client blinks slowly as well, say...]

That's it.

And as your eyes close... That's it... That means you are ready to *relax even deeper.*

Take a deep breath. Breathe in... and breathe out. Breathe in... and breathe out.

And as you do, your mind can open more and more to that peaceful and relaxing place you've been before.

[Client's head drops forward]

And as you go into that deeper and deeper process of [said slowly] re–lax–ation you might find your head tilting forward... and that's fine. That's just your body agreeing to your mind's decision to let go and relax.

As you create a mental picture in your mind of somewhere relaxing and quiet... somewhere warm and peaceful...I want you to *allow your body to experience a tremendous amount of relaxation.*

[pause. Wait for out–breath] That's it.

Feel your heart rate slowing. Feel the oxygen being pumped throughout your body. Simply let every muscle in your body go limp and loose.

[pause]

You can start with the muscles in your face, your temples... around your eyes...

Relax the muscles in the neck and back. Any where you feel tension, simply *let that tension disappear...* as you relax.

[pause]

Envision the sensation of relaxation in your body doubling with each breath you take.

Not only can the body... [wait for out–breath] relax, but the mind can relax, as well. And as the mind relaxes, the wonderful thing... is that it's impossible not to let go of stress and tension. You cannot be as relaxed as you are now and not let go of that. Breathing in relaxation. Breathing out any tension. Your relaxation doubling with each breath you take.

In your mind, *let your thoughts become absorbed* in the scenery of that warm, relaxing place that you have created.

[pause]

You will always be able to hear the words that I use, but as your mind becomes absorbed in the imagery you've created... perhaps you won't focus on the words that I use, but only those words that your subconscious needs to hear.

[pause]

As you relax, perhaps there are outside noises or distractions...if you hear anything... that keeps your mind from being able to focus on what is important and relaxing in that image you've created... simply use that noise as a reminder to bring your attention and your awareness back to the place of peace and tranquillity that you have created.

[pause]

This is hypnosis that you are enjoying, right now.

You could think to yourself, "If I wanted to open my eyes, I could." But you don't do that because it feels so good to simply relax... and *feel your mind and body...* become one, as you experience... *total peace...*

Commentary

Fractionation is the process of taking clients in and out of trance in order to deepen the hypnotic experience.

Each time a client returns back into a trance, they will go even deeper than the previous occasion. As a result, it is not always necessary to use a separate deepener with this induction.

If there was a justification for using a covert induction, the fractionation conversation can potentially fit the bill. You can make it obvious what you are doing, or you can simply start the conversation and allow your client to feel the hypnotic effects. Whether you stop before the deepener and simply say something like, "so that's sort of what hypnosis often feels like," or carry on with a deepener into a formal hypnotic experience will depend on you, your client, the setting and their outcomes.

One potential scenario for the covert use of the fractionation induction would be during a free-flowing pre-talk. If the client is engaged and has previously given their consent to be hypnotised, then the pre-talk effectively becomes an induction.

We will discuss fractionation in more depth later in the book (a number of times, in fact). Suffice it to say that it is a very effective hypnotic tool and this induction is a useful way to demonstrate that.

Tips

You may have noticed that the hypnotist adds an extra step that he does not mention. Speaking about experiences of 'trance' that the client may have previously experienced in their every day life, can be trance-inducing in itself.

Just as it is possible to talk about head-lice in such a way as to cause someone to scratch their head, it is not unimaginable that a hypnotist could describe a scary experience – or even simply the feeling of being afraid – so enticingly that a client would feel hairs rising on their arm, or a shiver run down their spine.

In this transcript, we see the hypnotist say:

> You've had that, haven't you, when you get home, or you reach a certain landmark along the way and you think, "how did I get here?"

This question already invites the client to think of previous trance experiences and possibly go inside to access the recollection of that feeling.

That would mean that when the hypnotist has the client close their eyes as the first step, it is actually the second. They have already, potentially, dipped inside.

One of the things that a transcript does not fully capture is the verbal or physical 'theatrics' of the hypnotist. With this induction, that can include the sense of 'flow' that the hypnotist helps generate. The aim of the induction is clearly not to merely educate the client on the steps involved in hypnosis. Instead, the hypnotist's intention is to progressively – and repeatedly – allow the client to experience going into and out of hypnosis.

When I am using this induction, as I move onto each new stage I make a gesture that conveys that we are continuing in a process. It can be difficult to describe, but imagine that someone is hesitantly telling you a story, unsure if they should say more and labouring every point that they make. Can you picture the sort of gesture that you might make to encourage your friend to keep going and keep talking?

That is the sort of gesture I make as we move to the next stage in the fractionation conversation. It's my way of expressing that these stages are not unconnected and that the client is in fact progressing through an experience.

I should perhaps be explicit about the fact that I make such gestures regardless of whether or not the client's eyes are open or closed. Do not underestimate what your client might pick-up on, regardless of their 'state.' And do not underestimate how much your body language is expressed through the things that you actually say and do, thus reinforcing both.

My Friend John

Introduction

This induction and deepener is a version of Milton Erickson's "My Friend John" method. As Stephen Brooks describes it, this is an induction disguised as an analogy about another patient. The hypnotist describes a hypnotic induction that has happened – or is happening – to someone else. As the therapist describes the induction, he directs embedded suggestions more and more towards the client.

The version of My Friend John seen here includes elements of dissociation and mild confusion, as the client shifts focus from my previous hypnotee, to their friend, to themselves and also from past tense and present tense.

I am so passionate about *My Friend John* that I have written an entire book devoted to the induction – and its flexible variations. You can find the details in the Bibliography at the end of this book.

Transcript

There are two common questions regarding hypnosis. The first is, what does it feel like... and the second is, how does it work. It's good to ask questions like that, isn't it?

– "Yes, I think so."

So, before you go on to be hypnotised, I thought I would

explain to you how I put other people into trance. Is that OK?

– "Sure."

And I think the best way to do this – so you can get a sense of both sides of the process that you're interested in – is if I describe for you how I hypnotised a friend just recently. And whilst I'm doing that, you can follow my directions and imagine that you are hypnotising someone else.

So, just imagine that there is someone sitting on that sofa in front of you. Form an awareness of how they look and how they go into trance whilst sitting there. And as I describe how I hypnotised my friend, you can pass on those instructions to your friend. You can do it in your mind, if you like.

I started by having them relax. So, what you can do is... tell them gently to relax... I say to them... Relax... let your shoulders drop... let your arms flop... imagine how the arms could just lie heavy and relaxed... as if they were made of lead...

And then I said to them... and you can tell your friend... let your legs relax now... just allow your legs and feet to be so relaxed that they feel heavy and totally relaxed now...

I tell them, focus on your breathing. In your mind... say to them... focus on your breathing... now... and with each breath out... you can find yourself... relaxing more and more... and each gentle breath will take them deeper and deeper... more and more relaxed...

Just focus on each breath... and allow each breath to make those arms and legs... more relaxed... and you might even wonder just how relaxed a person could get...

And in your mind imagine what it would feel like for them

to be so relaxed that they could hardly keep their eyes open... imagine them relaxing... [clients head began to drop forward slightly] head sinking comfortably... imagine how their eyes could be so tired that every blink gets longer... [wait for next blink] and the eyes stay shut longer... [wait for next blink] that's right... and imagine what it might be like to close those eyes... think what it would be like to feel your eyelids getting heavier and heavier and how nice it would be to allow them to shut and relax too...

Then I say, imagine saying to the person... and you might be able to feel the little muscles around your eyes... those weak little muscles that control your heavy, heavy eyelids... how tired they are... right now... and notice how heavy the eye–lids feel... [wait for next blink] ...that's right... and you don't need to close those eyes until you're ready to go right into a deep trance.

[Wait for eye–closure]… that's it. All the way… deeply relaxed… drifting down.

Then I said... focus on those little muscles around your eyes... the tiny weak little muscles that control your eyelids... and what would it be like to pretend that those eyelids were so relaxed that they just won't work. How would that look... if those eyelids were so relaxed, so at ease that they just can't open.

And say... focus your awareness on those eyes... and how it feels when those eyes just will not open... when it feels as if they are locked tight shut... and just will not work...

[Wait for next out–breath, saying at the same time:] Deeper down...

Tell them to imagine going down a staircase... I tell them to imagine (...imagine...) going down and down... with each step, becoming more and more relaxed... from ten to one... and as each number passes, they go deeper and deeper... more at ease.. more comfortable. So, I might count for them... and you might count... and you might count for your friend...

Ten, relaxing deeper

From the ninth step... to the eighth.

8, more relaxed, more at ease

From seven to six...

The sensation of relaxation doubling with each step... Allowing your mind to drift... And your body to relax.

Six to five...

Deeper... and deeper.

Five

Doubling the relaxation... with each step... [wait for out–breath] as you go further down.

Three...

Two...

One...

Sometimes, I might do that a little bit differently. With you...or with your friend... I might just say, with each breath you go down further and deeper. And you don't need me to count because with each breath you take, [wait for exhalation] now, your imagination is able to hear me counting inside your head. So, your first breath in [wait for exhalation] and out would be number 10. Your next breath [wait for exhalation] would be nine, and so on. And with each breath you take [wait for exhalation] that's right, you go further down that staircase... now... and as each number passes [wait for exhalation] go deeper and deeper... more at ease... more comfortable...

[pause]

Now tell your best friend to breathe slowly, and deeply, in and out... deeper and deeper.

And now... allow the mind to focus on the hands... allow the mind to become aware of the left hand and the right hand... what they are feeling... where they are... and allow the mind to choose one hand or the other hand and you might become curious as to which hand will be chosen... and when the mind has chosen...

One finger or a thumb will lift on its own... entirely without effort... or it might be a hand or a wrist or something else...

Tell your friend, that those fingers are lifting ever so slowly, ever so gently, off his lap [or wherever the hand is resting], and it is beginning to float all the way up.

And when that hand touches his face you will go into a very deep trance. You will hear everything that I say but you will feel so comfortably relaxed that you just want to sink deeper and deeper down into that wonderful feeling.

Commentary

As with The Fake Induction and The Fractionation Conversation, My Friend John is ideal for gently leading someone into trance. After all, with no obvious induction directed towards them, the hypnotee has no reason to resist.

My Friend John is simple and flexible, relying on good pacing and leading from start to finish. Each time I deliver this induction it looks different. Sometimes I may describe doing a Progressive Muscle Relaxation, particularly if I think that the client could benefit from learning the skills involved in a PMR. At other times, I may use Eye-fixation, or Sensory Overlap. In fact, I probably use elements of different inductions thrown in each time. That makes it effectively an induction within an induction!

You will most likely have noticed those places where I was able to give direct suggestions to the client, cloaked as suggestions to John, precisely because I was describing someone else that I had hypnotised.

In the transcript above, you will also see a hand-levitation. This is an effective gauge of how well the client is responding. I would expect that by now they are taking everything on board themselves, having effectively forgotten about "John" or their own friend. So, their own hand should begin to lift, encouraged by pacing and leading.

However, it may not always be obvious when to stop the pretence of hypnotising someone else. In this example, it was during the arm levitation, when my choice of words expressed the change of focus:

> And when *that hand* touches *his* face *you* will go into a very deep trance.

I sometimes take eye-closure as the termination point. However, I will more often keep going until some hypnotic phenomena has been achieved, even if that is simply eye catalepsy.

The important point is that you want to reach a place where you are confident that the client is now responding directly to your suggestions. When that occurs, there is no longer any need for 'John.' You may even choose to make this transition explicit by using your client's name at that point.

Tips

When you first start practising the My Friend John induction, you may feel like your intentions are being broadcast in bright neon lights. You might feel like your client will never fall for what you are trying to do. And that is a sign that what you are trying to do – and your reason(s) for doing it – needs some tweaking.

I almost always use My Friend John in a clinical setting. So, people have come to see me to get hypnotised. I therefore think of it as being conversational, rather than covert. Of course, it is not initially overt, but it is not as if I would be embarrassed if I was caught out. After all, hypnosis is what they are here for!

An analogy that springs to mind is of a child who is struggling to relax enough to go to sleep. You might offer to read them a story to *help them sleep* and no doubt your dulcet tones would have the desired effect. Yet, that is a very different scenario to one where a child does not want to go to sleep and they feel their head dropping from time to time, gradually beginning to suspect that you are attempting to *trick them into sleep*. If your clients feel like that after experiencing My Friend John – as if you had tricked them into trance – then I would suggest that you find a way to frame it that at least implies the possibility of something hypnotic taking place.

In my experience, rather than complaining about the subterfuge, the outcome that is more common is that a client will realise what is happening part of the way through the induction. However, by the time they are at that point, they are in such a pleasant state of mind that they are more than happy to continue being guided by you.

Some people just will not go all the way into hypnosis using My Friend John. This is usually because they are unclear on their role and are not sure what you want them to be doing. However, this is by no means insurmountable.

Some client's will require explicit permission, unless you have previously told them what will take place:

> "That's right. And you can go inside with them, allowing yourself to enjoy that experience."

Alternatively, you might simply lead them through the induction all the way to the end and then say, "So, let's do this..."

As far as your client knows, you have simply demonstrated how you hypnotised someone and now it is their turn. The lovely thing about such times is that the My Friend John will have prepared them and they will experience something of a fractionation as you lead them *back* in to hypnosis. They are likely to go quite deep in response to whatever induction you choose to use next.

However, you intend to use it, I thoroughly recommend becoming fully acquainted with My Friend John. It is a useful exercise and a powerful induction.

Thain Wrist-lift

Introduction

Barry Thain's Wrist-Lift Induction is a thing of beauty. I consider it to be a variation of Erickson's Ambiguous Touch handshake, but I actually use Thain's version more often. That's simply because for ease-of-use and effectiveness, it is difficult to beat.[29]

I am grateful to Barry Thain for permission to include this induction and for personal correspondence on the subject. However, the transcript below – though clearly very heavily influenced by Barry – is a record of when I have used the induction and varies slightly from the original. My version is slightly less authoritative than Barry's, so anyone hoping to see the real thing should pop over to his site and purchase his DVD, *Hypnotism for Hypnotherapists.* You will most certainly not be disappointed.[30]

Transcript

Did you ever find yourself day-dreaming at school, or at work, looking out of the window, staring, and your mind has just gone a million miles away?

– "Yeah."

29 Having said that, you might enjoy the *Auto Wrist-lift* discussed in a later chapter.

30 The DVD is currently available for purchase at https://www.mindsci-clinic.com/fb/products/dvds/hypnotism-for-hypnotherapists/

...Like, you're now just lost in a world of your own?

– "Ye..." [Interrupting the client, with the next statement...]

In a moment, I'm going to lift you arm up by the wrist and when I do, you don't need to help me.

What's important is that I would like you to find a spot on the back of your hand, and focus on that. And it doesn't even matter if you focus all of your attention on that spot and allow yourself to [touch the hand as you say] become absorbed in that.

And you can look at that, whilst I do this sort of thing... [Said whilst moving the arm around]

Look at that spot. Focused. Absorbed. Looking at that spot... And just let whatever happens, happen.

[Feel around, as if looking for the right place to hold. Lift up arm. Move up, slightly down and let it gently shift from left to right, occasionally up and down. After a while, it stops moving.]

[Pass fingers down in front of client's eyes.]

Sleep. Deep down, deep asleep... into that place where you dream. Drifting away, sinking down.

Now, in a moment, when you are ready to go twice as deep as you are now, you will find your arm begin to lower down towards your lap. That's it, going down, way deeper, resting down in your lap, all the way.

Twice as deep...

In a moment, I am going to count down from 10 to 0. I

want you to picture that Zero in your minds eye, like the "o" in the word "Hypnosis." And as I count down from 10 to 0, you get closer and closer to it... closer and closer. And as you step through, on the other side of that "o", you will find a state of comfortable yet profound hypnosis. In that state of profound hypnosis you can create new realities and see them come true before your eyes. Imagination, creativity and possibility let loose. In fact, every suggestion I make to you, to empower you, can become your reality instantly and immediately. And it feels great! You can see what I tell you to see. Hear what I tell you to hear. And feel what I tell you to feel. In that place, you can dream dreams and we can see those dreams come true.

As I count down from 10 to zero, watch that zero and on the count of zero you pass through, through that "o" and into that enjoyable state of deep profound hypnosis.

10... closer and closer

9... going in and down into that state

8... deeper and deeper

7... more and more excited about passing into deep hypnosis

6... closer and closer

5... each breath

4... like a step down

3... the closer you get, the more you can go there

2... down and deeper down

1... All the way in.

And my voice can go with you, as nothing else really

matters. Just the sound of my voice... and the future you are creating for yourself now.

As you step through to... 0... That's it.

Commentary

The arm catalepsy occurs because your clients are unsure what is happening to the hand, or where it belongs, creating a sense of dissociation. When the hand then rests in the air, which they do not feel themselves doing, that creates a moment of openness as their "subconscious" mind has been primed to follow your suggestions already.

This transcript also included Barry Thain's original *O in HypnOsis* deepener.

Tips

It is important to remember that this is a descriptive transcript, not a prescriptive script. The "instructions" that are included are simply the kind of touches that you will employ when you perform this naturally and competently. This induction is therefore far more simple than the transcript might imply.

Instruct them to focus their attention on the back of their hand and to allow that hand to absorb all of their focus. As that happens, your ambiguous movements cause a slight bemusement. This provokes an internal search for the meaning of what's happening, allowing their focus to "absorb" more fully from the hand into their inner experience.

Although my version of this induction is gentler than Barry's, it is vital to give clear direction at the moment of deepening. After all, a part of them is briefly aware that you're the only person who seems to know what is happening.

The Bandler Handshake

Introduction

The Bandler Handshake is perhaps the easiest and most effective of all the handshake inductions. With practice and confidence, you'll find that you can quickly and easily put people deeply under your hypnotic 'spell.'

Transcript

[Hypnotist offers out their hand, as they say…]

Thanks for coming along today.

[The client puts their hand out to shake hands. A split second before their hands meet, the hypnotist takes a hold of his partner's wrist with his other hand. He then swings the arm up and round, such that the palm is toward his partner's face.]

Look at your hand...

[Said whilst pointing at the hand that originally went in for the hand-shake.]

And rest your eyes on one spot on that hand...

[The hypnotist is employing tiny movements, invisible to onlookers, as he moves the hand slightly up and down, backwards and forwards for a few seconds.]

Look at your hand, focus on your hand, and as you become aware of your eyes...

[Hypnotist blinks]

... and the changing focus of your eyes

[Hypnotist blinks]

...they can close now

[At the same time as saying, "they can close," the Hypnotist's pointing hand moves down]

...as you allow yourself to drop down inside and go to a deep place of peace...

[Hypnotist senses that the hand is staying-up of its own accord, so lets go of hand, which stays in place.]

...a place of comfort and relaxation.

And you can go into a deep place of inner resourcefulness and relaxation, knowing exactly what level of trance is needed for you to find those resolutions you are looking for.

And you can find that you will drift deeply into that place, only as quickly as that hand comes down to a resting position at your side...

Commentary

There continues to be a debate over who this handshake should be attributed to. Bandler and Grinder originally credited Milton Erickson with its creation. However, Bandler has said in recent years that Erickson was not able to physically perform the induction as usually described. He claims to have given the glory to Erickson, as a sign of respect to the one who inspired this version. Whether that matches the facts, even as recorded in the early writings of Bandler and Grinder, I'll leave for you to decide.

We have chosen to use the common description "Bandler Handshake" not to imply that we accept that Bandler was its creator, but to simply use the most widely recognised title. This helps distinguish it from the Ambiguous Touch Handshake, which is what people more often refer to when they speak of the "Erickson Handshake." Either way, there's no denying that Bandler has popularised this induction more than anyone else.

The induction usually falls under the category of "pattern interrupts." This is based on the idea that there are specific patterns of behaviour that our minds run as programs or strategies, as if on auto-pilot. Every person, in fact every sub-culture, has developed their own patterns – tasks that run on auto-pilot. Obvious examples would include a handshake (whereby in many cultures if you stick out your hand to someone they will stick out their hand to shake it without really thinking about it), a verbal greeting routine ("Hi, how are you?" generating the response, "Fine, thanks. How are you?"), high-fives, waving, expressions of manners ("please," "thank-you," "you're welcome," "bless you,") and so on.

One theory is that if you interrupt a pattern with some unexpected stimuli then the subconscious becomes temporarily confused and has to briefly pause to consider which course of action to take. Obviously, this happens in the blink of an eye and eventually the conscious mind takes control again. However, for a split second, you have an opening, an opportunity to hi-jack the confusion and provide the direction which the subconscious is looking for.

I discuss this understanding of pattern-interrupts in a later chapter.

There are actually a number of variations of the Bandler Handshake, though the five following are the most common:

- The Floating Hand: Their hand floats up to or towards their face [Think of this as the magnetic forehead!]
- The Falling Hand: Their hand falls down to their face (or sometimes their side) [Think of this as the gravity variation]
- The Frozen Hand: Their hand remains cataleptic, in front of their face, where you placed it after the handshake. Usually followed-up with a falling deepener [This is the cataleptic Bandler original]
- The Focused Hand: No handshake is used. You simply ask your partner to look at their hand. This can result in either of the three outcomes above [This is Jonathan Chase's "Shapes" version]
- The Fast Hand: This is the Derren Brown rapid variation [Think of this as the flashy or face-palm version!][31]

Tips

This induction really can be picked-up very quickly. However, there are a few things you might want to look out for. Firstly, ensure that you are experiencing and projecting the appropriate state yourself. Obviously, if you are anxious and do not think it will work, you will end up communicating this through your body language, tone of voice, etc.

Visualise the induction working perfectly and then do exactly what you saw yourself – and your client – doing in your visualisation. Speak and act with confidence. Know that it will work.

Finally, never forget that the induction is only the beginning. This is especially true of rapid or so-called instant inductions. Interrupting

31 See *The Hypnotic Handshakes* for transcripts of each variation.

the handshake is only the beginning; what comes next is the vital part. You have a window of opportunity to lead them into trance. A very common mistake with beginners who use inductions like a handshake or arm-drop, is to perform the interrupt, achieve the beginning of hypnosis and then sit back to watch their entranced subject simply open their eyes and wonder why they were being stared at.

It is vital to flow straight from interrupt into deepener and suggestions. This does not necessarily mean rushing through it like a speeding bullet, because that can be jolting and just as distracting as saying nothing. It means that you need to give their mind something to focus on, even if that is nothing more than a count from 5-0, or their own breathing. A smooth delivery trumps quick technique.

On occasions, you will come up against someone who seems to intentionally resist your attempts to transform a handshake into a hand up in front of their face. There are a couple of reasons why this may be.

Firstly, you are opposing their natural movement. This comes down to avoiding direct oppositional movements in favour of circular blending ones. That is, the client should feel as if the hand has naturally flowed into its new position, utilising the energy that they put their hand forward with. They should *not* feel as if you have attempted to twist their arm into place.

Additionally, someone trained in martial arts – particularly Aikido, Ju-Jitsu, Wing Chun or Tai Chi – may be highly sensitive to variations in touch, especially around their wrist and forearm. In that case, the Bandler Handshake is not the most appropriate induction to use, unless you opt for the focused hand variation, or have a high pain threshold!

If you feel as if your partner is resisting, it may be because they sense something unusual is happening – which, from your perspective, is the whole point! – and they do not realise that it is part of the hypnosis.

I see absolutely no reason to hypnotise someone without at least some level of agreement. So, a useful pre-talk can eradicate multitudes of problems that unexpected or impromptu hypnosis can cause. Part of your pre-talk can even include something like, "I may touch your hand, arm or shoulder at different points and in different ways; that's all part of the magic. [Smile] Okay?" You then have consent to touch them, as well as an expectation from them that if you go on to touch them on the hand/arm in strange ways, it is all part of the process.

When they agree, you can say, "Thanks, I appreciate that..." as you go to shake their hand.

If you are at all concerned about the timing/execution of a pattern-interrupt, it can be useful to start by becoming proficient with the Focused Hand variation. Once you are comfortable with that, it will most likely feel like a small step to begin incorporating pattern-interrupt variations.

Thumb stare

Introduction

This induction can be thought of as a cousin of the Coin Drop, seen later. It lacks the coin drop's kinaesthetic quality, but adds a more explicit note of eye–fixation.

Transcript

You can just shuffle around a bit until you're comfortable. Then, when you're comfortable and ready to slip into trance, we'll get started. Okay, you're ready, now?

– "Yes."

That's good. What I'm going to ask you to do now is just raise your arm up like this.

[Demonstrate, by raising you arm so that it is level with your forehead and your thumb is pointing up.]

That's it, just a bit higher.

And you can just look at the back of the thumb, perhaps fixing your gaze on the fingernail, or one of the creases on that knuckle. Okay?

– "Yeah."

That's good. So, as you look at that thumb there, I'd like

you to keep your head still, but don't take your eyes off of that thumb. As you fix your gaze on it you will notice that the other fingers tend to fade out of focus and you've already begun to notice tiny movements in your arm...

[Wait for next twitch, or slight downwards motion. If none occur, wait until you are convinced that their gaze is fixed on the back of their thumb.] ...That's it.

And as those tiny movements continue, you arm begins to feel heavier and heavier, as your body and mind prepare to enter into a deep state of relaxation. [Wait for movement.] That's right.

Now, I don't want you to go into trance yet. You will not go into a deep state of relaxation until that arm reaches your lap. When it does, your eyes will close and you will carry on going deeper into trance.

Keep concentrating on that thumb... [Wait for movement.] That's right... and notice that the arm gets heavier and heavier and heavier, as you become more and more relaxed. And the more relaxed your mind becomes, the lower it allows your arm to lower.

Slowly going down, down, down... That's it... Preparing to go into trance. Nearly there... relaxing into a deep and profound state of relaxation as the arm lowers all the way down. Going down, down, down, deeper, deeper, deeper.

That's it... and the eyes can close.

[Proceed to the Deepener...]

Commentary

The client's arm is placed just above eye-level, in a position where fatigue will eventually cause it to come down naturally. However, the hypnotist links the tiring of their gaze + the downward motion of the arm with the client going deeper into trance. That is, when you detect that your client's arm is tired and about to lower, you might say, "as you go deeper now, that's it, further into trance..."

As their arm does lower in time with this, it gives them the message that they must be going into a deep(er) state of relaxation or trance – just as you said!

Then, as they continue to relax, their arm and gaze tire even more, and the cycle continues!

Tips

In this transcript, I suggest that the client doesn't lower their head. This helps their eyes to feel like they are closing, as they follow the arm down. Some hypnotists, however, like to instruct the head to lower with the arm, adding to the physical sensation of going deeper.

It's essential to time your suggestions with the actual movement of the arm, but this soon becomes second nature. In fact, the ideal is to make your suggestions exactly at the same time, if not slightly before. So, learn to pick up on the signals they give you.

This will make even more sense when we later discuss pacing and leading.

The Hand–Drop (8 word induction)

Introduction

In its shortest form, this is a powerful and reliable induction that can consist of only 8 words, "Press on my hand. Close your eyes... Sleep!"

To successfully execute the hand-drop, you will want to make use of a good pre–talk. Clients need to understand that hypnosis is safe and natural. They must also understand that it is important to follow your instructions.

Transcript

[NOTE: Unlike other scripts here, this one consists of mostly directions. After all, there really isn't all that much speech to include. The clue is in the title!]

Place your hand, palm side up, in front of the client.

"Press on my hand."

While they are pressing down, have your client close her eyes, giving the client two tasks to focus their attention on at once.

"Close your eyes."

Whilst the client is pressing down on the therapist's hand with her eyes closed, the therapist's hand is suddenly removed, creating the startle response which lasts for a very short period of time, two seconds at the most. During this "instant" your client is in a state of high suggestibility.

Then say the word, "SLEEP" in an authoritative tone and delivery, instantly inducing a deep state of hypnosis. However, if this suggestion is not immediately followed by further suggestions for deepening, your client will emerge from trance.

"Go limp and relaxed, continuing to relax further with every breath. As I gently rock your head, your neck relaxes and that feeling of relaxation moves through your entire body."

Commentary

Shock inductions should be approached with the appropriate level of care and caution. As the 8-word induction involves a hand drop which initially startles your client, it is not advisable to use it on someone who is suffering from shoulder, back or neck problems. Likewise, it should be avoided for clients with a history of heart problems.

Personally, I never use a shock induction (which I differentiate from a surprise induction, e.g. Bandler Handshake) the first time I work with someone. I tend to only use it after a certain level of rapport has been developed and a returning client maybe asks to experience something a little different. However, your mileage may vary.

There are a number of theories abounding as to why and how shock inductions work. From the "window of opportunity" idea that some people associate with pattern-interrupts, to PGO spikes in the brain as a result of the shock. The latter may require some clarification.

The theory is that when someone is shocked, this causes an electrical impulse that runs through three key brain regions: the pons, geniculate nucleus, and the occipital lobe; i.e. PGO. Such electrical surges are sometimes referred to as PGO spikes. PGO activity is believed to be associated with dreaming, learning and even hallucinating.

So, those who hold to the PGO spike theory tend to assert that a shock induction temporarily puts the brain into a 'state' where it is simultaneously looking for direction, open to learning and ready to engage creatively.

It might not surprise the reader to learn that I am not completely convinced by the PGO explanation. It is certainly interesting – and ticks all kinds of boxes – however, it is still very much an unproven theory. In fact, to date, scientists have not even proven that PGO spikes occur in human beings!

Yet, even if PGO spikes do explain what is happening in the brain of someone being shocked, they hardly provide an *experiential* description of shock inductions at work. After all, if you asked a client to describe what had just happened, I'm fairly certain that none of them would say, "Well, I experienced an electrical surge run through my pons, geniculate nucleus, and the occipital lobe..."

The following analogy provides an experiential description of what takes place, as well as giving a nod to the neurobiology involved. Use it with caution though, as I am not arguing that this is what is happening in the brain. I am merely describing how many people experience it.

I sometimes explain the effect of shock inductions by referring to the brain's fight or flight reflex. Many people are aware of the idea that our ancient ancestors evolved this response to deal with perceived threats. They would see a dangerous wild animal and automatically – without thinking – either attack or run to safety.

The thing that some people may not be aware of is that the full response is known as the 'fight, flight, or freeze' reflex. For freeze, picture a rabbit caught in the headlights of a car.

I sometimes suggest that a shock or surprise induction provokes something like the freeze response. (It might not, neurologically, but it works as an analogy!) It's automatic and is not a reflex we really get to choose or reject. It is as if our brain instantly goes into a 'wait and see' state and looks for some form of explanation, or at least which steps to take to become unfrozen.

Splash a glass of water in a friend's face and they are going to be shocked, look at you and say, "What the ****?!" As you were the root of the shock, they naturally look to you for an explanation, direction or apology.

Now, imagine splashing a glass of water on another occasion and before your friend has a chance to look at you and object, you immediately say, "duck!" whilst ducking down yourself. The chances are very much in your favour that your friend will duck down too.

Something unexpected has happened and your friend looks to the person (perceived to be) in the know for an explanation.

PGO Spikes are not necessary to explain the phenomenon of shock inductions. It seems that an experiential approach (albeit one informed by some psycho-social ideas) gives us a credible and reliable understanding of what is taking place.

What this demonstrates is that unexpected and/or out-of-place behaviour can create brief moments of expectant openness, curious confusion, or simply anticipation for a meaningful explanation or direction. This would seem to be a fair description of what client's experience, regardless of any particular brain activity.

I will say more about this when discussing pattern-interrupts later.

Tips

When first using the hand-drop or 8 word induction some people find it difficult to know when to pull away their hand. It can be helpful to wait until the client seems to be thinking, "I can't push any more/harder..." At that point, they are often slightly confused, helped by the two commands that they are concentrating on at once.

It is then that you interrupt by swiftly moving your hand away.

It is widely thought that the weakness with the 8 word induction is the lack of a test for depth, as we would find with, e.g. The Elman induction. Cal Banyan recommends borrowing from Elman, after the initial deepening ("Go limp and relaxed... As I gently rock your head...") has been performed. For example, suggest that the client now relaxes their mind, by counting and relaxing the mind increasingly with each number, until they have faded away to nothing. Banyan then recommends that you perform a simple deepening, like counting down from 1 to 5 with the suggestion of going deeper with each number.

A noteworthy practical tip is that you do not pull your hand away by dragging it forward (i.e. toward you). This can cause your client to lean forward in an attempt to keep connected to it. Neither do you whisk or slide your hand away and up. This can cause shock, but does not lead to a naturally workable physical position.

Instead, the hand drops instantly down. It should feel to the client as if your hand has instantly vanished. Then, as they physically 'drop' forward, you are well-placed to offer them suggestions (as well as keep them physically safe!).

Deeper Sleep

Introduction

The Deeper Sleep induction is a DIY rapid induction. It was designed to provide the experience of a rapid induction, without some of the razzmatazz. The bottom-line is, it works!

Transcript

In a moment, I am going to use the word, "sleep." And I'm sure you know that when hypnotists talk of sleep, they do not mean normal sleep. They mean something more like that day–dreamy phase where you're not quite asleep, but you're not your normal awake self.

And so when you hear a hypnotist command, "sleep," that's a signal for you to let go and drift off into that day–dreamy state.

- In a moment, I will say sleep and you will close your eyes

- and when you close your eyes, your head can drop forward

- and as your head drops forward, you can go off into that state.

Okay? Ready?

[Stare intently. Then perform a physical movement[32] and say, "Sleep!"]

That's right.

Drifting off... Dreaming... Pleasantly...

And your subconscious mind knows that there is a level of sleep lower than this one.

So in a moment, I am going to have you open your eyes and close them. When you close your eyes, you can take yourself down into a *deep* state of hypnosis.

Open your eyes... And close them. Sleep again... deeper down.

That's it. [Pause]

And your subconscious mind knows that there is another level of sleep lower than this one. So in a moment, I am going to have you open your eyes and close them. When you close your eyes, you can take yourself down into a *deeper* state of hypnosis.

Open your eyes... And close them... into a deeper state of hypnosis.

[Spoken on the client's exhalations:]

That's it... Drifting... Deeper... Dreaming.

And your subconscious mind knows that there is a level of sleep even lower than this one. So in a moment, I am going to have you open your eyes and close them. When you close your eyes, you can take yourself down into the *deepest* state of hypnosis.

Open your eyes. And close them... *into the deepest state of*

32 This can be a simple nod of the head, or a hand gesture.

hypnosis.

That's it... All the way now.

Commentary

The induction seen in this transcript is essentially a (rather unique) rapid induction followed by deepening.

The Deeper Sleep induction can almost be thought of as a training process. Some clients will know that when a hypnotist says sleep, that is when their head flops forward and they demonstrate the typical 'tranced-out' behaviour. They may not consciously do that, but their expectation is so high, that they do it nonetheless.

However, other clients might simply stare at the hypnotist and wonder why he is shouting that it is bed-time!

The second group of clients are not necessarily 'resistant.' They are more likely simply unclear what is meant to happen next and the role that they are to play in that.

So, the Deeper Sleep induction takes Dave Elman's adage that 'all hypnosis is self-hypnosis' and applies it to a (relatively) rapid induction.

Tips

This induction can be thought of as a stream-lined version of PHRIT, discussed elsewhere in this book. Like its predecessor, it relies heavily upon fractionation. So, the client goes into hypnosis, then out, then into deep hypnosis, then out, then into deeper hypnosis, then out, then finally into "deepest" hypnosis.

The beauty of this induction is that the whole debate around 'depth' of trance is completely irrelevant. Personally, I do not believe that there is any real differentiation between hypnosis, deep hypnosis, deeper hypnosis and deepest hypnosis. However, thanks to the power of fractionation, the client will experience going 'deeper' each time they close their eyes. This serves to confirm your words, providing extra expectation that what you say will take place.

After the client goes back 'in,' I pause before stating 'And your subconscious mind knows that there is another level of sleep lower than this one.' The length of pause increases with each additional 'depth' that has been reached.

The logic behind this is that if you pause too long when they first close their eyes, they will wonder if it has worked, or if they did what they were supposed to do. However, by the 2nd or 3rd round, not only have they got a grasp on what is taking place, but they are enjoying the increasing 'depth,' so why not let them enjoy that?

I may also add in brief suggestions or metaphors during each stage of 'sleep.'

Modified Wicks

Introduction

The core of this induction was originally developed by Graham Wicks and published in 1982 ('*A rapid induction technique, mechanics and rationale*,' in the Australian Journal of Clinical & Experimental Hypnosis). It has been modified and updated by Graham Old, whilst respecting the rationale and appearance of the original technique.

The original pure induction – as conceived by Graham Wicks – had the hypnotist keep hold of the client's hand (and lower it themselves), regardless of the presence or absence of catalepsy. The modification added later was to allow the arm to float down on its own, if catalepsy was initially achieved.

This is a rapid hypnotic technique, devoid of any shock. It is phenomenal at its core and incorporates kinaesthetic confusion. It's a beauty!

Transcript

Are you left–handed or right–handed?

– "Right–handed."

Okay, well let's use your left arm then, just to give it a bit more attention. And it's fine for me to touch you on the wrist, as I lift up your arm?

– "Yes."

That's good. Thank you. And you have full movement and good health in your wrist, your arm, your shoulder?

– "Yeah."

And, lastly, you're happy to go into hypnosis quite quickly this afternoon?

– "Yes, I am."

Great!

[Hypnotist takes the client's arm by the wrist and extends the arm all the way above their head...]

Close your eyes. Take a deep breath. Hold it...

[As you say, "hold it," let go of the arm almost completely, with it just resting on your thumb. At this stage, if their arm is cataleptic, after a couple of seconds continue:]

Let the breath out. And let the rest of your body relax completely... In a moment, your arm will slowly begin to float down to your lap. As it comes down, you will feel yourself going more and more deeply into hypnosis. But I don't want you to go all the way in, until that hand has come to rest.

[As the arm begins to float down:]

That's right, coming down only as quickly as you go deeper into hypnosis. The deeper you go, the better you feel. And the better you feel, the deeper you go. All the way...

[Once the hand has come to rest in their lap or by their side:]

And you can go all of the way inside now. Every beat of your heart, every word that I say and every sound that you hear, causing you to go deeper and deeper.

[If their arm was heavy when you said, "hold it," instead of being cataleptic, after a couple of seconds continue as follows:]

Let the breath out. And let your body relax completely... Your arm is now deeply relaxed and heavy and it will get heavier and heavier as I allow it to descend. And as your arm moves down, you can go deeper and deeper into that relaxation. But I don't want you to *go all the way into hypnosis,* until that hand has come to rest.

[As I move the arm down, taking between 10 and 20 seconds, I may include words like:]

That's right, getting heavier and heavier, going deeper and deeper. And the deeper you go, the better you feel. And the better you feel, the deeper you go.

[Once I have brought their hand all of the way down, I say:]

And you can go all of the way inside now. Deeply relaxed. Loose and limp.

[Said as I drop the hand for the final half inch.]

And every beat of your heart, every word that I say and every sound that you hear, causing you to go deeper and deeper.

Commentary

This induction relies on the almost instant catalepsy that is established at the beginning. However, it includes a fail-safe for the occasions when this is not achieved.

The induction is preceded by a simple 'yes set,' which we allude to a little later in the book. Included in these affirmations is the rather blatant suggestion that hypnosis will be achieved "quite quickly."

Tips

The way that you "place" the arm when it is fully extended can have a surprising effect on whether or not the catalepsy takes. It may not be obvious to onlookers, but it is possible to almost place the arm onto an imaginary hook when it is extended. This may not even be discernible to the hypnotee, but if nothing else it serves to increase the hypnotist's congruency.

You say, "hold it," at the exact moment that you almost let go of the arm. It is left resting on your thumb at that point, to such an extent that you will be able to detect wherever you or they are keeping the arm up. The linguistic ambiguity of what you mean by "hold it" contributes to the success of the catalepsy.

If you feel that their arm is coming down too quickly, you can increase your "patter" as it is coming down. You may even want to say something as blatant as "nice and gently now, only as quickly as you are going into deep hypnosis." If all else fails and you feel that the arm comes down far too quickly – and does not match their internal experience – you can simply act as if this was fully expected and confidently say, "And to ensure we have got balance, we will repeat this on the other side too…"

Coin Drop

Introduction

This technique can be employed using either a pen, a pencil or a coin. It is generally considered particularly effective for children.

Ask the subject to get a coin and hold it out in front of their body between the thumb and index finger. Tell them to grip it in a secure way.

Transcript

> Now close your eyes and think of that [pen or pencil, or] coin between the thumb and index finger of your right hand...
>
> Now breathe in deeply and exhale slowly five times ... Each time you inhale you bring more oxygen into your lungs. It passes from your lungs into your heart, and your heart pumps it into your circulatory system. It moves through your whole body, and each time you exhale you keep relaxing, becoming even more calm and more peaceful.
>
> That relaxation is moving through your whole body, and through your right shoulder, down your arm into your hand and fingers... soon the fingers on your right hand will become so relaxed that the coin will slip from your hand and drop to the floor.

As you hear the coin dropping to the floor, it may seem a little funny at first, but it will cause you to continue relaxing even more... you'll enjoy the feelings of relaxation that are coming over your whole body.

That relaxation is continuing to move through your whole body. You are relaxing from the top of your head to the tip of your toes…

Your arm beginning to float down now, as you go deeper with it into that relaxation…

You are continuing to relax and feel more at ease. You are sensing, feeling and imagining peacefulness, comfort, and calmness all through your system... You are relaxing deeper and deeper in a way that is just right for you… letting go...

And as you notice the rest of your body relaxing even more now... the finger and thumb holding the coin continue relaxing and the coin will soon slip from your hand and drop to the floor

[Pause...]

When the coin drops from your fingers, you will move into an even deeper hypnotic state, and you will keep your eyes closed until I ask you to open them

Commentary

Everything we said when discussing the thumb-stare applies here. The only difference is in letting your client (usually a child) know that it is not a problem when they drop the coin.

When working with children, I might often have them keep their eyes open. The fixation on the coin then produces eye fatigue, which can be paced to occur at the same speed that the arm gets tired.

As the arm tires, the child is able to feel that the induction is working, as the coin feels like it is getting heavier, just as you said it would.

If I am working with adults, I might be more inclined to invite them to close their eyes (as seen in this transcript). They can then be encouraged to focus on the feeling of the coin between their fingers.

Tips

To avoid any concern a child might have over dropping the coin, you might want to start by informing your client that it often happens.

It can aid attracting attention and absorbing awareness, if there is something particularly interesting about the coin. Alternatively, badges or medallions are a suitable alternative. However, even a simple pen works well.

Floating Candle

Introduction

The Floating Candle was created as a variation of eye–fixation, for those seeking to use their imagination during the induction.[33] It includes a built–in hallucination.

Transcript

> What I would like you to do is just imagine a candle, up on the wall. It could be on a shelf, on some kind of old–time candle–holder fixed to the wall, or just floating in mid–air, over there.
>
> And just let me know when you've got it.
>
> – "I can see it."
>
> Good. And all I really need you to do…
>
> [Hypnotist begins to speak more slowly, mainly on the client's exhalations]
>
> ...is keep your eyes resting on that candle and noticing whatever you notice.
>
> And I wonder, is that candle lit?
>
> – "Yes, it is."

33 See https://howtodoinductions.com/inductions/fixation

And is that flame still, or flickering? What do you see?

– "It's flickering, but only slightly. It's mostly kinda still."

That's what I had guessed.

So, now, let your eyes…

[Waits for the next blink]

That's right… just continue to rest on that candle. You may even find your focus narrowing even more, as you focus on that flame, just over there… and just look at that point.... just keep focusing on that spot, without moving those restful eyes...

And while you keep looking at that spot, perhaps your eyes wonder around a little bit, and always coming back to it in a gentle easy going comfortable way, you can become aware of the muscles around your eyes.... how they are holding your eyes up.... that's right... and your eyelids... and how they feel…

You may [waits for them to blink] blink a bit more frequently [waits for them to blink again] that's right... and your breathing might get deeper, as you relax.

Now, as your eyes are resting on that flame over there, attracting your focus, your mind wrapped around the idea of that flame on that candle where your eyes are resting now, the eyelids may perhaps become heavy… or your eyes want to close. But I don't want you to close them just yet.

Let them remain open.

And lots of people, as they begin to go into hypnosis, find that their focus becomes increasingly fuzzy... vision getting dim and misty... And as you look at that flame you might see that it begins to waver... or maybe you see it blurring...

[Pause]

That's it...

You may not even have noticed what is happening with the rest of your body... your arms and legs getting heavy, just as your eyelids get heavier and heavier. And as you think about how nice it would be to allow your eyes and eyelids to relax... and close those tired eyes...

I would like you to conceive of that flame as a doorway, a portal if you will to your special place. You know that place... of peace and calm, safety and serenity... some people see a beach, some see a bench in a park, or a picnic by the river, resting in a hammock, or merely lazing on the sofa on a Sunday afternoon... It's *your* special place... of peace and calm, safety and serenity.

And as you focus your eyes on that flame and as they become more tired and more heavy and more restful...

When you are ready, you can step through that doorway, as you... close your eyes.

And closing those eyes means you can relax straight into that special place... And whilst you are there, you may as well take the time to look around. See what you see, hear what you hear and feel what you feel... Notice whatever it is that you notice in that special place... Perhaps colours stand out to you, sounds that you can hear... maybe an idea pops into your head... Take this time to allow your subconscious mind to collect whatever resources it feels it wants to, to bring back with you, to assist you and empower you to be all that you intend to be...

[Pause]

[Deepen, move to therapy/phenomena, or awaken.]

Commentary

The unique feature of this induction is the hallucination of a floating candle. That may be a candle on a shelf, a candle in an old-fashioned candle-holder, or whatever else you or your client come up with.

Interestingly, if that initial phenomena is not achieved, then it simply functions as a typical eye-fixation induction and is just as effective.

Tips

It can be helpful to ask clients if the flame is still or moving. However, you have no real way of knowing if this is a genuine hallucination or not.

Either way, stepping "through" the flame like a portal is a natural way to proceed to a deepener.

Sensory Overlap

Introduction

Sensory Overload Inductions are a classic way to work with so-called analytical clients. Usually, the hypnotist uses whatever is happening around them, directing the client to focus on each input as it occurs, without giving them time to deal with any one sensation before moving on. The theory is that the analytical mind is overwhelmed with trying to keep up with everything, gives up and retreats into trance.

There are a few problems with this approach. Firstly, it does not take account of people's descriptions of what it is like to be overloaded. Secondly, it relies on the assumption that the hypnotist will be able to out-run or out-think the client. And finally, it requires the hypnotist to function in a way that may not be the most therapeutic.

The transcript that follows is slightly different to the usual presentation of this induction. In this case, the analytical client's ability to "over-think" is utilised. Rather than seeking to overcome the client's brain, this version of a sensory overload embraces it.

Transcript

Take as much time as you need to get comfortable in that chair... I am going to be talking about various things and you might want to keep track of them... or you might not... it's up to you...

[The hypnotist is talking mainly on the client's exhalations, almost from the beginning.]

I don't know if you will be able to concentrate on what I am saying better with your eyes open, or closed... so you can go ahead and do whatever is most comfortable to you...

[Client closes eyes.]

And as you relax into that comfort, I am going to invite you to pay attention to the sound of my voice... and to notice the sound of the words that I am using... As I'm talking to you, you might even picture the words that I am saying... perhaps you can imagine me writing them down as you think about the shape of the words... and hear my pen or pencil scratching on the paper as I make the shape of those words with my writing...

As we go on, you can become aware of the other sounds around you... the gentle in and out of your own breath... the sounds close-by... the ticking of that clock in the background... the creaks and groans of the heating system... as well as the sounds outside that come and go... those every-day normal sounds that tell us that life goes on as usual... as you continue to listen to the sound of my voice and the sounds of my words...

And as you allow yourself to rest in that chair... settling into that comfort... you may also become aware of how you are sitting... your feet flat on the floor... your hands resting on your lap... as you pay attention to the sounds of my voice and notice the sound of the words that I am using... As you imagine me writing these words down and the sound of the shape of these words... you can be aware of the sounds close-by... and the sounds outside that come and go… as you listen to the sound of my voice…

And I don't know how aware you are of your body in the chair… as you feel the back of the chair on your back and the weight of your legs and how your arms are lying relaxed in your lap… as your body relaxes, your arms and legs getting heavy… as you hear the sound of my voice…

And you might even become aware of the feeling of your feet on the floor… and they may feel numb and heavy… or how they usually feel, as you relax… aware of the sounds and words around you, relaxing your arms and your legs…

You might focus on your breathing now… aware of how your breath is allowing you to naturally and effortlessly… relax more and more.. to let go and go deeper and deeper as you relax into the chair now… your shoulders loosening, your muscles relaxing, as your feet and arms and legs relax… and the sound of the world outside continues… with the sounds of the heating and the ticking of the clock… and the sound of my voice and the shape of my words… whilst you relax now deeper and deeper…

[The hypnotist's voice is now slowing down, reflecting the gradual reversal of the earlier energised and overloaded state.]

And maybe those gentle steady breaths can remind you of those times you ignore everything… as you settle down to sleep, to let go… and allow your mind to drift away… dreaming, sinking, floating… like a dream-cloud taking over, enjoying the feeling of release… and calm…

Everything can settle down in its own time… settling comfortably now, those sounds relaxing you… soothing you… as you pay attention to the sound of my voice and your body continues to relax… deeper and deeper… sinking further and further, into that pleasant dream…

nothing to do now... except drifting down and enjoying the feeling... how easily you let go when you want to go...

more and more relaxed... feeling your whole body... as you focus on your breathing... sinking deeper and deeper into that relaxation...

And that relaxation can drop into your feet... nice and heavy and relaxed... and you can notice that your thighs and your knees and your calves and your feet and your toes feel heavy... nice and heavy and relaxed... And you can sink into that and enjoy it...

And if you would like to... you could even imagine those feet being too heavy to lift... as you allow yourself to enjoy that relaxation... and go ahead and imagine that... knowing what it would feel like... if your legs were too relaxed to lift... if your feet were so heavy they could not be lifted... sticking further to the ground... enjoy that feeling and embrace it... and if you want to feel that feeling even further, when you... know that your feet are too relaxed, too heavy to lift... you can go ahead and try and lift those feet... as you do, finding that it helps you sink into that relaxation... finding that they just feel heavier and heavier..."

[Client smiles as they appear to attempt to lift their feet.]

And then you can just stop trying... and let go... and let that pleasant calm relaxation... spread throughout your body and mind... that's it...

Commentary

We have called this variation Sensory Overlap. Common examples of this type of induction might be seen as seeking a break-down moment, a sort of crash when the overload has become unbearable and the client seeks refuge in trance. That is not the case here. In this version, the overlap is used as a means of leading the client gently back down to a state of calm.

You might think of the overlap in this induction as like the muscle tension that takes place in some versions of a Progressive Muscle Relaxation. The tension in itself is not the goal. Neither is it meant to be so painful that the client avoids it. Instead, the tension offers a comparison and in fact a spring-board to the relaxation.

In this induction, the overlap is like the application of tension. Then, as more items are added, the tension increases a little, then a little more, then there is a brief mention of relaxation as more tension is applied, then the tension increases, then a little more... and then a long slow sigh is let out as the tension gradually subsides, as more and more items are let go, until the only focus that remains is on the resulting relaxation, which the client sinks deeply into.

There is no uncomfortable breakdown, or retreating into trance, just a gradual increase of sensory input that provides a pleasant experience as it is all reversed.

Tips

As the term implies, a Sensory Overload Induction is intended to overwhelm someone (usually so-called analytical clients). The goal is to overload them with sensory input, to such a degree that they essentially burst and jump into trance as a way to break free. This is not a way that I am particularly keen to work with people.

Sensory overload is an uncomfortable experience for many people, e.g. some people on the autism spectrum. So, if I think such an approach would ever be useful, I opt for a sensory *overlap* instead. This is essentially a gentle, comfortable and less explosive version of a sensory overload induction.

I often think of it as a conductor introducing additional instruments to the sound of one haunting violinist. At first, the sounds may complement the violin, but after a while it becomes indistinguishable noise as more and more sounds are added. Imagine listening to that cacophony and having the power to reverse the actions of the conductor, removing each additional sound that was added, one by one. As you get down to 3 or 4 instruments, your ears will seek out the sound of the violin. Then, as the remaining instruments are removed, the sound of that violin will become more prominent and desirable. Finally, there is the relief that is experienced as you are left with that lone violin, focusing intently on that sound.

There is no crash or distress to escape from. Instead, you take a skill that the client has – to think and analyse what is taking place – and you build on it. You accentuate that skill and then you relax it. You are effectively pacing and leading from one state, up into an accelerated state of multi-focus and then working backwards into a state of singular focus on the first sound that was heard – the hypnotist's voice.

When I am using this induction with clients, I often imagine circling the room in ever decreasing circles, switching from one sensory input to another. I'm not sure that the spiral-type focus adds anything to the client's experience, but it helps me keep track of where I am!

Sinking Spot

Introduction

The Sinking Spot is another variation of the classic eye–fixation. It includes a built–in hallucination and uses the physical occurrence of the eyes lowering to suggest going 'deeper' into a hypnotic experience.

Transcript

All you need to do is keep your head still and follow my finger–tips with your eyes. Okay?

– "Okay."

Right, so, look here…

[Hypnotist holds up his hand at eye–level in front of the client, his hand in a Cub Scout salute, with his forefinger and middle finger pointing straight–up. He taps the fingertips of his upright fingers, to emphasise where the client is to focus.]

I am going to move my fingers back and forth like this...

[Hypnotist waves his arm in front of the client, from left to right, causing the client to look fully to the left and fully to the right.]

And up and down, like this...

[Hypnotist moves his arm down, in line with the centre of his client's body, until the client's eyes are fully extended looking down.]

And you can just keep your head comfortably resting and still, following along with your eyes. Okay?

– "Yeah."

[The hypnotist then moves their hand all the way along the horizontal axis, from the far left to right, twice. Encouragements such as, "that's right," or "keep following," are offered from time to time.

After the horizontal axis has been covered twice, when the hypnotist next reaches the centre, he then moves his hand down and up again.]

Now, down and up, that's it...

[The hypnotist is effectively drawing a large uppercase T in the air. This is repeated twice more.

As the hypnotist's hand comes up for the third and final time, the hand comes up slightly higher than the client's eye–line and the hypnotist then taps the air firmly.]

See that spot staying there, floating in the air. You might picture it as a coloured dot, or a small ball... [The hypnotist takes his fingers away, as he says...] keep your eyes resting on that spot.

And as you focus on it, I don't know if it is solid or transparent. Perhaps it is a 3D sphere, like a marble, or flat like a coin or a sticker. However, you see it, rest your eyes there, on that spot.

[Hypnotist begins to match the client's breathing.]

It may be that the colour changes, as your focus shifts in and out. Perhaps you notice more detail. It may be textured, I don't know. Or it may begin to blur and wobble slightly.

And while you keep looking at that spot, wondering around it but coming back to it with your eyes in a gentle easy going comfortable way, you can become aware of the muscles around your eyes.... how they they are holding your eyes up.... that's right... and your eyelids... and what they feel like....

You may [wait for them to blink] blink a bit more frequently [wait for them to blink again] that's right... and your breathing might get deeper, as you relax.

And after some time, you might notice as the spot seems to be too heavy to stay up any longer. It may start sinking, slowly, slowly, ever so slowly down.

And you can follow it with your eyes... as it moves slowly lower and lower, as it gets heavier and heavier.

You may have already noticed that as that spot gets heavier, you can be aware of your body relaxing deeper and deeper, your eyes heavier, moving lower and lower... sinking down with that spot.

And blinking [wait for them to blink] that's it, even more frequently now. But I don't want you to allow those eyes to close until the spot has come all the way down, as you come down with it.

That's it...

You may have noticed your arms and legs are getting heavy, as your eyelids get heavier and heavier. And as you think about how nice it would be to allow your eyes and eyelids to relax... the spot continues to sink... and I don't want you to relax all the way, or close your eyes and *go all the way inside*, until that spot has sunk all the way down.

As you focus your eyes on that spot and as they become more tired and more heavy and... more fatigued...as they follow that spot down...

As they reach the bottom, you can allow your eyes to close.

[Pause briefly]

And closing those eyes means you can relax now.... It feels so good... so peaceful... as you *really let yourself relax*...

Breathing–in and out, allowing that relaxation to double throughout your entire body. Going deeper... and deeper, that's it... all the way... all the way...

Commentary

You might think of the Sinking Spot as eye-fixation + phenomena. One of the nice features of this induction is that if the phenomena (positive hallucination) is not achieved, then it simply functions as a typical eye-fixation induction.

The movement from left to right adds to eye-fatigue. However, it also serves a few other functions.

If clients are familiar with processes such as EMDR or IEMT, then this induction might feel like it is doing more than simply tiring the eyes. Clients have been known to inject their own meaning into what is happening, as they can be aware that something extra is taking place.

On a related theme, parts of this induction involves what we have elsewhere referred to as "re-posturing." There are movements or actions that suggest something meaningful is happening, without saying what that meaning is. Such actions often lead clients to think, "Well, that clearly means something and must do something..." even when it is not specified what is actually taking place.

Tips

After you have performed a series of upside-down letter Ts, you "place" the client's focus on a specific point. You will have already achieved a certain level of eye-fatigue, along with expectation and confusion.

The next stage involves leading the client's focus downwards. This is most effective when the client feels that they are directing the downward movement (or at least, the sinking spot is). However, in reality, you are pacing things based on how quickly you sense the client desires to lower their gaze.

When your timing is accurate, you can shift seamlessly from apparently taking your lead from the client, to matching their timing and on to leading them. They will gradually begin to feel as if you are telling them that the spot is getting heavier (i.e. their gaze is lowering) and they are merely following your suggestion.

The Leisure Induction

Introduction

Stephen Brooks teaches this induction on his Diploma course. I will never forget the day I saw him sit down with a stranger and simply talk them into trance. I now use it regularly and it has rarely failed me.

This is a great example of overt conversational hypnosis, that can incorporate a number of different elements from other inductions in this book. It relies heavily on revivification and the recognition that people experience trance (or at least something like it) numerous times in their daily lives.

Utilising those experiences is non–threatening, educational and enjoyable for the hypnotee.

Transcript

> Tell me about a time when you found yourself doing something you were totally engrossed in. Something you enjoyed, something you did where you are relaxed and yet totally absorbed. You know, where you *maybe lose track of time for a while* & your level of awareness seems to change?
>
> – "Yeah, sure. I get that whenever I paint."
>
> Ah, you paint. And what is it that you enjoy about painting?

– "I don't know. The colours. The creativity. It feels a bit like everything slows down while I kinda get in this creative zone."

Everything slows down. It's funny that you said you don't know what you enjoy about it, because clearly on one level you do.

– "Yeah."

You enjoy slowing down in that zone.

– "Yeah. Definitely."

Is this something you do on your own or with others?

– "On my own. I've always gotta be on my own?"

Because...

– "It's just part of the whole peace and quiet thing. I can focus then and just get, like, lost in the moment."

Hmmm... Lost in the moment. What a great phrase.

– "Yeah."

So, what is that like, that 'lost in the moment'?

– "It's like..."

Wait, hold that thought. Before you go there, are you painting inside or outside?

– "Ah, inside. But by a window. So, I'm painting outside scenes, but I'm in the comfort of the inside." [Laughs]

Well, comfort's important. [Both laugh]

So, *you're comfortable*, slowing down, getting *in that zone...* And what more is there to getting lost in the moment? What does that feel like?

– "It's just peaceful. A time to escape."

And you value that peacefulness, that 'time to escape'...

[Begin to match their breathing, speaking on the exhale]

What else is there that feels good about that slowing down... getting in that zone... just peaceful... time to escape?

[Client pauses, looking off to the left corner of the ceiling]

[Nod slowly, as if to affirm their 'lost in thought' experience]

You look like you're escaping now.

– "Yeah." [Laughs] "I'm just thinking about slowing down and how that feels."

And have you noticed the changes in your breathing yet... slowing down?

– "I hadn't, but, yeah." [Laughs] "That's weird."

How did you know... that slowing down... changing your breathing... is the first part of going into trance?

– "I don't know."

That's right. You really don't know, do you? You're only just beginning to learn the things that you know, that you didn't know that you know. And I wonder, do you find it easier to increase that 'peaceful, slowing down', as you recall painting and all of the feelings associated with it, or if you simply *escape right into that zone* that painting takes you to now?

[Client does not answer, but stares off into space]

That's right. Muscles relaxing. Body slowing down. And as

your body slows down, your mind can escape... into that zone... Peaceful.

[Client's breathing has slowed dramatically, with a couple of very deep exhalations. Their gaze had frozen off in the distance, but now their eyelids appear to blink rapidly.]

[Said with a slight shift of the head, as if speaking towards the corner of the room that the client got 'lost in thought'] That's it.

And as your eyes begin to blink more, you can find yourself going deeper into that. But I don't want you to close your eyes... until you are ready to *fully return to that place...* See what you see. Hear what you hear. Feel what you feel. Enjoying that, slowing down... getting in that zone... just peaceful...

[Clients eyes close]

That's it... Time to escape.

Commentary

Many leisure activities involve, create or even require the practitioner to enter a state of receptivity and absorption. Many also produce states resembling relaxation, but that feel like a deep day-dream. "Spaced-out," or, "in the zone," would be good descriptions. Whether that is a reader getting lost in the plot of a story, or an angler whose whole person is drifting in tranquillity, the result is the same: trance.

This induction works by leading people to recall their leisure "trances," showing them the gradual steps that they take towards trance. By feeding-back the information they give you, they verify it internally and thereby relive aspects of their experience. This step-by-step revivification produces the frustration and fractionation that increase the desire to return to the previous state of trance.

In many ways, this is the core induction in this book. It is one of the simplest, yet also rewards true mastery of the principles and skills at work. I would recommend becoming intimately acquainted with it, yet still returning to it time and time again once you have finished the book.

Tips

We have devoted an entire book to the topic of this induction.[34] In *Mastering the Leisure Induction*[35] we provide the following framework to describe the basic process seen in this transcript:

1. Ask your client to tell you about an activity or pastime that they enjoy

2. Ask questions to gain more information: what, when, where, why, how, etc.

3. Repeat back to them what they have said to you

4. Help them feel the memory in the present moment

5. Move from an external focus to an internal one

6. Say what you see [e.g. minimal cues]

7. Let the client go into hypnosis

There are two skills it is necessary to develop if you want to truly master this induction: Observation and utilisation. (We will have *much* more to say of these vital skills later in the book.)

You will need to learn to observe how the hypnotee responds as

34 In fact, it was the first induction chosen to feature in *The Inductions Masterclass* series.

35 Old, G. (2014). *Mastering the Leisure Induction*. Milton Keynes: Plastic Spoon.

they say and recall certain aspects of their previous experience. You will also need to learn to observe their 'minimal cues,' the common signs that people display as they enter more fully into their internal world.

As you observe these things, feed them back to the client and allow them to wonder what it means. At the same time, ask questions to enable them to 'paint' a fuller and clearer picture of the leisure activity. This causes them to switch between an external and internal state. In the same way as My Friend John, the client does not initially realise that they are entering trance, but as soon as they feel it developing, they usually let go and enter into it. After all, they've just spent 5 minutes telling you how much they enjoy it!

Along with Observation and Utilisation, you will also want to become competent at Pacing and Leading. This includes your use of temporal language. Notice that at the very beginning, I planted the idea that this could be a present experience, as well as past recall. Then, I progressively moved from past tense to present tense until the client was fully reliving their earlier trances.

Mirror Mirror

Introduction

This induction probably belongs in the My Friend John family of inductions. Like almost everything in this book, it relies on observation and utilisation, along with good pacing and leading.

Transcript

> As you sit there, arms on your lap, shifting around to get comfortable, I would like you to imagine a mirror in front of you.
>
> And in that mirror, you can see your reflection. So, go ahead and look in the eyes of your reflection. And you can notice that you can see yourself reflected back in your eyes.
>
> So, you will notice as you, that's right, get more comfortable... as you breathe in and out, breathing in peace and calm... and letting go of any stress and tension. And you can see what it looks like as your breathing changes, there, for you here.
>
> And as you see your reflection in the eyes of your reflection, you might notice each time that you blink. That's it. And you will be able to see, as well as me, that each blink seems slighter slower than the one before, as if your eye–lids are becoming just a little bit reluctant to

open each time you close them.

That's right.

And as your shoulders drop as you continue to relax, you might notice those further changes in your breathing, getting deeper now, slower, more relaxed.

And you may have noticed your eyes blinking more quickly now, a sure sign that they are preparing to close, so that you can let go and go inside.

Keeping your focus on that reflection in your eyes in that reflection, breathing slowing down, blinking more quickly, eyes ready to close... That's it.

And you can go all the way inside now...

Commentary

The Mirror Mirror induction relies on the same principles as My Friend John. In effect, you describe someone going into hypnosis. However, in this case, you are describing the client themselves.

Tips

Mirror Mirror makes good use of pacing and leading. As you begin, you are merely describing the behaviour of the client in front of you. They can "see" the stated behaviour in the reflection in front of them. This creates an element of dissociation and has a "trancey" feel about it.

After you have described the client's current condition (pacing), you can begin to add some instructions (leading). These can be direct or indirect, depending on your style. A recommended approach is to be indirect in the beginning, gravitating towards being more direct.

You will see some element of confusion in the transcript provided. This is not a necessary feature, though you will find that it can occur naturally as an aspect of the dissociation your client is going through. It was included in this example precisely to enhance the experience of dissociation.

The induction also incorporates a rather blatant example of eye fixation. This can be a fun induction to work with – as can most variations of My Friend John – and it can be tempting to drag it out as you enjoy the dissociation your client is clearly experiencing. However, be aware of the eye fatigue your client may be feeling. It is usually advantageous to allow the eyes to close when (or soon after) they are ready to, in order to avoid any unnecessary discomfort or pain.

Post Hypnotic Re-induction Training

Introduction

PHRIT began as a simple yet effective way to set-up a post-hypnotic re-induction. It is useful for teaching clients to respond to post-hypnotic suggestions, as well as saving time in subsequent sessions.

It works by essentially teaching the client how to respond progressively. As such, it is perfect for hypnotists who lack experience in working with post-hypnotic suggestions, or who worry that they lack the confidence to pull off a quicker re-induction at a later time.

Transcript

> [Begin by inducing a light trance, or simply helping the client to relax. Then say:]
>
> Now that you've seen how quickly you can relax, I would like you to know that the next time you take four deep breaths, on the 4th breath out you can say the word "relax" in your head and allow your eyes to close. You can then bring yourself right back to this place.
>
> The next time you take four deep breaths, on the 4th breath out you can say the word "relax" in your head and allow your eyes to close. You can then bring yourself right back to this place.

And you can nod your head to let me know that you understand and accept this idea.

[Client nods head.]

So, as, I count from 1–3, when I reach 3 you can open you eyes and we can carry on talking. 1, 2, 3.

[Client opens eyes]

How was that? You seemed to be enjoying yourself.

– "Yeah! That felt great."

Okay, so when you're ready, you can take four deep breaths and as you breathe out the 4th time you can say the word "relax" in your head and allow your eyes to close and take yourself back into that pleasant experience.

Take four deep breaths and on the 4th exhalation you can say the word "relax" in your head and allow your eyes to close and take yourself back into that pleasant experience.

[Client takes four deep breaths, closing their eyes on the fourth breath.]

Now that you know just how powerful your mind is, and how easily you can return to this deep and pleasant state, I want you to know that the next time you take four deep breaths, you can let those eyes close on the fourth breath as you say the word "relax" in your head. You can then allow yourself to come right back to this place.

Just nod your head to let me know that you understand and accept this idea.

[Client nods head.]

And I will count from 1–3, and on 3 you can open you eyes... 1, 2, 3.

[Client opens eyes]

And when you're ready to return, you can take four deep breaths, say the word "relax" in your head and allow yourself to go back.

[Client takes four deep breaths, closing their eyes on the fourth breath.]

And now I want you to know that the next time you take four deep breaths, saying the word "relax" in your head on the fourth exhalation, your eyes will close and you'll come right back to this place, if not even deeper.

The next time you take four deep breaths, saying "relax" in your head on the fourth breath out, your eyes will close and you'll come right back to this place, if not even deeper.

Nod your head to let me know that you understand and accept this idea.

[Client nods head.]

And now, as, I count from 1–3, on 3 you can open you eyes... 1, 2, 3.

[Client opens eyes]

Now, go ahead and take 4 deep breaths…

Commentary

With PHRIT you train someone to move from an active response all the way through to an automatic one. The four stages are:

1. Active
2. Permissive
3. Passive (Observer)

4. Automatic

Whenever I intend to set a post-hypnotic suggestion (PHS), I now always start by doing a suggestion for re-induction. That way, the client knows that they are capable are doing this and does not doubt or question the realism of the suggestion.

Once PHRIT has worked, I find that all other PHS (all expressed in a similar progressive or repetitive way) are accepted much more easily.

In reality, this is so much more than an induction. In fact, understood in the fullest sense, PHRIT can be viewed as:

- A tool for establishing anchors
- An APPROACH to establishing re-inductions
- A means of setting-up post-hypnotic suggestions

Tips

This method of installing a post-hypnotic suggestion for re-induction initially works very permissively. The suggestion is made and agreement is sought. The client is then brought back and taken "under" again. The suggestion is made again, only less permissively.

This proceeds until the re-induction is accepted – and experienced – as a clear and direct suggestion.

In addition to teaching the client how to progressively accept the suggestion, the repeated experience of being taken in and out of hypnosis usually results in the client going 'deeper' each time. The benefit of this is that it is possible to start the PHRIT process with only a very light level of relaxation.

It is possible to add a variation to PHRIT, where one less breath is taken on each re-induction. This can culminate with the re-induction being triggered with the simple word "relax" (or whatever word is chosen).[36]

To further explore the theory and practice of PHRIT, see the second book in my Inductions Masterclass series, *Revisiting Hypnosis.*[37] However, you will also see it cropping up in various guises throughout this book.

---

36 Experimentation with this idea is what lead to the later creation of the *Deeper Sleep* induction.

37 Old, G. (2016). *Revisiting Hypnosis.* Milton Keynes: Plastic Spoon.

Magnetic Hands

Introduction

We have already seen Magnetic Hands used as a Response Routine, but it functions very well as a basic induction. In fact, it was the first induction I was ever taught and I was hooked the minute I saw the hands beginning to move together.

This transcript, includes an example of a deepener. It also presumes that you've started with a brief pre–talk.

Magnetic Hands is far simpler than the detailed notes below would suggest.

In fact, the induction is incredibly flexible. It can be used as a rapid induction, where some hypnotists like to push the hands together and down as they are just about to touch. Or it can be used to demonstrate phenomena, such as the hands sticking together once they have touched. However, the induction itself is incredibly simple and there's no reason not to get practising with this one right away!

Transcript

[Begin with a Pre–Talk, then say:]

Now, just place your hands out in front of you, like this...

[Demonstrate by placing your hands about 12 inches to a shoulder width apart, palms facing each other]

What I'm going to do in a moment – relying on the power of your imagination – is I'm going to place an incredibly powerful magnet here [touch the palm of their left hand with your fingertip] and another one here [touch the palm of their right hand with your fingertip]. When I do, you'll begin to feel the pull between your hands...

[Gently push their palms together, whilst saying...]

And as your hands get closer, your eyes can close and then you'll go deeply [gently apply a little pressure on the top of their hands so that they feel a very slight downwards push] into a nice relaxing trance.

Okay?

"Yes."

Good. So, just to make sure it's clear... You'll place your hands out... [wait for them to put their hands in the right position.] That's it. And I'll place a strong magnet here [touch the palm of their left hand with your fingertip] and here [touch the palm of their right hand with your fingertip]. And as you become aware of that magnetic pull between your hands, your hands will begin to come together.

[Gently push their palms together, with them probably helping a little this time, whilst saying...]

And as your hands draw closer together, you'll feel a wave of relaxation, your eyes will close and you can let your head drop forward as you sink into [apply a little pressure on the top of their hands] that nice relaxing trance.

Got it?

"Yes."

Great. So, to recap... Your hands are out... [wait for them

to put their hands in the right position.] That's it. And I place a strong magnet here [touch the palm of their hand with your fingertip] and here [touch the palm of their hand with your fingertip].

And as you concentrate on that magnetic field, that area between your hands, your hands begin to come together...

[Very gently push their palms together, if they haven't already begun to do so.]

You'll feel a wave of relaxation as your hands pull closer together... your eyes will close [wait for their eyes to close] as you begin to enter trance...

[If their head doesn't drop slightly forward at that point, say...] And your head can drop forward as you drop down... deeper [apply a little pressure on the top of their hands, if they haven't begun to go down] into a nice relaxing trance.

Okay... So as you place your hands out... you can feel the power of those magnets ... [touch 1st palm and then the 2nd, as you say...] ...Nowwww.

Focusing on that space between the palms [Wait for movement in the hands] ...that's right. Feel the pull. You don't have to force it. You don't have to fight it. You can just enjoy the relaxation that comes over you as you see your hands coming close and closer and closer... [Wait for next movement in the hands] ...that's right.

And as your hands touch... [Look for the slightest movement of the eyes, or a blink] your eyes can close... that's right. As the wave of relaxation floods every fibre of your body. Your hand dropping to your lap... as your head falls forwards and your sink down into that trance. Sinking, floating drifting... more and more relaxed.

[The Deepener:]

I'm now going to count and each number I mention, and every breath you take, and every beat of your heart, doubles that relaxation you are feeling now. Focusing on my voice; all other sounds only serving to deepen that relaxation that you're already feeling, until all you can hear is my voice.

Ten, deeper and deeper.

Nine, every number doubling the sensation of relaxation.

Eight, every breath taking you further down.

Seven, every beat of your heart, deeper and deeper into that place.

Six, more and more relaxed.

Five, four, three, two,

And... One.

That's it. All the way into that experience... into that peaceful place.

Commentary

In reality, this induction is incredibly simple. However, I have included added details that you will grow to appreciate as you experiment with it more. If you have taken your client through a pre-talk then, in some cases, they may already be in a light trance. Either way, they will know exactly where to go when they close their eyes.

This version of the magnetic hands induction, includes elements of rehearsal. As well as preparing them to expect it to work, this creates muscle-memory as their hands get used to coming together. It also means that their eyes and arms may be tiring and be more likely to drop down.

[Read more about the *Rehearsal Induction* to get more insight into some of what is happening there.]

The terminology that I have used, like 'feel the pull between your hands' and 'focus on the magnetic field' is simply another way to get them to focus on the space between their hands. Focussing there, rather than on anything they can or can't feel in their hands gives their imagination more to play with, as they want to move the hands together so that they can actually feel something where they are focussing.

Many people perform this induction by having the client close their eyes first. (Or, sometimes, after one rehearsal.) The benefit of this is that their hands seem to go together quicker, perhaps due to making things easier on their imagination. However, I love the look on their faces as they actually see their hands coming together!

Tips

I normally start by giving an instruction, like "Just place your feet flat on the floor." This is an example of re-posturing that we have discussed elsewhere, establishing co-operation right from the start.

Make sure the subject doesn't rest their arms or elbows on their lap, as they will need free movement.

One delightful addition that a member of our team came up with was to ever-so gently push the palm slightly as he placed the magnets on his client's palms. This is so gentle as to be practically imperceptible to the client, yet it results in their hands bouncing back inwards, so they are already moving in the desired direction.

Don't worry if their hands take some time to come together. Simply encourage every small movement that you see. If their eyes are closed, they don't know quite how much their hands are (or are not!) coming together, so feel free to exaggerate how impressed you are as you say things like, "That's it! Just like that – closer and closer."

If you feel the need to, you can always encourage the movement by gently touching the outside of their hands and giving them a helpful push inwards. Or, perhaps suggest that you are placing rubber bands around their hands, such that they are being pulled from the inside (by magnets) and pushed from the outside (by the rubber bands). However, be aware that sometimes the hands are moving slowly, because the client is so absorbed in the experience. You will learn to recognise when this is the case.

If you're nervous about their eyes not closing (and there's no reason why you should be!), either have them close their eyes first or adjust your initial wording to something like, "...And at that point, as your hands touch, you can just close your eyes and let your head drop..."

When it comes to the deepener, it can have a positive impact on your pacing, if you say the numbers on each exhalation. Additionally, you will see that some people associate the release / relaxation of breathing-out with the numbers that you are counting down, reinforcing the sense that your words – and the process that you are taking the client through – are having a verifiable effect on their experience.

Rehearsal Induction

Introduction

This induction is based on one outlined in John Overdurf and Julie Silverthorn's masterpiece, *Training Trances.*

The Rehearsal Induction links raising the subject's arm with going into hypnosis. The hypnotist raises their arm, makes some suggestions and places it back down. This process is repeated a couple of times, with more steps (and extra pacing/leading) added, apparently just to demonstrate how the hypnotist will later lead them into trance. However, it is during the actual process of rehearsals that the client slips into trance.

If you're new to this induction, I confidently predict that you will soon count it among your favourites.

Transcript

> Before you go into trance, I'll just demonstrate how this is going to happen. Okay?
>
> — "Yes."
>
> All I'm going to do is reach over and gently take your wrist and I'm going to lift up your arm and at a certain point it will stop all by itself. And that would be the point at which you go into trance.
>
> ...Then I'll move it down and you eyes would open and

you would come out of it...

So, it would be like this... I'd reach over and pick up your hand like this [take by wrist]. And I don't want you to go into trance just yet, because I want to explain this to you...

...because this will be something that will assist you later in going into trance.

All you're going to notice is that I'm going to pick up your wrist like this [slowly lifts wrist, so hand is in the air and elbow is bent at 90 degrees]

and

[speaking more softly, but still conversationally]

I'm going to talk to you in a certain way, and as that hand reaches a certain point, you'll notice a number of things happening that will let you know you're going into trance...

...and then to have you come back out of trance, we'll move the hand back down like that... [move hand back down]

Good.

So, if now was the time for you to go into trance, I just want you to get the feeling for this, all I would do is reach over like this, I would pick up your arm... and stop at the point... when you would go inside, notice then that your eyes would close at a certain point. Then I would move it back down again. Okay.

So, what I'm doing is adding a few steps there. Now, if we were going to actually do it again, all I would do is reach over and I would lift that arm up like that, and when that arms stops by itself... that's right...

[arm remains suspended without assistance]

...you noticed the tendency ...for your eyes to close, and you would go deep into a trance, and once you go into trance, all that we would do to have you come back out would be that I would push that arm back down like that.

So that the next time when I reach over, like this

[client anticipates and begins to lift arm herself] ... that's right...and as that arms lifts, like that, as your eyes close,

...and it would stop by itself... [arm stays suspended]... and you would know what to do...all the way in...that's right... and your unconscious mind can follow perfectly the suggestions with your conscious mind paying attention, or going off anywhere it wishes.

...As each breath that you take...that's right...and every word that I say takes you deeper and deeper.

All the sounds that you hear, the everyday surroundings, serve to focus you and enable you to continue going deep and deeper into trance.

...That's it... All the way in.

[Proceed to Deepener, if required]

Commentary

I first encountered this induction in Anthony Jacquin's influential book, *Reality is Plastic*. I later found it in *Training Trances* and it remains one of the most reliable inductions I have come across.

As with My Friend John, The Fake Induction and the Fractionation Conversation, this induction is excellent for so-called 'resistant clients.'[38] This is for the simple reason that it leads them into trance before you've even officially begun!

The Rehearsal Induction creates catalepsy in the client's arm as you repeatedly go through the steps that you will be using. It's name comes from the fact that you rehearse the induction as many times as needed, with them falling into trance during the rehearsal.

Tips

It is important to be pacing and leading the client's experience as you rehearse. Pick up on what is happening to them and mention any aspects of their behaviour that would support trance formation. Do this, increasingly, with each rehearsal.

Their arm will probably lift on its own by the third or fourth rehearsal, as you are reaching over for it. At that point, just give a small amount of encouragement, perhaps using your thumb on the underside of their wrist.

Most of the time, the arm will remain suspended when it stops. However, you could just slowly release all of your fingers, leaving just your index finger touching the back of their wrist. This gives the impression that the hand is still being held. This also gives you the opportunity for added ambiguous touches, if their arm is not yet completely cataleptic.

The best advice I can give is to rehearse!

38 See *Hypnosis with the Hard to Hypnotise* to learn why I do not generally recommend viewing or labelling clients in this way.

Elman Handshake

Introduction

Dave Elman originally referred to this as the 'catalyst induction.' However, it did not always involve a handshake. In fact, in his classic book *Hypnotherapy*, Elman teaches this induction via three puffs on a cigarette!

Transcript

Just take my hand, and look into my eyes. That's it. Fix your eyes there.

[The following instructions are given whilst the hypnotist continues to hold their partner's hand.]

Here's what is going to happen: I am going to shake your hand 3 times. The first time I shake your hand, you're going to relax so much that your eyes are gonna start to feel tired. They are going to get quite heavy. You know the feeling when you're reading a book late at night and you're struggling to keep them open?

— "Yeah."

That's going to happen the first time I shake your hand. But I want you to fight it and keep them open.

The second time I shake your hand, there will be a really strong urge for your eyes to close, but I want you to try and fight it. If they do close...

[Partner blinks]

That's right... I want you to try to open them again... until, the third time I shake your hand.

And the third time I shake your hand, your eyes will close, your head will drop forward slightly and you will enter into that daydream place of hypnosis.

Okay?

— "Yeah."

[Begins Handshakes. The hand is shaken continuously as the hypnotist repeats what will happen. That is, each "handshake" is actually a series of shakes. The hypnotist only stops shaking between the instructions]

The first time I shake your hand now, your eyes are gonna start to feel tired, beginning to feel heavy...

[Waits for a blink]

That's right... But I want you to fight it and do your best to try and keep them open.

The second time I shake your hand now, there will be a strong urge for your eyes to close, but I want you to fight it.

[Waits for a blink]

That's right...

[Partner slightly closes their eyes]

But I want you to do your best to open them...

[Partner opens their eyes, blinking repeatedly]

That's right... try to keep them open.

And now the third time I shake your hand, your eyes close, your head drops forward...

...And sleep!

[Hypnotist pulls hand further down and forward on the downward shake as they say, "Sleep."]

That's right... relaxing all the way down.

[Follow with an arm-drop deepener, such as:]

And as this arm just plops into your lap [or falls to your side], you can go ten times as deep...

[Hypnotist lets arm go]

And as your other arm just falls by your side, you can go twice as deep into that experience...

[Hypnotist picks up the other arm and just drops it into their lap.]

All the way down... sinking, drifting, floating, deeper into that pleasant experience...

Commentary

The Elman Handshake can be described fairly easily:

- Tell your partner to look you in the eyes.
- Tell them that you will shake their hand three times.
- Explain that on the first shake, "you can allow yourself to relax. You know what it feels like to really let go. Want that and you can have it."

- Explain that on the second shake, "you will relax so much, that your eyes will want to close, but fight it. Don't let them close just yet."
- Then say that, on the third shake, "you can close your eyes and let go completely as you go inside."
- Take their hand and explain again what will happen with the first shake. Shake their hand 2 or 3 times. Let go of the hand.
- Take their hand again and explain what will happen with the second shake. Shake their hand 2 or 3 times. Let go of their hand.
- Take their hand a third time and explain again what will happen with this shake. Lift their hand up as you begin a hand-shake. However, as the hand is coming down, tug it down and forward slightly as you say something like, "Sleep..." or "Close your eyes and go inside."

The 'tug' on the third shake is not necessary, if that is not your preferred way of working. However, it does add an additional element to the induction. Even if you do choose to employ it, you can be shaking their hand the third time until you see their eyes close. At that point, it is natural to have some kind of climatic action to confirm that they are now in hypnosis. So, a gentle pull down *as the hand is naturally coming down* from a shake will be more than enough.

Finally, some people object to the word "sleep" being used, as hypnosis is not sleep. That is a natural enough objection, but it is also one that is easily addressed. During most of my pre-talks, I talk about hypnosis being like going to the land of day-dreams, where all kinds of possibilities are within our reach. I emphasise that sometimes in a daydream we can still hear everything and everyone around us, but then at other times, we are a million miles away, as if our teacher is calling out our name, but we are just too absorbed in bliss, staring out the window in a dream, to pay it any attention. I then say that hypnosis is not the same as being asleep, but that I still sometimes use that word because it is a good signal to our brains to return to the land of day-dreams.

(If you wish to keep using the word 'sleep,' feel free to steal my explanation, or simply say that hypnotic sleep is not sleep as we know it!)

There are a few principles that make this induction work. Firstly, you tell your partner to fight certain experiences. To do this effectively involves them 'locating' those experiences. This is akin to the 'do not think of a pink elephant' exercise that we refer to elsewhere. However, in this instance, it is as if you are saying to them, "When I shake your hand, whatever you do, you have to make absolutely sure that you do not think of a pink elephant." You are actually inviting them to put extra effort into the activity that will bring about the very thing they are avoiding.

Secondly, you utilise your partner's responses, acting as if each one is exactly what they were supposed to do. They will naturally blink at some point and you will acknowledge it as them fighting the urge to close their eyes. They will exhale and you can welcome it as a sign that they are relaxing. Then, finally, their head will come slightly forward on the final shake as you direct them, "That's right, all the way down..."

Thirdly, the predominant principle that this induction relies upon is the element of expectation. As each shake produces the results you said it would, expectation is increased that the following shake will be equally effective.

Tips

Some people who use this induction, do not have their partner look them in the eyes. Instead, they ask them to look at the cheek bone just below their eyes. Or, they might instruct them to look at their earlobe. Both of these options result in a situation where the subject feels that someone is looking into their eyes, yet although they are very close to returning the gaze, they are not quite there. This is a powerful if disconcerting experience, which simply serves to confirm that something unusual is happening.

If you do ask your partner to look into your eyes, I recommend practising your hypnotic gaze. I like to have my left eye focusing just in front of their eyeball, whilst my right eye looks through their eye to the back of their skull. This will give a defocused effect and will cause your partner to be unsure whether you are looking at them or not. However, this is not an essential element, as long as your hypnotic gaze conveys assurance and expectation.

You may have noticed, that as the handshake is being pre-explained, it is unclear if the client is being told what will happen, or instructed as to what to do. This is intentional. The second time that events are explained, just before the handshake, you may want to be more direct and make it clear that you are making a direct suggestion as to what will happen.

Your own style and preferences will dictate how you word things – and how you want your partner to experience them. However, we have found this ambiguity to be useful.

Reg Blackwood teaches a nice element to this handshake. He suggests, during the first two handshakes, saying, "fight it" when or if you see nothing happening. This then encourages them to produce the phenomena they are told to fight against. Secondly, he says, "That's it," when their eyelids flicker, or begin to close.

I tend to say "that's it" even if all they do is blink. However, you can also simply nod your head as they blink.

Perspective Induction

Introduction

This induction grew out of discussions around Milton Erickson's influence on solution-focused therapy. In 1954, Erickson wrote a paper entitled, *Pseudo-Orientation in Time as a Hypnotic Procedure.*

Later, as Steve de Shazer and his team continued to work with pseudo-orientation in time, they discovered that, 'simply describing in detail a future in which the problem is already solved helps to build the expectation that the problem will be solved and then this expectation, once formed, can help the client think and behave in ways that will lead to fulfilling this expectation.'[39]

In solution-focused therapy, we are less interested in what someone is trying to avoid and more in what they are looking for instead. Where do they want to get to? And what would life look like if they were there? --- And that last question is key...

Transcript

Want do you hope to get out of this session? I mean, how will you know when this has been a valuable use of your time?

– "Well, I am learning to drive, but I keep freaking-out in the car and just can't keep going with the lesson."

39 *Clues: Investigating Solutions in Brief Therapy*, p.5.

Freaking out?

– "Yeah, like a panic attack... My whole body gets like flooded with fear."

So, how will you know that coming here today was a good decision?

– "I won't do that any more. Like, my fear of driving will have gone."

And what will have taken its place?

– "What do you mean?"

Well, you've done a good job of describing what you *don't* want – that fear of driving. However, I'm also interested in what you *do* want. What do you want *instead* of that old fear?

– "I want to drive with ease, effortlessly, almost like I'm in the flow."

In the flow, that's nice.

– "Yeah."

I'd really like to hear more about that flow. So, what we could do now, is imagine that the door there out of my office is a portal into an alternate world... You'll of heard all about the multi-verse and films like Sliding Doors, right?

– "Yeah, love that film."

Really? Me too! Okay, so, that door there is a portal into an alternate world, parallel universe, different time-line, however, you like to imagine it now. And what I want you to know is that when you step through that door, it can be as if you are stepping into another world for you. And the only thing that is different about that world – everything else is the same – the only thing that is different is that that old fear has now gone. When you leave through that door, you will know that coming here was a great decision on your part, because you will find that you now drive with ease, effortlessly, like you're in the flow.

So, that's something to look forward to, now, isn't it?

– "Hell, yeah!"

Paint the picture for me then. Imagine that you've gone through that portal, that old fear is gone, and you're driving tomorrow, next week, six months time – how can you tell that you now drive with with ease, effortlessly, like you're in the flow?

– "I'm just like, not even really thinking about it. Just driving."

You're not even really thinking about it.

– "Yeah, you know like, on auto-pilot. Not obsessing or getting worked-up."

So, like on auto-pilot, not even really thinking about it. What's that like?

– "That's the flow I was talking about. Just, there's just like an ease to it. It's natural."

It is natural. And what's *that* like?

– [Laughs] "Oh, it's great! I love it."

[Laughs] And it's an interesting experience, isn't it? How we can drive effortlessly, with ease, like we're on auto-pilot, but we're still driving safely, seeing the road signs, stopping at the lights, yet somehow still enjoying that feeling of driving naturally.

– "Yeah, it's great."

So, if I was driving past you, how would I know you are loving it, driving with ease?

– "Um, I guess, the look on my face? I'd look relaxed?"

Relaxed.

– "Yeah."

Driving with ease, effortlessly, naturally, relaxed. And what does that feel like?

– "I just love it. So calm and peaceful. It just all flows."

It does, doesn't it?

– "Yeah."

Now, if I was the Sun shining down on you, what would give away to me that you were loving driving, so calm and peaceful?"

– "You'd see it on my face again, but there's just no tension. I'm not like gripping the steering-wheel…"

In the flow. Not gripping.

– "Yeah."

And how is that?

– "It's good. It's nice."

And, if I was a fly on the other side of the windscreen, how would I see that it's good, it's nice? What would that look like to me?

– "You'd see me just driving easily. No big deal. No stress, no tension, no panic..."

The old panic's gone.

– "Yeah, and I'm just driving, like effortlessly."

How would any cars driving safely behind you know that you were just driving effortlessly?

– "I wouldn't be jittery with my break pedal, or anything like that."

So what would you be?

– "Calm, confident. Safe and at ease."

That's good.

– [Takes deep breath.] "Yeah."

And if I am sat in your passenger seat – let's pretend I didn't know that old panic has gone – what would give me a clue? What would be a hint that, 'Oh, just a minute, things are different now…'?

– "Oh, you'd know, for sure! There's a big difference. I'm just… there's no issue. You could just tell."

How could I tell?

– "I'd be driving calmly, happily. Yeah, that might be the main thing. You'd see that I was happy. Yeah."

So, I'm sat next to you [Hypnotist's voice has been slowing down slightly, matching the physical changes he is noticing in his client] ...and I'm seeing that you are happy...

– "Yeah."

Driving with ease, calm, confident…

– "Yeah, definitely."

Safely, effortlessly. In that flow.

[Client opens mouth as if to speak, but stays silent.]

And how is that relaxed, easy, effortless, calm, flow, right now?

[Client smiles, but still stays silent.]

That's right...

Commentary

This is not a basic induction. It's certainly not an "if you want to induce hypnosis, do this..." series of steps. However, this transcript is an example of how an induction can be a part of the therapeutic process in and of itself.

The idea of trance may or may not be useful, yet there is no denying that clients can sometimes approach therapy with their thinking locked-in around their problem. That is one reason that some therapists speak of helping clients move from a problem-trance to a solution-trance. Personally, I actually prefer to talk about moving from a problem-trance to a *possibility*-trance, helping clients discover hope and – through further discussion – the realisation that the problem was neither insurmountable, permanent nor unchanging.

This induction – through use of a 'portal,' or 'miracle question,' or crystal ball, or any means of stepping outside of the problem - invites clients to view things from a completely different perspective... from the perspective that their problem has been resolved.

And part of that is to see the impact of the removal of the problem, to really understand how life – the whole of life – would look without the problem. If this client had a partner, I may have pictured them in the passenger seat. And I may have focused on their children in the back, rather than a car driving behind.

The Perspective Induction has clear similarities with the Leisure Induction. However, instead of revivifying a past experience, you lead your client to associate into a future one.

There are also some similarities with my Sensory Overlap induction, gradually moving round and round – with different perspectives – until you move inside. This is partly to enable the client to thoroughly consider what their preferred problem-resolved future would be like (from all sorts of angles), but also to function as a mildly disorienting means of circling round in ever-decreasing circles until you are then focusing on the client's current experience.

Tips

I don't know if you really think about your opening question or statement when a client comes in. Some people might ask, "What seems to be the problem?" However, that clearly risks reinforcing the problem-trance.

Or, "How can I help you?" Yet, if we want to quibble, it could be argued that such a question implies that *we* are the ones going to be doing the work, rather than our clients. As in, "how can I help YOU?"

So, practitioners coming from a more solution-focused position, might be inclined to ask something more like:

> "What needs to be accomplished by the end of this session (or this series of sessions) so that you can say that coming to see me was useful and meaningful?"

Or, more simply: "What's your best hope from coming here today?"

I've spoken above of circling round until you reach the client's current experience. It is possible to stretch the induction even further than seen in this transcript. For example, other examples of this induction might include something like:

> How would I see that you were beginning to relax?

– "My breathing would have slowed-down."

How would your breathing know that was a sign that you are relaxing...?

It is possible to reach a place where the client does not know how to answer. (It is the hypnotist's role to recognise if the client would experience this as a useful minor confusion, or just annoying nonsense.) However, if you are asking questions about the Sun's perspective and the views of a fly on the windscreen, it makes as much sense to wonder how their breathing would perceive things.

Of course, if you are discussing your client's physical reactions, it is important to be aware of the appropriateness of the situation. If a female client answered a question by referring to their breathing changing in their chest, I would obviously not say anything like, "And if I was looking at your chest, how would I be able to tell...?"

Instead, I might reference the fly on the windscreen again (who might be seen as less predatory than a male therapist!), or even ask how the rest of their body knew the changes in their breathing meant they were beginning to relax more and more now.

You will most likely have seen the temporal shifts in the transcript. At times, I am talking about something in the future. Yet, at other times, I speak of things as happening now. You may choose to work consistently and gradually move from the future to the here and now. However, with this induction, I prefer to switch between the two, almost leaving the client unsure if the change has already happened (and they experience it as if it has), or if it is something that will kick-in when they walk through that portal.

I would not tend to follow this induction with an explicit deepener. Instead, I would eventually end the experience and talk about it and any lessons learned. Then we might do the whole thing again, but instead of starting in the car, they are future-pacing and rehearsing the world without their problem. So, fractionation will play a role in deepening, which could be utilised if it was felt necessary for some reason.

Incidentally, usually, if the problem/miracle scene was somewhere like this (i.e. in control of a vehicle), I would likely not proceed as I did here. I might have them experience the initial difference, but then have them step out of their body and float off to somewhere else where it is perhaps more appropriate for them to e.g. close their eyes when/if they want to.

From that safer scene, they can go through the same induction dissociated. Then, later in the session, outside of any experience of trance, have them associate into the happy driving version of themselves to confirm and cement the changes. I would just rather avoid implicitly suggesting that someone goes into a deep trance experience whilst actually driving a vehicle.[40]

40 This does not need to be an issue at all, even with the driving example. The whole induction can be an eyes-open, 'up-time trance,' experience.

Slam-dunk Induction

Introduction

The Slam Dunk induction is another great offering from Barry Thain. If that is not enough to pique your interest, perhaps reading the following transcript will do the job.

Transcript

> Take a deep breath and... as you breathe out... relax and allow your eyes to close.
>
> Now... look through your eyelids at your left thumbnail... keeping your eyes closed... look at your left thumbnail... and keep looking at it as you lift it up and hold it six inches in front of your face...
>
> Now let it go down again and... as it goes down... your arms gets twice as heavy... And every time you lower your arm it gets twice as heavy until... soon... it's so heavy you can't lift it at all ...
>
> Still looking at that thumbnail... with your eyes closed... lift it up to your face... and let it go down and your arm gets twice as heavy again...
>
> Keep doing this until their arm is so heavy you cannot lift it at all ...

[Wait until the arm stops moving. Once the arm stops, continue.]

Good... Now with your eyes still closed... look at the thumbnail on your right hand...

Every time you lift that up to your face you become better able to accept and act on my instructions... automatically...

And when your hand stops... between your lap and your face... you will be able to accept and act on my instructions... instantly and immediately... using your powerful mind... to create a new reality...

So keep looking at your right thumbnail and... bring it up to your face... better able to follow my directions... automatically...

Now let your hand return to your lap...

Keep doing this until your hand stops between your lap and your face.

[Wait until the hand stops.]

You are now able to accept and act on my instructions... instantly and immediately... using your powerful mind... everything I say can instantly become your reality... here and now... for your own good.

Commentary

Here is Barry's own explanation for the induction:

'Several years ago I came to see the concept of rapid and progressive inductions as fundamentally flawed. It is *hypnotees*, not inductions, who are either rapid or

> progressive. I proved this in 2007. I started a progressive relaxation with 30 hypnotherapists, and stopped after one minute. Ten of them were already hypnotized.
>
> 'Theoretically, therefore, a so-called rapid induction might work equally well with a progressive hypnotee if you keep doing it for ten minutes or so.
>
> 'But how do you know if your progressive relaxation has worked after 30 seconds so you can avoid wasting the next ten minutes? And how do you know if your rapid induction would work if only you kept going for another ten seconds?'

The Slam-dunk induction is a perfect way to execute an induction that will be rapid for those who would respond rapidly and more progressive for those who take more time.

Whether or not Thain's theory that it is clients who are "rapid" or "progressive" is accurate, it is a significant idea and deserves much wider consideration.

Tips

It is, of course, completely acceptable to only use the first part of this induction. That would provide you with an arm catalepsy and the information required to ascertain if you client was a 'rapid,' or a 'progressive.'

Thain's approach is very direct. If that is not your style, I would strongly encourage you not to dismiss this induction as a result. There is much here that can be experimented with, adapted and utilised to match your approach and your client's needs.

Heavy Ball

Introduction

This is a lovely pressure-free induction that achieves phenomena (in this case, a hand stick) almost instantly and effortlessly.

Transcript

I'd like you to rest your hand on your lap like this, as if you're waiting for me to put something on it, or maybe give you a present [hand placed palm-up]

Have you ever been swimming? [Client nods]

You know that feeling in water, where you might kick or punch, and it's all much harder and slower?

I'd like you to imagine the weight of water on that hand. Not uncomfortable, but too heavy to push against.

Or imagine a bowling ball in that hand. And it is just too heavy to lift. It's not quite so heavy that it's uncomfortable. But it's just too heavy to lift. The exact weight. And when you have a sense of that, try to lift that hand and find that the ball is just too heavy.

Now I want you to take your other hand and find that you are able to squish and mould the ball. And I want you to mould and squash it down until it is the size of a marble.

And when you have that marble, lift it up as high as you can so that I can see...

[You can go in any number of directions after this. For example:]

Can I take that?

What colour is the marble? Is it transparent, or solid? Was it hot or cold or warm when you held it?

I am going to place the marble back into your hand... and I want you to imagine that every time you breathe out, it gets heavier... and heavier... and heavier...

Commentary

This is an open-ended induction, which can go in a number of directions.

As with the *Auto Wrist Lift*, this induction achieves hypnotic phenomena effortlessly and very early on. This in itself can have a hypnotising effect on some people. That is, rather then hypnotising them to elicit hypnotic phenomena, you achieve the phenomena in order to hypnotise them.

There are various theories as to why this can happen. One of the most common theories is the idea that certain phenomena occur at specific levels of trance. Thus, producing such phenomena means that someone is at – or takes them to – a particular level of trance.

Aside from questioning the notion of levels of trance, or the belief that certain phenomena occur at specific levels, this explanation fails to account for inductions like this, where phenomena is achieved at a 'waking level.' It also ignores the fact that hypnotic phenomena is experienced in our ordinary everyday lives, outside of hypnosis.

A more satisfactory explanation might involve considering the effects of phenomena on someone's expectations or perception of hypnosis. So, if a client associated certain actions with being 'in' or 'under' hypnosis, experiencing such phenomena might lead them to conclude that they had therefore been hypnotised. They may then find themselves thinking and behaving precisely the way a person does when they have been hypnotised – effectively hypnotising themselves in the process.

Auto Wrist-Lift

Introduction

This is a phenomenal induction. It is intentionally open-ended and can go in a number of directions.

The Auto Wrist Lift shares a number of features with the *Heavy Ball Induction.*

Transcript

I would like you to find a spot on the back of your hand, and focus on that. And it doesn't even matter if you focus all of your attention on that spot and allow yourself to become absorbed in that.

Now, I would like you to use your other hand to lift that hand up by the wrist, like so.

[Demonstrate, bending the lifted arm at 90 degrees at the elbow.]

Now, hold it gentler. Now, gentler. In fact, I'd like you to hold it as gently as you possibly can, with the arm still remaining in the air...

Gentler... Hold it so gently that you cannot even feel it...

And when you are confident that you arm will stay up on its own, you can remove the other hand and see what that feels like... just floating there, of its own accord...

Commentary

This induction is intentionally open-ended. Once you have achieved the phenomena of catalepsy, you can proceed in any number of directions, depending on your style and your client's goals.

As with the Heavy Ball, this induction achieves hypnotic phenomena effortlessly and very early on. This can have a hypnotising effect on some people and means that rather then hypnotising them to elicit hypnotic phenomena, you achieve the phenomena in order to hypnotise them.

Tips

Due to the open-ended nature of this induction, you can use it in all sorts of situations.

You might want to carry on in an "Eyes open" / "Waking trance" way. This relies on the recognition that once your client has their arm floating in the air, presumably of its own accord, they are fully engaged with the process and open to your instructions.

If this is a route you choose to go down, I would suggest not spending too long waiting after you achieve catalepsy. I like to give my clients time to be amused by what is happening, often asking them something like, "How are you doing that?" or "What's that like?"

Rather than bringing them out of their experience, these questions tend to take them further into it as they accept that the arm is floating and begin to enjoy what is happening.

However, I do not ask more than one or (at the most) two questions. I do not want to risk them over-analysing or trying to actually figure-out why and how their arm is floating on its own. If you wait too long, you will find some clients take a step back from the experience, viewing it as some kind of magic trick that they want to figure out. When that happens, the magic is often over and they become an objective investigator, rather than an active participant.

This need not be the end of things. You could treat the wrist lift as simply preparatory phenomena and proceed by saying something like, "Okay, well now that we know you can easily do that, let's do that on the other hand and use that as a means of going deeper into this experience." I may also offer some pseudo-science nonsense about e.g. seeing how both sides of their brain can respond to my suggestions and therefore knowing that she can go deeper into hypnosis easily and effortlessly. (Of course, saying she can go deeper carries the implication that she has already begun to enter hypnosis.)

Then, after we achieve the same effect on the other wrist, I simply invite them to close their eyes and "go fully into that experience."

Alternatively, rather than proceeding in an eyes open fashion, once they achieve catalepsy on the first wrist, I might say:

> "Now, go ahead and close your eyes and simply allow yourself to drop deeper into this experience. And your arm might want to begin floating down slowly in its own time. And the further your arm comes down, the further you will go into this state you are now enjoying. But I don't want you to *go all of the way inside* until that arm has gone all of the way down and rested on your lap."

The Old Finger Lift

Introduction

The Old Finger Lift was developed as a means of progressively – and flexibly – enabling someone to shift their focus in a variety of ways (whilst appearing quite repetitive, aiding relaxation and/or fatigue).

Transcript

> Just plop your hands down on your legs like so [demonstrate, by placing one hand on each thigh/knee]... and just rest them there.
>
> I am going to ask you to look at each finger, in succession, as I count from 10 to 1.
>
> And each time you look at a finger, I would like you to take a nice deep breath, and let it out. It will be as if you are letting out any stress, or tension, just letting it go. So, effectively, you will be relaxing a little more with each breath you take.
>
> Okay?
>
> And after you've done that, on the last finger, you can let your eyes close.
>
> [Then, point to each finger in turn, counting down aloud

each time that you do. Wait for them to exhale after each number, before moving on. As they close their eyes at the end, say:]

That's it. Just letting it all go.

Now, with your eyes closed, I will ask you, as I count from 10 to 1, to lift each finger in turn and then put it down. And I want you to allow each finger to feel heavier than the last. Imagine that and you can experience it.

Ready?

[Count down from 10-1, watching your client lift their finger and then put it down. Make suggestions with each successive finger, that it is getting heavier.]

And this time, I am going to lift each finger slightly, one by one. And each time a finger drops down, you can find yourself dropping deeper into this experience.

[Count from 10-1, lifting a finger as you do so, then let it drop.]

[Finally, touch the back of each finger – 10 down to 1 – as you say the following.]

Now, you can allow yourself to float, drift and sink fully inside, exploring that world of inner resources that you have within, reaching further depths than you may have encountered previously, as you enjoy this inner journey into the strongest and most creative aspects of who you are.

Commentary

This is a fairly straightforward induction. It helps to think of it as a 4-stage countdown to internal focus.

The 4 stages can be:

- Look at each finger, as the hypnotist counts
- As the hypnotist counts, lift and lower each corresponding finger
- The hypnotist lifts and drops each finger, 1-10
- The hypnotist taps the back of each finger as he makes suggestions...

When I first used this induction, I would pre-explain all four steps before beginning. This has the benefit of increasing expectation. However, it also makes it more difficult to go "off-script" if the opportunity arises.

You may want to explicitly allocate a specific function to each individual countdown. For example, the first one is to relax the body. The second is to quiet the mind, etc. There are plenty of opportunities to be creative here.

Tips

Phenomena that sometimes arises automatically, or that you might want to look out for and encourage, includes:

- Their fingers may be too heavy to lift (in the 2nd round)
- A finger may become cataleptic and remain in the air (in the 3rd round)
- Their Hand(s) may be stuck to their leg (after round 4)

Tension Observation

Introduction

The Tension Observation induction is a rather blatant variation of a Progressive Muscle Relaxation. It also includes elements of body awareness (for example, noticing those places where we may carry tension without being aware of it) and acceptance of our present experience.

As such, it is an inherent Therapeutic Induction.

Transcript

> If you go ahead and get yourself comfortable... as comfortable as you can... And just experience this however you experience it.
>
> So, if you imagine that you are willing or able to become slightly less tense, just imagine what that might do to your eyelids. Some people's eyes might close, gently. Others might kinda half-close, as they relax. Other people's eyes might stay open. However you respond to that is perfectly fine.
>
> And just become aware, as you breathe, of that tension in your body. Some people imagine that as they breathe out, they are letting some of that tension go. And you don't have to *make* that happen. That may just happen

automatically, by itself.

Now, what I'd like you to do – and this may sound slightly strange – I'd like you to intentionally locate a point of tension in your body... Just one tiny point. Maybe about the size of a 10p coin, or a Quarter.

Just find a spot of tension, maybe in your shoulders... maybe somewhere in your back. Maybe one of your legs... maybe your big toe. Just *focus-in on one small spot of tension.*

And, no doubt, this is a feeling that you know well.

So, notice whatever it is you notice about that tension... There's no right or wrong way for your body to respond to this... You can simply experience what you experience...

But notice what that tension *feels* like. Is it moving? Is it still? Is it buzzing? Does it change? Can you maybe picture it a particular colour?

Become fully acquainted with that tension, that we often spend so long resisting... and fighting against.

I'd like you to almost – even if just temporarily – *welcome that tension.*

And now... I'd like you to find another spot of tension. And maybe imagine the two linking up...

Maybe now... you can become aware of another spot of tension... this tension that you carry so well.

And you can either allow those points of tensions to link-up, like they're becoming a network in your body... or you can just allow the general feeling to spread... Not so it's uncomfortable... but so it's that old familiar tension you know well.

And when you've really got a handle on that... you can just allow it to fade back, reverting back down to one small spot of tension.

And as you breathe out... you can let the rest of that tension go... and focus in on that old spot of tension.

Now I'd like you to find another place in your body... it could be anywhere... where you feel a *lack* of tension... And I don't know what that feels like for you... it's often different for everyone. But just notice an area – again just the size of a small coin, to start with – an area where there's a lack of tension...

And notice how big that is... notice if it's still... is it variable... is it moving... buzzing... does it have a colour? Become fully acquainted with that lack of tension.

Now maybe allow that to slowly spread. You don't have to make it happen... Maybe each time you breathe out... you become more aware of the lack of tension, or more familiar with that feeling... Maybe it can spread from that one spot... or maybe you can notice more than one spot of lack of tension and they begin to link up...

Allow that to increase... And become fully acquainted with that. Feel what you are feeling. Experience what you are experiencing.

And you may already know that people refer to this lack of tension by different names. Some people call it ease... some people call it comfort. I know some people who would call it relaxation. What you call it isn't really relevant. The important thing is that you *know this feeling*... and you get to become more comfortable with it, and acquainted with it. And it begins to feel as natural to you as your own breathing.

> And just allow that relaxation to continue spreading… in its own easy way… throughout your body…
>
> [Proceed with deepener, therapeutic story/metaphor, or phenomena.]

Commentary

Many versions of the Progressive Muscle Relaxation begin by having the client tense an area of the body and then let that tension go. This enables the client to become familiar with their body relaxing (as the tension dissipates).

The Tension Observation induction utilises tension in a slightly different way. It begins by asking the client to locate a small example of tension and to become fully familiar with it. This all takes place in a non-threatening way, with the client invited to pause and even accept the tension.

The client is then lead to find another small point of tension and connect it to the first. This may take place a third or fourth time. The whole process is then reversed until the client is back with just one point of tension. This implicitly demonstrates how tension can be released, as well as narrowing the client's focus.

The next stage is for the client to locate a small point of 'lack of tension.' This is generally easier and more intuitive than e.g. finding a point of 'relaxation.'

Tips

Asking your client to locate an area of 'lack of tension' is far more accessible than telling them to relax. You are not asking them to remove all tension from their body, or to e.g. relax their entire torso. You are merely making the easily accepted suggestion that there must be at least one tiny spot of 'lack of tension' somewhere in their body.

Spreading the 'lack of tension' can take place in a number of ways. I sometimes find enough spots of 'lack of tension' that I can ask my client to notice them linking-up. (I often use the visual example of a map of the London Underground.) If I am working with children, I might talk about drawing dot-to-dot and asking them what the picture looks like. With adults, I may do something similar, but have them imagine stars in a constellation and ask what they can see.

Alternatively, I may invite my client to imagine the 'lack of tension' spreading out from the initial spot. As they do this, they might notice it spreading out to include additional spots of 'lack of tension' they had not previously been aware of, or it may simply spread progressively, moving out from the first spot to fill their body.

I personally find that a good therapeutic story works as a natural and effective deepening process. After the story, or any additional therapy, I may close the session by having the relaxation shrink and return to its initial point of 'lack of tension.' This takes place with the suggestion that the client has now learned how to find their 'lack of tension' point and to amplify and spread it whenever they so desire.

Hazlerig Cat's Paw

Introduction

James Hazlerig developed this induction after spending some time thinking about bi-lateral stimulation.[41] In many ways it can be thought of as a directed self-hypnosis experience.

The Cat's Paw includes elements of bi-lateral stimulation, eye-fixation, fractionation and progressive muscle relaxation. The induction has similarities to the Old Finger Lift and the Dr. Flowers Induction.

Transcript

Just hold your hands up, like this, with your palms out.

[Demonstrate by placing your own hands just below eye-level, palms facing out.]

And now pick a spot above your head, at about a 45 degree angle and look at that spot.

Now you can go ahead and tense your right hand…

[Demonstrate by making a fist with your hand]

…focus all of your attention on your right hand, keeping your eyes up there on that spot. And let the rest of the body relax, whilst your right hand becomes tense.

41 http://hypnoticstorytellingcourse.com

Then relax that hand and release the tension.

[Demonstrate by unclenching your fist]

Now go ahead and repeat that with your left hand.

[Demonstrate by making a fist with your left hand]

Tense that hand and focus all of your attention on it, keeping your eyes up there on that spot. And let the rest of the body relax, as that hand becomes tense.

Now relax and unclench that hand.

Okay, now just let your eyes close down, and you can still picture that spot up there.

And tense up that right hand again. And with each number that I count, we are going to alternate which hand is tense.

So, we start with the right – 10. Then let it relax.

9 – as you clench the left hand…

8 – letting the left relax, as you tense the right…

7…

6…

5…

4…

3…

2…

1…

0…

Good. Take a deep breath. Let your eyes gently open up

and kinda try to find that spot up there.

Now, we are going to do this again. So, go ahead and close your eyes down. And let's repeat that process, starting on the right...

10...

9...

8...

7...

6...

5...

4...

3...

2...

1...

0...

You're doing great. Now let your eyes just gently open up, just a little bit, doesn't have to be very much.

You might find them wanting to stay closed. In a moment, if you wanted to, you could just go ahead and keep them closed. But for now, let's do this again.

Close your eyes and, starting with the right...

[Count from 10-0, with the client clenching alternate hands with each number.]

And if you want to, you could struggle and strain to open up the eyes, or you could just let them stay completely shut...

as we do this again...

[Count from 10-0, with the client clenching alternate hands with each number.]

and if you're ready to, you could just let those eyes just remain closed, as we do this just one more time and go even deeper...

[Count from 10-0, with the client clenching alternate hands with each number.]

And just let yourself relax down deeply, take a nice deep breath and let it out...

Commentary

Although – as we have previously stated – this induction shares some similarities with a few other inductions, it is also unique in a number of ways.

By having the client focus on a spot above them, whilst clenching alternate hands, the bi-lateral stimulation involved can provoke a slight dissociation.

When the client initially has their eyes open as they look at the spot, this can cause the eyes to become tired relatively quickly. This, coupled with the effect of switching between hands and opening/closing their eyes between the rounds of counting, can result in a powerful and fairly unique experience of fractionation.

This induction easily sits within the Therapeutic Inductions approach. The built-in bi-lateral stimulation, along with the muscle tension and release, mean that this induction can be far more than a means of leading someone into hypnosis. The Hazlerig Cats Paw induction can potentially be a therapeutic tool in and of itself.

We have used the induction with a number of clients struggling with anxiety. We had them think about the issue that causes them anxiety and to "try" to keep thinking about this as we went through "a quick hypnotic process." The following bi-lateral stimulation, coupled with attempting to focus on a number of things at once (the anxiety, the spot above their head, the tension in their hand and the relaxation in the rest of their body), meant that the experience of going through the Cats Paw induction had a significant impact on their anxiety. And that was supposedly before we had even got to the therapy part!

Expectancy Induction

Introduction

The Expectancy Induction presented here has been provided by John Cleesattel.[42] It is indisputably an application of the principles inherent in the Elman Handshake.

Transcript

> So, you can begin by getting yourself comfortable. And you can shift around to get even more comfortable any time you choose...
>
> If at any time, or for any reason, you find that you are not comfortable when being in trance, simply say the word "Exit" out loud and you will immediately be made to feel comfortable and will be taken out of trance.
>
> Hypnosis is all about desire, permission, and being able to follow instructions. If you want to be hypnotized, and you allow it to happen, and do what I say, you can be.
>
> Now, there is nothing that you need to do to help me. You can't make it happen, but you can *notice it when it does.* This is kind of like goose bumps. You can't make them happen, but you can notice them when they do.
>
> In a moment, I will be saying the names of some colours. I

42 http://www.wizardoftrance.com

won't let you know what colours I am going to say, but when I say the first colour, you will notice a nice warm glow in your chest. It will be very soothing and will feel very good. Let me know when you feel this, and we will move on.

Is this okay with you? [Wait for positive response…]

Are you ready? [This is important to say, as it sets the expectancy.]

Green. [Snap your fingers and then wait for them to tell you they feel it...]

Feels good doesn't it?

Are we ready to move on?

Okay, when I say the next colour, you will notice this warm glow will spread all over your body, relaxing you very much and feeling absolutely wonderful.

You will notice that your eyelids have become very heavy.

It is up to you if you close them or not, but you will find it is much easier to relax if you do.

When you feel this, let me know and we will proceed.

Is that okay with you? [Wait for positive response…]

Good.

Are you ready?

Orange. [Snap your fingers and then wait for them to tell you they feel it, or you see them struggling with their eyes...]

Are we ready to move on? [Wait for positive response…]

Good.

When I say the next colour, you will notice your eye lids are so relaxed that they will no longer open.

When you are sure they are that relaxed, I want you to try to open them, and give them a good try.

You will notice that the harder you try to open them, the more firmly they remain closed.

Is that okay with you? Good.

Are you ready?

Blue. [Snap your fingers and then wait for them to test their eyes]

[When you see them trying to open them, tell them...]

That's good, now stop trying and feel yourself drifting deeper into trance.

Notice how good that feels. And the deeper you go, the better you feel. And the better you feel, the deeper you go.

That's it...

Commentary

Cleesattel expertly utilises the principle that when we expect something to happen, our imagination prepares us for the expected event.

As each colour you name produces the results you confidently said it would, expectation is increased that the next stage will be equally effective.

As with all inductions in this book, your role is to utilise your client's responses, acting as if each one is exactly what they were supposed to do.

Tips

This induction can lead to some useful "waking trance," or "hypnosis without trance," type of experiences. We have already seen with things like the Auto Wrist-Lift and Heavy Ball inductions that it is possible to achieve hypnotic phenomena almost from the beginning of your interaction. So, in that sense, nothing here is exceptional.

However, moving progressively through the stages of this induction (which already involves responses, i.e. feeling something when a colour is announced), which culminates in more explicit hypnotic phenomena creates a very unique experience for the client.

I do not generally engage in finger-snapping, or other dramatic gestures. Yet, in this induction I think that they actually serve quite a useful purpose. After all, the induction progresses so naturally and easily that your client may need just a little bit more than the name of a colour. They may benefit from something 'hypnotic' and a finger-snap is a good societal stereotype of something strange about to take place. It adds to the expectation that your client has already begun to generate and escalate.

If this is the first time you have encountered the Expectancy Induction, I recommend that you test it out. It is well-suited for the clinic, stage or streets.

Dr. Flower's Induction

Introduction

Dr. Sidney Flowers created an incredibly simple yet effective induction, that rightly bears his name and is a favourite of many therapeutic hypnotists.

The Dr. Flowers induction utilises eye fixation, expectation and fractionation. It is particularly useful for situations where physical touch is not appropriate (meaning that inductions like the Elman, for example, might not be allowed).

The induction is recognisable by the fact that the client opens and closes their eyes as the hypnotist counts down. Some variations have the hypnotee open-and-close between numbers. Others might have them close on (e.g.) even numbers and open on odd.

Transcript

> I would like you to start, by picking a point on that wall, where you can focus all of your attention.
>
> Look at that wall, almost as if you can see through to a perfect calm and soothing scene. You may even feel like you are looking into a daydream. Either way, simply rest your eyes on one spot on that wall.
>
> [Wait until your partner's eyes appear to have fixed on one spot, ideally appearing slightly defocused.]

That's right. Now, bring all of your attention to that spot, as you rest your eyes over there.

Soon you'll find all of the muscle groups in your body will relax. Your facial muscles will relax. Your arms will relax. Your legs will relax. Your whole body will let go.

And soon you will close your eyes… and go into a sound, peaceful hypnotic rest.

Hypnosis is not a state of unconsciousness, but rather a state of dreamy relaxation where the mind is open to new experiences.

Are you ready?

— "Yeah."

In a moment, I am going to count backwards from 20 to one. With each number I say, you will close your eyes. And in between the counts, you'll open them.

So, for example: 20 – close your eyes… and open them. 19 – close…open. 18 – close…open. And so on.

And what you will begin to notice is that it increasingly feels like too much effort to open your eyes. You would rather keep them closed, enjoying that scene, over there, drifting into that experience.

And sometime before I reach 1, maybe at five, maybe at ten, maybe even at fifteen… You'll close your eyes and go into deep, sound hypnotic rest.

Okay?

— "Yep."

Perfect. Let's begin.

20… 19… 18…

Notice now how easily you can sink into this process, just allowing yourself to enjoy that experience...

As you begin to feel that relaxation spreading throughout your body...

[Client's facial muscles relax and drop.]

That's right.

17... 16... 15...

And you can be aware of that sense of relaxation, and as you do you can notice how it becomes more and more inconvenient to open those eyes...

14... 13...

[The hypnotist notices their partner struggling to open their eyes, so interrupts the usual pattern of counting in threes...]

And when it becomes too difficult to open them, or just too easy to keep them closed, you can keep them closed; simply imagining that you are opening them.

12...

That relaxation spreading throughout your body, as you drift deeper into that rest. And the deeper you go, the better you feel... and the better you feel, the deeper you go.

11... 10...

[The client does not open their eyes between 11 and 10.]

That's right.

9... 8... 7...

Enjoying that deep deep rest...

6... 5... 4...

And with each number now, you can find that relaxation doubling, going deeper down, twice as deep.

3... 2...

And... 1...

That's it... Any remaining stress or tension, just disappearing, evaporating from your body...

And in a moment, not yet but in a moment, I am going to say the number "zero." And you can even picture that big round number in front of you... like the 'O' in the word, 'hypnosis.' And when I say that number, you will step through into deep hypnosis... completely relaxed in mind and body... stepping into that calm and soothing scene your own mind has created for you...

Get ready...

Zero...

And you can go straight through that big round number, stepping into a deep hypnotic rest... as you let go all the way down...

Commentary

This is a great induction if you are working online, with a group, or in situations where physical touch is prohibited.

Dr. Flowers is easy to learn and a good and reliable induction for beginners. However, that does not mean it is not suited to more advanced practitioners. It is a flexible induction and can be delivered in a number of different ways, to match the style of the hypnotist and the needs of the client.

Many versions of the induction start by building expectation, telling the client what is going to take place. The next step builds compliance by directing the client to follow a number of simple instructions.

The opening and closing of the eyes can have a fractionating effect, meaning that all other responses (e.g. expectation, eye-fatigue relaxation, compliance) may be enhanced.

Tips

To be completely honest, nowadays any induction that involves opening and closing the eyes might be referred to as "Dr. Flower's induction." A number of versions start by having the client visualise a scene. For example, they may instruct the client to look at the wall, but then follow it up with an invitation to look "through" the wall to a beautiful garden on the other side.

This can be a useful tip to achieve eye-fixation in a less obvious way than instructing someone to focus on e.g. one specific spot on the wall. Additionally, having the client focus on a spot/scene on the wall, but also to follow instructions and notice a growing relaxation, may result in a sense of dissociation.

The countdown should be timed to pace and lead the client's experience. Normally, this will involve counting more slowly as you get further down the count. Additionally, you may find that it feels natural to leave longer gaps between the numbers, so your client's eyes are shut for a longer amount of time.

When they stop opening their eyes, you can continue counting down, adding suggestions for relaxation and/or trance until you get to zero.

EXERCISE

Which inductions in this section are most appealing to you?

Do you prefer quite formulaic inductions, or more conversational ones?

Consider if you – or your clients – would benefit from familiarising yourself with the sort of inductions you would not normally use.

What Can We Learn From 30 Inductions?

You might, quite fairly, wonder what you are now meant to do with 30 inductions.

Do I expect you to learn and master all 30 Inductions, so that you are never left without a tool to use? No, not at all.

Although I have enjoyed using and teaching all of the inductions in this book, in reality, I probably limit myself to using 4-6 inductions with any degree of regularity.

So, why have I gone to the bother of sharing so many inductions in this book? There are a few reasons.

Firstly, the 4-6 inductions you might choose to master could well be different to those that I use. So, I have provided multiple options for you to choose how you are going to stock your toolbox.

Secondly, it can be helpful to learn variations of your favourite inductions. You may have been well aware that you could induce hypnosis via eye-fixation, but had you considered having your client hallucinate a candle flame, or use that as a 'portal' into hypnosis?

You may have been aware of inductions like the thumb stare, but had you considered utilizing physical elements – along with the feeling of letting go – seen in the coin drop?

I also think it is helpful to have knowledge of a variety of different induction categories, such as relaxation-based, surprise, confusion, or physical phenomena. This simply provides you with a broad knowledge base from which to work.

Finally – and building on the previous arguments – knowledge of a variety of inductions, grants the hypnotist a great deal of variety and flexibility. For example, if you were using a hand-drop and your client's hand didn't move, you might be able to proceed as if it is a modified wicks, or an arm levitation.

Knowing how inductions work – and how they are experienced – significantly increases your knowledge of the realm of hypnosis and the options available to you as the 'dream pilot.'

EXERCISE

Select 4-6 inductions that are from different categories (e.g. eye-fixation, relaxation) and practice with a partner.

Practice experiencing the inductions as the hypnotee, as well as the hypnotist.

Does your experience (as the hypnotee) of any particular induction change your opinion of it?

DEEPENERS

Many hypnotic practitioners feel as if the induction does not do enough to get their clients properly 'into' hypnosis.

Similarly, their clients might report feeling as if they were not quite 'there' yet.

It is as if the response routine opens their window on reality, whilst the induction opens the door on a whole new world. Yet, what does it take for them to step through that door and begin to inhabit this new world of possibilities?

Is this what deepeners do? Are they needed?

And, if so, what sort of deepeners might we employ?

Do we need Deepeners?

The Purpose of Deepeners

What do hypnotists mean by a 'deep trance' or indeed 'hypnotic deepeners'?

Some schools of hypnosis assert a direct relationship between hypnosis and particular brain-wave activity. For quite some time, it was popular to present hypnosis as the point when a client's brain went into 'the alpha state.'

Later, predictably enough, some people began to teach that reaching 'the delta state' was a preferred deeper level of hypnosis (with the implication that more could be achieved in such a state).

It might not surprise you by now to learn that, despite the commitment that some practitioners have to such models, the evidence for such a position is far from conclusive.

Yet, even if the research thoroughly supported such approaches, it is as far from an 'experiential model' as we could get. So, as I teach things, the purpose of deepening hypnosis is not to literally get to a 'deeper' level or hypnosis, or attain special brain-wave states. Instead, it is to 'deepen' a client's experience.

What do I mean by that?

As we saw with the A4 + 2 description of the hypnotic journey, hypnosis can be thought of as an experiential process by which clients learn that reality is pliable and their current experience of it can be altered. Yet, given that hypnosis can be perceived as a fluid experience in this way, it can be helpful to assist clients to learn that this is not necessarily fleeting.

After all, they may experience their hands being magnetically pulled together and think, "Well, that was a crazy 4 minutes! Anyway, back to normal now..."

Deepeners – in terms of the journey that a client goes through – help to strengthen, stabilise and sustain what is fundamentally a fluid experience. Through prolonging and potentially increasing each previous aspect of A4 + 2 (expectation, attention, absorption, imagination and emotional arousal), we assist our clients to continue with the final aspect of altering their experience.

Some practitioners believe that deeper levels of hypnosis are required to achieve 'deeper' phenomena, or therapeutic goals. We will address this belief when we look at the Suggestion Pyramid and the Chain of Command.

For now, it will suffice to say that deepeners help to intensify, ratify and secure a client's current experience of hypnosis.

Understanding the Examples that Follow

We have already seen some deepeners in action, with some of the induction transcripts. These include the O in HypnOsis, the Relaxing Staircase and making use of your client's Special Place.

Generally, you will want to use a deepener that follows naturally and organically from the preparation work and induction you have used. After all, it would be counter-productive to use, for example, an induction that emphasised relaxation and then jump to a deepener that was all about dissociation, or confusion. Instead, your client should feel as if everything they have experienced is one flowing and developing journey.

Performing your Deepeners

Some of the following chapters contain transcripts, yet without the commentary and tips of the induction transcripts, Other chapters simply describe a deepener, a series of deepeners, or important deepening principles.

Using a deepener – for the client – should feel less like the next stage and more like a fluid continuation of what they are already experiencing. It is important to recall this to avoid creating a disjointed or staccato experience for your client.

EXERCISE

Prior to reading this chapter, how would you have described the purpose of deepeners?

Are deepeners necessary for therapeutic hypnosis?

If so, how would you describe the role or purpose of deepeners within the journey of hypnosis?

Reflect on the idea that the deepener can flow organically from the preparation and induction that have preceded it.

Deepening Staircase

Introduction

The deepening staircase is a classic deepener – and rightly so. Not only is it flexible, with numerous elements that can be changed, it can also be prefaced in different ways and also terminate in different places, for various reasons.

The transcript that follows is a basic example of the deepener in action.

Transcript

> As you sit there, very comfortable and very relaxed – you become aware of a staircase – a beautiful staircase with a polished, ornate banister running down alongside and a deep, rich carpet underneath your bare feet.
>
> As you look down the stairs you notice that there are ten steps leading gently down – ten steps leading down, and down, and down; these are the steps that will lead you deep into dream–time – deep into relaxation – and in a moment I'd like you to walk down those steps with me and I will count them off for you one at a time, and you will find that the deeper down you go, the more comfortable and the more relaxed will you become.
>
> So when you are ready to walk down the stairs I want you to gently place your hand on the banister and begin to

slowly descend the stairs as I count them off from 10 to 1.

10 – deeply relaxed, deeply comfortable,

9 – deeply relaxed, deeply comfortable,

8 –more and more and more relaxed,

7 – deeply relaxed, deeply comfortable,

6 – nearly half-way there,

5 – more and more and more relaxed,

4 – deeply relaxed, deeply comfortable,

3 –more and more and more relaxed,

2 – almost at the bottom now, just one more step to go, and

1 – going deeper and deeper down into hypnosis now, all the way down – to that deeper, healthier level of mind.

And as you reach the bottom step you can let the stairs and the ordinary, everyday world, further and further down – as you go deeper and deeper

You are now standing at the bottom of the steps and feeling very comfortable, very relaxed and at peace with the world. In front of you is a large, oak door. The door is closed, but you can open it. You have the key to this door. And you really want to go through the door and see what is there on the other side, for you somehow know that a wonderful place is there waiting for you.

So move now toward the door. Push it open. Push the door open. Push, push and push – and suddenly the door creaks gently open, and you push it even further open and walk through.

Now close the door behind you and turn and find yourself in a very special place... a place of calm, safety and serenity...

[Proceed to describe the special place, or leave them to imagine it with vague descriptions they can fill–in for themselves]

Passing Clouds

Transcript

I'd like you to use your imagination for a few moments now. I'd like you to imagine... to think about... yourself lying down... outside... you might be on the grass… or on the most comfortable piece of furniture you can imagine...

It is a warm, gorgeous day… The sun is just beginning to set... The temperature is just right, just the way you like it... Best of all, there are no insects anywhere to distract you... It is as if this place were made just for you...

You find yourself alone and completely safe… comfortable... So go ahead and imagine the softness of the grass… or that piece of furniture that you are on right now... Describe it to yourself in detail... What is the colour?... The size?...

The texture?... Get it clear in your mind so it becomes real to you... It is more comfortable than the softest feather bed...

And as you lay there, you are gazing up at the beautiful dusk sky... You notice the colours... the shades of reds… blue... and yellows... The many colours, as they dance upon the few scattered clouds...

As you continue to gaze... effortlessly at the sky... You watch the clouds begin to form into shapes... Some look like animals... Some look like trees... All different shapes that let your imagination begin to roam... When suddenly you notice one of the clouds that is nearly above you begin to form into the shape of a number... It looks just like the number... 25

... and as the soft breeze blows on it, you see it begin to dissolve and blow away as easily as it formed...

Then you notice another cloud coming by that forms into the number... 24... and that one begins to dissolve in the soft breeze too...

You notice that this keeps happening... slowly... as the clouds form in to the number... 23... then dissolves away...

and then... 22... and it continues this way going down... down... in numbers... very... very... slowly...

21... and you notice that in between each numbered cloud... as it blows away and as the next one forms...

20... that you are becoming soooo ... soooo ... very comfortable... peaceful... and at ease...

19... sooo... sooo relaxed... and you enjoy this wonderful relaxation...

18... and you find yourself, even allowing yourself, to let go completely...

17... You give yourself the permission that this is what you want to do...

16... as you continue to see the clouds forming into the numbers...

15... and you continue to observe them... slowly on your own...

14... and with each one... as it goes by...

13... you become twice as relaxed... twice as much as the one before...

12... as you observe them...

11... dissolving... just passing by...

10... you are so comfortable... soooo open...

9... deeper and deeper... in to this wonderful relaxed state...

7... All outside sounds... seem to help you to let go even more...

6... as you allow yourself... to be there completely...

5... totally relaxed...

4...totally safe...

3... and completely at ease... You fall into a wonderful dreaming state...

2... until finally you see the last cloud form into the number...

1... and as it dissolves... you allow yourself to let go completely... deep... deep... so very relaxed...

The Sweet Passage of Time

In reality, most hypnotic experiences are similar to sleep in that you do not stay at one level for the entire experience. Sometimes you're 'deep,' other times your 'shallow,' and sometimes you are somewhere in-between.

Often, you might find your clients going deeper simply by virtue of already being in hypnosis. The longer they are in 'trance,' the deeper they may naturally go – especially if that is suggested to them:

> And many people find that as they enjoy this experience, you will gradually, naturally and effortlessly find yourself drifting even further into this.

When this is coupled with fractionation – which can also occur naturally, due to the fluctuating 'levels' of the experience – allowing your clients time to soak and indulge in their hypnotic journey can be an effective and straightforward way to enable them to go deeper.

You can aid this by reassuring your clients that the rising or lowering of their experience is perfectly normal:

> And you may even find, as you come up and then down, that after you drift back down you can, over time, float deeper down on each occasion. That's right.

Fractionation as a Deepener

Hippolyte Bernheim discovered that the more that patients came to see him, the deeper they would go into hypnosis. He stated that when patients came in for their fifth session they went into a much deeper state of hypnosis. Off the back of this, Dave Elman reasoned that if the patients returned for five days in a row (rather than five weeks), they would reach this deep state more quickly. Then he thought that the visits could be just an hour apart. Finally, he discovered that this could all be experienced within one session, allowing Elman to achieve in three minutes what it took Bernheim five weeks to do.

The process of repeatedly taking someone into and out of hypnosis has acquired the label, Fractionation. It functions as a natural deepener and is disarmingly powerful. You have already seen this at work in the Elman induction, PHRIT and the Deeper Sleep induction.

Those three inductions can be seen as rather overt examples of fractionation. That is, you tell your client that they will go deeper next time they go 'in.' However, with the Fractionation Conversation, the client simply experiences this taking place naturally.

Other ways to allow fractionation to function as a deepener, without declaring it as such, include asking questions of your client – to cause them to come 'up' a little to answer – or conducting a series of short blocks of hypnosis (perhaps interspersed with conversation or other techniques), rather than one long session.

The Mind's Eye Closure

Michael Yapko has developed and championed a simple deepening process which he refers to as 'the mind's eye closure.' This process employs the familiar notion of our imagination acting like some kind of 'mind's eye.'

When I am using this as a deepening process, I prefer to employ it after an induction that has incorporated eye-closure as a hypnotic effect, or even an eye-lock (e.g. Elman).

Here is how Michael Yapko describes the method in his seminal book, Trancework:

> '.... just as you have physical eyes that can see the world around you, you have an inner eye that we can call the "mind's eye"... and it can continue to actively see images and process thoughts even as you relax deeply... and you can think of your mind's eye as having an eyelid... and like your physical eyes your mind's eyelid can relax and gradually grow more tired and heavy, and it can begin to drop... and as it begins to close it slowly closes out stray thoughts and stray images and can leave your mind perfectly quiet and open and free to experience whatever you'd like... and it's closing more and more... and your mind grows more quiet, more restful... and now your mind's eye can close... and close out any stray thoughts or images allowing you to focus on how relaxed and attentive you are becoming...'[43]

43 Michael Yapko, *Trancework* (5th ed.), p. 267.

In my experience, this can be a simple and effective way of helping clients to turn-down (or even silence) potentially distracting internal dialogue. For some clients, especially those for whom such internal dialogue can feel continuous and even unpleasant, this is a useful step in reaching deeper levels of hypnosis.

Sunset

Introduction

The following transcript demonstrates a time that this deepener was used with a client who had described their 'special place' as a café, on the beach, that they had enjoyed during a family holiday.

However, the only real essential elements are the description of lights going out. You could describe a sunset from various locations, the lights on various floors of an office block being switched off, or so on. In reality, this is simply a visual way to experience the deepening effect of something like the relaxing staircase.

Transcript

> So, as you're sat there, relaxed and relaxing, I wonder if you can imagine looking out to Sea... And it might be late afternoon, or early evening...
>
> You're relaxed, calm, settling down... enjoying the experience... as the day begins to draw to a close.
>
> And as the waves come in, [wait for exhalation] and out again, you can allow yourself to notice the natural ebb and flow of the day... thoughts come and go... waves come and go...
>
> Perhaps as the waves [wait for inhalation] come in, you can breathe-in peace and calm... and as they [wait for

exhalation] flow back out, you can let go of any stress and tension.

And I wonder how well you can recall that Mediterranean sun… at that time of day. That soft, warm, relaxing sun…

Perhaps you can recall the soothing sensation, of the sun beginning to set. Café lights are on, calm and soothing… not too bright… just enough… just right.

And that sun continues to set… those glorious calming colours across the sky… as the day settles and the Sun itself continues to rest.

Notice, with a peaceful appreciation… and enjoying that sense of rest… how the Sun lowers… the brightness of the day giving way to the soothing evening lights of the café…

And that sun continues to set… the sky softly going to sleep now… as that sun comes down… deeper and deeper…

You may become more and more relaxed as the sun sets further down, or you might notice how calm you are becoming as the sky softens… sun setting all the way now…

Café lights keeping you calm and relaxed… those soothing lights… as the sun… moves down… setting all the way… gone now...

Various Brief Methods

Deepeners do not need to be long drawn-out events. At times, their purpose may simply be to provide a transition between the initial experience of altered reality and a more sustained and cemented affair.

Utilisation

> And any sounds that you hear will only serve to remind you what a natural process this is, allowing you to sink deeper into that experience.

Or:

> And at times you may hear the ticking of the clock in the background, or the hum of the air conditioning. And as you do so, you might find that you can take that as a signal to let go and drift deeper into hypnosis.

Contingent Upon Client's Experience (Pacing and Leading)

> And every breath that you take, and every word that I say and every beat of your heart will cause you to go deeper and deeper into that state.

Or:

> And as you notice that change in your breathing, you might become aware of your body relaxing. And as you become aware of your body relaxing, you can notice how your mind sinks deeper into relaxation with it.

This principle also applies to hypnotic phenomena. We can see examples of this with the Modified Wicks induction. It is inevitable that the client's arm is eventually going to tire and come down. Therefore, you use this prior knowledge to connect deepening with the event about to happen.

Physical Signals

There are certain physical signals you might want to employ, to tell the client that they can now go deeper.

These can include a hand-drop:

> And as I lift up your arm and drop it into your lap, you can go deeper into this experience…

Or something as simple as a tap on the knee/shoulder:

> When I tap the back of your hand (knee/shoulder, etc.)... you can instantly find yourself even deeper... ten times deeper... just like... [tap] that…
>
> [Repeat twice more.]

Self-Perpetuating Deepeners

Finally, you might choose to use the client's current experience as a self-perpetuating cycle of deepening. For example:

> "And the better you feel, the deeper you'll go. And the deeper you go, the better you feel."

The Super Suggestion

I first discovered the useful tool known as the 'Super Suggestion' in the writings of Jonathan Chase. However, Chase suggests that it was known at least as early as 1867.[44]

The fact is that if you are seeking to reach a place where your client is most open to responding to your suggestions, then it makes sense to simply suggest that they follow your suggestions. However, use this too early and you risk a rejection. After all, it is the hypnotic equivalent of asking someone to agree to whatever you ask of them before you say it. If you have not already established a 'deep' enough engagement from your client then the Super Suggestion may be rejected and you can even find yourself retreating a few steps back up the pyramid.[45]

The Super Suggestion, as I encountered it, comes from the realm of Stage Hypnosis. However, it need not be restricted to that arena. If you have proceeded in the way this book suggests then the Super Suggestion can function to make explicit the client's engagement with the process so far.

The following example of the Super Suggestion is as blunt as that employed in a Stage Hypnosis[46] or Street Hypnosis[47] scenario. However, it fits comfortably with most therapeutic inductions and is designed to avoid any kind of rejection by your clients:

44 See Jonathan Chase, *Deeper and Deeper*, p. 101.
45 This metaphor will make more sense when we look at hypnotic phenomena.
46 ibid., p. 101.
47 Anthony Jacquin, *Reality is Plastic*, p. 70.

> From this moment on, you can accept everything I say to you, every single thing I say. Everything I say will instantly become your reality. You will know what I say you know, feel what I say you feel and do what I ask you to do. Everything I say is instantly your reality without doubt, question or hesitation because you have such a powerful mind. You can follow perfectly every direction I give you.
>
> Just nod your head to let me know you understand and accept this suggestion.

This, like all suggestions, benefits from repetition. After having repeated the suggestion a couple of times, I find it helpful to ask the client to visibly accept the suggestion by nodding their head.

Of course, it is possible to develop less authoritarian versions of the Super Suggestion. These may make it less fitting for a Stage/Street situation, but more acceptable in a therapeutic environment:

> And you have done so well, that from this moment on, you are free to accept everything I say to you. Everything I say can instantly become your reality. As you have shown yourself to have a powerful subconscious mind, you can – when you are ready – allow yourself to know what I say you can know, feel what I suggest you can feel and you can find yourself able to do what I ask you to do.
>
> Knowing that you are here for your good, and that you have taken the decision to regain control of your life – and demonstrated that you have the resources to do so – everything I say can instantly become your reality without doubt, question or hesitation... because you have such a powerful mind... you can follow perfectly every direction I give you.
>
> And you can nod your head when you are ready to let me know that you understand and embrace this suggestion.

When I include a version of the Super Suggestion, it tends to be very permissive. I also find that it works well after other simple, quick deepeners.

It is effectively a way to ensure that clients understand that the pliable reality they have been experiencing is here to stay for (at least) the rest of the hypnotic encounter.

EXERCISE

What do you think of the concept of depth as it applies to hypnosis? Do you think this is a useful description of the client's experience?

Do you tend to use the same deepener (or types of deepener) all of the time, or do you vary depending on your client and/or induction?

Experiment with both longer deepeners (e.g. the Passing Clouds) and shorter deepeners.

Practice using the Super Suggestion with a partner, both the authoritative and permissive versions. Which feels most natural to you?

Which version do your practice partners respond most favourably too?

HYPNOTIC LANGUAGE

To the uninitiated, hypnosis might seem like an exercise in words, the result of the correct spells cast in the right way.

Hopefully, by this point in the book, you are more aware of the importance of creating magical experiences for our clients.

However, words are obviously a part of this world-making endeavour and might help or hinder our efforts to open up new possibilities for our clients.

The chapters in this section are not meant as rules to be obeyed. Instead, think of them as ideas to consider, additional tools that you might utilise to your clients' advantage.

The Hypnotic Voice

One of the first things to say about hypnotic language refers to the so-called 'hypnotic voice.' Depending on when you first learned of hypnosis, this might have seemed like a major or insignificant aspect of effective hypnosis.

For a good few years, '*the hypnotic voice*' was considered *the* primary secret on the hypnosis scene.

Then, in large part due to the resurgence of Street Hypnosis and impromptu performance, the idea of a hypnotic voice was largely discredited, if not mocked. Hypnosis was seen as a simpler and far less convoluted affair.

Yet, my experience has taught me that the notion of a hypnotic voice is both natural, reasonable and beneficial. And this is not hard to appreciate. After all, do you not speak to your children, your spouse and your co-workers in different voices?

I am not suggesting that when you begin apparently hypnotising someone, that you speak in a deeper or mysterious voice. However, some (even indistinguishable) change in your voice can benefit you. I remember telling-off one of my children at a time when I was feeling incredibly chilled and stress-free. Yet, something about how I spoke to them caused them to burst into tears. This confused me until I learned the power of conditioning.

When a parent comforts their injured child, they use a different voice to when they are motivating them to tidy their room. To learn more about this, you may want to read the chapter on anchoring.

EXERCISE

Do you think that the concept of the so-called 'hypnotic voice' is out-dated?

Practice inductions that begin conversationally – such as My Friend John, or the Leisure induction – and change your voice as your intentions become more hypnotic.

Ask your practice partner later if they noticed any changes in how you were with them.

Is it a fair or realistic comparison to describe use of the 'hypnotic voice' as an example of conditioning or anchoring?

What other ways, apart from tone of voice, might it be possible to adjust your voice to have a hypnotic effect?

Pacing and Contingent Suggestions

Pacing, Leading & Contingent Suggestions

We now turn to a language pattern that experienced hypnotists may employ throughout their speech, even when they are not aware of it. That is, *pacing current experience* and *contingent suggestions.* (These are often taught as two different skills, but I feel that they belong together as they most effectively function as one coherent whole.)

If you look back at the transcript of the Leisure Induction, you might notice that although this skill is used throughout the induction, it actually serves different purposes at different points. For example, at the earliest stages of the induction, it increases the sense of flow and process of what is taking place. Yet, when it is employed later, it helps with *pacing and leading* and deepening your client's experience.

Continuing with the Leisure Induction as our example, when our clients are providing information on the experience they are recalling, if we do nothing more than repeat back their words to them it can cause the induction to feel staggered and even disconnected. So, to avoid this, we use *linking language* to create smooth transitions, increasing the feeling of a flowing process:

> "So, you're comfortable, slowing down, getting in that zone... And what more is there to getting lost in the moment?"

This implicitly reminds the client that all of these events are not unconnected, but are part of a process that previously lead (and now re-leads) them in to trance. Moreover, it places them back in that process much more easily than if we were simply reading out a bullet-point list of each aspect of their recollection.

The extent of the linking used in the example above is not completely conveyed in written form. The pace and rhythm of what was said was just as important as the content to express the smooth transitions from one thing to the next. This is why we have not simply labelled this section "Use Conjunctions." In reality, your language *could* be very static (even the aforementioned bullet-point list!), but the delivery – including your body language – can still convey the sense of a progressive flow.

However, if you so choose, you can make the linkages explicit, even including them in your questions:

> Client: "I like laying in my hammock."
>
> Hypnotist: "Laying in your hammock. And what is it that you like about laying in your hammock?"
>
> C: "Um... I can just let go and be." (Smiles)
>
> H: "So, as you're laying in your hammock you can just let go and be. And then what?"

Asking "and then what?" is effectively the same as asking "What else?" but it feeds into the feeling of process and keeps it flowing.

When such language is used throughout the induction (for example), it begins to feel completely natural to both the hypnotist and the client. One benefit of this is that the later employment of pacing and leading language does not appear obtrusive.

Observant readers may have already realised that this skill is yet another example of utilisation, which we will discuss (once again!) in the next section. The idea is to build a link between what the client is currently experiencing (pacing) and what you would like them to do next (leading). To use this language pattern unobtrusively, you can also employ it as a 'Yes set,' which we can think of as a patterned response of accepting what you are saying. Establishing an agreeable frame of mind in this way enhances rapport whilst also planting a receptiveness to continue to respond in an affirmative manner.

Another example demonstrates this perfectly:

> "So, as you're laying in your hammock, you can just let go and be. And your body sinks into it as your tension begins to float away… And as you leave the worries of the day behind, you can allow yourself to drift deeper into that bliss now."[48]

You will note that this suggestion incorporates feedback, nominalisations, a Yes Set *and* contingent suggestions. The suggestion at the end piggy-backs the response of 'drift[ing] deeper into that bliss' onto their ongoing experience.

The hypnotist observes the client's non-verbal responses (their 'minimal cues') and includes them within the suggestions. For example:

> H: "I wonder if you realise that as you go deeper into hypnosis that your eyes have started to blink more..."
>
> C: "Ummm…"
>
> H: "and as your eyes start to blink more you can go deeper into hypnosis, but I don't want you to close those eyes just yet, not until you are reeeaally ready now to feel happy and peaceful and calm. And as you..."
>
> (Client closes their eyes and breathes out deeply.)[49]

There is even a contingent suggestion used just at the end, yet hidden as a negative. Ordinarily, contingent suggestions are as simple

48 See Old, *Mastering the Leisure Induction,* p. 99.
49 Ibid, p. 31.

as saying, "As you X, then you can Y." However, as seen here, words such as "until" can also be used when prefixed by a negative, effectively saying: "don't do Y, until you X."

EXERCISE

A common approach when first learning to "pace and lead" is to start with three pacing (P) statements, followed by one leading (L) suggestion.

For example: "And as you sit there (P), your eyes blinking (P) and your breathing slowing down (P), you can begin to wonder just how much of that 'calm peace' you can continue to feel now (L)."

The next step, for practice purposes, is to repeat the entire process each time giving fewer paces and more leads.

So, you might start with 3 paces and 1 lead, moving on to 3 paces and 2 leads, 2 paces to 3 leads and finally even 1 pace to 3 leads.

What other ways can you think of practising and developing your *pace and lead* skills, either overtly or covertly?

Nested Loops

Later chapters will introduce the idea that *pattern interrupts* can be used for more than inductions. They are actually an effective tool in therapy, self-help and almost any kind of human interaction.

The common example given for a pattern to interrupt is one that we have already seen - a handshake. Of course, this makes sense in cultures where a handshake is a common social norm. However, there is far more that can be interrupted.

Any kind of socially expected (and therefore ingrained) behaviour is a pattern that can be interrupted. A high-five, saying "bless you" to a sneeze, someone returning a smile and so on. In established relationships, you may have witnessed couples where one says, "I love you" and the other replies, "I love you too," without an ounce of affection in their voice! It was an habitual and automatic response.

Stories are another example of a pattern that can be created and then interrupted. For starters, it is the case that most fictional stories follow very similar types of formula and structure. Introducing new directions, diversions or unexpected detours can cause an experience of excitement, expectancy or confusion in the reader's mind. However, even in therapy, stories can be used and interrupted effectively.

Nested loops can be thought of as stories within a story, though they can be as small as metaphors within a metaphor or even ideas within an idea. An example could be starting to tell a story with a familiar feel to it, perhaps it has a *Little Red Riding Hood* vibe, meaning your listener can fairly accurately predict the direction in which you are heading. Then, at an unexpected point, you veer off into another story. For example, you might say something like:

> "My own grandmother once told me about a time when she was a little girl..."

Or:

> "I actually knew a wood-cutter once. He would always sing this song about..."

You have successfully taken the energy from the pattern (i.e. the familiarity of the plot), blended with it and redirected it.[50]

In this example, we are *now* talking about when my grandmother was a little girl and I could perhaps talk about some lesson she learned or some antics she got up to with her best friend Eleanor. At that point, I could interrupt again, perhaps even mid-sentence, with a new direction, which this time contains a direct suggestion:

> "Eleanor Roosevelt once said, *Do one thing every day that scares you.*"

I would then go back to finish the story about my grandmother. Then, when that "loop" was completed, I would finish the telling of my Red Riding Hood-esque tale. Structurally, this might look something like:

- Begin Story 1
- Begin Story 2
- Story 3 / Suggestions
- End Story 2

50 This terminology will make more sense once you have read the chapter on pattern-interrupts.

- End Story 1

If your redirection at the point of Story 3, or the suggestion, is effective enough it will create a sense of confusion and/or expectancy within your client. Additionally, for many people, this nesting creates automatic amnesia for the suggestion, which may or may not be a desired result.

Nested Loops can be an effective way to make non-threatening suggestions to clients, often incorporating elements of what I later call *Trojan Horses.*

EXERCISE

Do you currently use nested loops in your hypnotic practice?

Is it possible to utilise nested loops in a less story-like way?

Practice using nested loops – in whichever way feels most natural to you – with a practice partner.

How did it feel?

How did your partner respond? Did they have any comments or reflections to make on the various loops?

It what ways might you modify your use of nested loops, based on your practice-partner's feedback?

Embedded Ideas

We have already briefly referred to the idea of 'embedded commands' a number of times. This is the idea, especially prevalent in NLP circles, of being able to drop commands into a conversation that will be missed by the conscious mind, but picked-up by the subconscious and responded to automatically. They are sometimes described, or presented as, the verbal equivalent of subliminal advertising.

I am mostly dubious of the claims of NLP trainers regarding their success with analogue marking and embedded commands, particularly in some of the ways they are presented. They tend to over-romanticise the subconscious mind and exaggerate the power of NLP. Although there is no doubt that human beings are suggestible, evidenced by the millions spent each year on advertising, there is no evidence at all that subliminal advertising ever worked on anyone.

Personally, I recommend focussing much more on embedded *ideas*, instead of embedded *commands*. Human beings are no more likely to respond to a command just because it is hidden. They still need a reason to respond and that reason is usually because it is meaningful to them in some way. However, embedded ideas have the benefit of being intrinsically indirect and are offered merely for the client to consider. So, instead of commanding them to relax, they are simply reminded that relaxation is natural and comfortable. And that idea can be expressed via insertive eye-contact (see below), in a metaphor, by a story and/or addressed to your friend, 'John.'

Embedded ideas have the potential of being repeated in a number of ways, precisely because they are less direct. If they are detected by the conscious mind, that is not an issue, as they are simply an idea you are sharing. There is not the same sense of potentially being manipulated or controlled.

To give a very basic idea of the difference I envision between embedded commands and embedded ideas, consider for a moment that I wanted someone to scratch their head. An embedded command in the form of 'analogue marking' might proceed as follows:

> I've got this friend, *scratch* that, had this friend. *Your* typical crazy kid, *head* not quite screwed on right...

An embedded *ideas* approach might look more like the following:

> [Scratches head]
>
> I've been wearing a cap all day. And you know when your hair gets all matted and your head gets warm. Feel like I need a nice shower and a bucket of shampoo!
>
> I used to go to school with this kid who always had bad hair. He was always scratching, you know? Eczema, I think. His fingers were always in his hair. He reminded me of my dad when he used to polish our school shoes. That was one of dad's Sunday evening jobs. He'd get the newspaper down on the floor in the kitchen and get our shoes and then polish them like his life depended on it. I've never seen hands move so fast! Backwards and forwards and side to side, rubbing and brushing, just really going to town on those shoes.
>
> There was this other kid, who had bad hair, he had long unruly hair, longer than most of the other boys in our class. And he always had head-lice, so he was always, you know, attacking his head and we'd sit and watch him and before you know it, we're all there – you can imagine, can't you – we're all there scratching away, like we can feel the little squatters on our own heads...

The second example is less dogmatic about the outcome. It is not a command that must be obeyed, but an idea to be considered. You will also notice that the specific idea was expressed in a number of different ways, not just by using the idea of scratching. Similar to the upcoming chapter on insertive eye-contact, the theme of scratching, or trance (or whatever it is that you hope will be accepted) is expressed in a number of different ways, increasing the likelihood of it being responded to.

EXERCISE

What advantages do you see in utilising the idea of embedded *ideas*, in place of embedded commands or suggestions?

Does it seem fair to describe some NLP trainers as over-romanticising the subconscious mind, or exaggerating the power of NLP?

How useful is it to be able to express an idea in a variety of ways, rather than giving a direct command or suggestion?

Are you comfortable with the notion of being less dogmatic about the outcome of your 'commands' or ideas?

Trojan Horses

My co-trainer Jon calls this the 'doggy treat technique.' However, it is more of a simple principle than a specific technique. Jon's idea is that this resembles someone trying to get their pet dog to take medication. A common practice is to hide the medicine (which they may not want) inside of e.g. a peanut butter sandwich (which they *do* want).

With an induction, we see this principle at work in e.g. the *My Friend John* induction. It is commonly viewed as a means to hide suggestions for going into trance. However, with a Therapeutic Inductions approach that's not really the point of the induction. So, My Friend John might instead hide a journey into relaxation by talking about someone else's experience of relaxation. This is especially effective with other hypnotists or nervous clients, who might view the induction as an attempt to hypnotise them. They notice you trying to surreptitiously induce hypnosis and might totally miss the fact that you are teaching them how to relax.

Another example is the 'Pattern-Interrupt Interrupt,' which you can find at howtodoinductions.com.[51]

Therapeutic examples of this might include having someone recall previous positive experiences as resource learnings to call upon. They could totally miss that you were also erasing previous phobic reactions. Or you might teach someone Autogenic Training[52] for dealing with stress, without them noticing that you had trained them to use glove anaesthesia for pain relief.

This technique can be particularly useful for people who might be

51 See https://howtodoinductions.com/inductions/pii

52 Cf. *The Seven Most Effective Methods Of Self-Hypnosis,* by Richard Nongard.

overly invested in unpacking the techniques you use. For example, if you work to address some of their anxious reactions, it is possible that they may be so inclined to over-focus on how you are doing it – perhaps motivated by fear – that they fail to engage with the technique and neutralise it. (This isn't always the case, of course. Sometimes such over-examination can make a technique even more effective!)

I recently worked with a very experienced hypnotherapist who was a self-confessed "control freak." I was very aware that anything I did might lead him to evaluate if I was doing it properly, how it should have been done, and what he would have done instead, etc.

On this occasion, we were working with a phobia that had historical precedent. As we discussed things a little, my client implied that his preferred reaction (which I always enjoy talking about more than what they want to stop doing) was to be able to dissociate from what was happening. However, I was concerned that if we attempted such a technique directly, he may unintentionally sabotage things slightly, especially if it was too obvious.

So, in the end I lead them quickly (too quick for them to dissect) through a serious of scenes and metaphors where they stepped aside from their current situation, whilst keeping one foot in the scene (so as to stay in control).

Part of this involved using scenarios they would recognise to see how easy it was to step aside from the phobia and see it from a dissociated position.

After we had finished they said, "when you were doing the rewind technique..." And I stifled a smile as I thought, "I didn't do the rewind technique."

And that is a long-winded description of an incredibly simple principle that I am sure you are already using in your own way!

Sometimes, particularly if you are working with fellow therapists or especially knowledgeable clients, it helps to hide one technique within another.

Predominantly Positive & Permissive

There's an idea that frequently does the rounds in hypnosis circles. That is the notion that "the sub-conscious cannot process negatives."

I am not sure where this idea originated from, but plenty of people reference the 'pink elephant' experiment. That is, if you say to someone, "Don't think of a Pink Elephant," most people have to initially think of the pink elephant before they know what to *not* think of.

There are a couple of problems with this. Firstly, it is not universally true. Some people *will* think of the Pink Elephant to clarify what they shouldn't think of. However, let's be clear, they are still ultimately *not* thinking of the elephant.

Even so, those who are aware of such challenges will intuitively know that when someone says, "Don't think of a pink elephant," the way to respond is to think of a yellow lizard. It's actually pretty easy.

Additionally, the very notion that there is such a thing as "the subconscious," rather than simply mental processes that take place beneath our conscious awareness, is hardly established fact. It may be, at best, a nominalisation.

Either way, that idea that seems so obvious to some people - that the so-called subconscious cannot process negatives – appears to me to be mainly without merit.

And yet, in what may seem like an ironic twist, I am generally in favour of keeping suggestions predominantly positive.

Positive Possibilities

The main reason I personally like to work with predominantly positive suggestions is because it is an aspect of how I am coaching clients. When they come to see me – perhaps due to how they think of therapy – they are already prepared to discuss all of their problems and how bad things are for them.

However, a large part of my work is in helping clients to shift from a problem 'trance' to a possibility 'trance.' That is, I aim to help them make the mental move from over-focusing and ruminating on everything that is wrong – along with the belief that it will always be that way – to the very reasonable stance of considering alternative possibilities.

Using predominantly positive language hopefully models for my clients a different way of being. It may seem like a small step, but there is a world of difference between saying, "You will no longer want to eat doughnuts," and "you can begin to find yourself enjoying the sweet and fulfilling enjoyments of fruit, remembering how they nourished you in the past and looking forward to the pleasures they can give you from now on."

Permissive Suggestions

Have you ever noticed that telling someone to "Calm down" rarely has the desired effect? And why should it? What makes us think that simply instructing someone to experience something different will achieve that for them? In fact, is it possible that promising, instructing or suggesting something that our clients are not currently experiencing actually makes it unattainable to them?

Perhaps there is another way to express the same ideas? In fact, it is possible that we can express the same ideas in such a way that they are more palatable and feel more achievable.

So, instead of telling someone to "Relax now..." I would tend to say something like, "Think about a time when you're relaxed..."

Or, to make it even more permissive, I might opt for:

> "I wonder if you can recall a time when you have been relaxed..."

I have no reason to fear that an implied question like that is less effective than, "I would like you to relax." After all, unless my client really does not want to relax, engaging with my words will enable them to relive a previous experience of relaxation.

Another example might include a direct suggestion such as, "Go ahead and bend your arm..." Your client may follow your direction, but the only real benefit that gives either of you is an example of temporary compliance.

It may be more beneficial – and educational – to explore the world of permissive possibilities and say something like:

> I'm curious what it would feel like if you were aware of your arm beginning to bend...

Such an approach may feel as if it takes a dose of courage – after all, you may not achieve your desired goal – yet when permissive language is used skilfully almost all risk is removed. After all, in reality, the full suggestion may have sounded more like:

> I'm curious what it would feel like if you were aware of your arm beginning to bend... [add examples of what that would feel like...], or how it would feel as the arm stayed where it is, solid, unmovable, like steel...

An added benefit of this type of approach is that each 'suggestion' can cause the client to go 'inside' as they seek to answer and respond to what has been said. After all, how would they know what it feels like for their arm to begin to bend, unless they fully consider and – at least to some degree – re-experience that sensation?

EXERCISE

Were you aware of the idea that 'the subconscious can not process negatives'? (And are you as amused by the irony of that statement as I am?)

Does the Pink Elephant exercise prove the alleged assertion?

Is the idea of the 'subconscious' as a nominalisation helpful or relevant at this point?

How do you feel about the idea that 'Using predominantly positive language hopefully models for my clients a different way of being'?

Do you feel that permissive suggestions are less effective than more direct or authoritative ones?

In what ways might passive or permissive suggestions be received as more palatable or feel more achievable?

Compounding Suggestions

You will have seen the principle of *Compounding Suggestions* used a number of times already in this book. However, it can be easy to underestimate what is really taking place.

Compounding suggestions is not simply making a suggestion more than once. That is just repetition, which – whilst helpful – is not quite the same thing.

For example, you might repeat the following suggestion to a client a number of times:

> "You are now a non-smoker..."

You might say that three, five or ten times. However, that is not compounding. It is merely repeating the suggestion a number of times. Compounding is much more. It involves repetition, re-experiencing, conditioning, fractionation and more.

The importance of compounding suggestions can hardly be overstated. In fact, Dave Elman wrote:

> 'This is the thing that makes Hypnosis work. From the beginning of hypnosis to its deepest state, it is all a matter of compounding. All you're doing at all times is developing a better state – a greater depth.'[53]

In contrast to mere repetition, compounding suggestions refers to the practice of repeating, reinforcing and *re-experiencing* suggestions. We see this at work in the Elman Induction. Where a suggestion is

53 *Hypnotherapy*, p. 108.

made, the client experiences the effects of the suggestion, you make the suggestion again – it is experienced again – and so on. It is not merely the repetition of suggestions, but the re-experience of suggestions being given and carried out effectively that is the essence of compounding.

This fits very well with my later ideas of *Pyramiding Suggestions* and the *Chain of Command.* Each time a client experiences a suggestion in response to the words of the hypnotist, it increases the chances of the next suggestion being equally as effective. This is true whether the next suggestion is for completely something new, or the same suggestion reiterated a number of times.

Compounding suggestions is sometimes stretched to include related ideas. For example, physical relaxation may be connected to mental calm which may be connected to physical heaviness which can be associated with mental absorption and so on. Depending on your model of psychology, you might think that the same 'state' is being suggested and this is why clients allow the suggestions to impact each other in that way. I tend to view it more as a result of associations and connections, which would seem to play a large role in how our minds make sense of experiences.

Nevertheless, compounding is taken to refer to the same, similar or related suggestions given, followed and experienced more than once. As we will later see, cascading suggestions builds upon this idea.

Double-Binds

Double binds are often referred to as giving the 'illusion of choice.' Ernest Rossi preferred to speak of Milton Erickson's use of double-binds as giving creative choices.[54] This slight nuance fits very well with my approach, which aims to empower clients with a whole new world of possibilities.

Clarifying our Terms

Strictly speaking, you can have Binds, Double-Binds, Unconscious Double Binds, triple Binds and more. I will briefly describe what the terms mean, or at least how they are commonly used.

Binds

A bind is when someone is simply bound to something, in this case, an agreement. So, in the context we are considering, a *single bind* might be something like, "Are you ready to go into hypnosis?" When the client answers yes, they are committing themselves to that course of action. They are accepting the obligation of going into hypnosis, even if they are not consciously thinking about things in that way.

Double Binds

54 Rossi in Erickson, M., Rossi, E. and Ryan, M. *Creative Choice in Hypnosis,* pp. x-xiv.

We encounter double-binds frequently in contemporary society. The last time I went shopping, the cashier asked me if I wished to pay with cash or card. The implication was that I am going to pay (i.e. that action is considered inevitable), but I was given a choice as to how I wanted to do it.

Double binds are statements that offer two choices that achieve the same outcome. So, it is not that we are saying to someone, "Do you want to pay or put the products back?" That is providing an alternative outcome (a topic to which we may return later). The choice is not between the two outcomes or two destinations. Instead, it is offering two paths, both of which lead to the same place.

Savvy parents may be wise to this technique, even if they didn't know what to call it. It's not rare to hear a parent say something like, "Do you want to go to bed now, or have a story first?" Yet, more hypnotic parenting might employ this even more skilfully:

> "Do you want to sing a song, or read a story, before you *put your toys away*?"

In clinical practice, a double-bind is more likely to sound like, "Would you like to go into trance quickly or slowly?" Or, "Would you prefer to go into hypnosis in this chair, or that chair?"

Unconscious Double Binds

An Unconscious Double Bind is one where the client does not consciously make a choice, although they may still 'bind' themselves to the choices on offer.

A common example might be to make a permissive statement such as, "And it will be interesting to see if it will be your left hand or your right hand that begins to rise as you go further into hypnosis..." Of course, until the client begins to 'go further into hypnosis,' they will not know which hand will begin to levitate first. However, by considering that either one is a possibility, they 'bind' themselves to the outcome.

Obviously, there are a number of little extras at work here. You will spot the use of expectation, an invitation to perform a TDS, as well as embedded suggestion. However, these often find themselves cropping-up in Unconscious Double Binds even when that is not the intention.

Triple Binds

Finally, a simple extension of the above is the triple bind. You might see this in a Street or Stage scenario, where the hypnotist confidently states:

> And you can begin to drift into trance within 5 seconds, 10 seconds, or .....*(long drawn out pause)*....NOW!

The Possibility of Choice

Despite the variety of terms and techniques, in reality, we are usually referring to a fairly basic process. And, given my preference for simplicity I tend to include all of the variations under the label of a double-bind.[55]

Like Rossi, I reject the idea of a double-bind as merely offering an 'illusion of choice.' Aside from implying a level of trickery or falsehood, when one is not needed, it also discredits our clients as possibly being easily fooled.

I see no 'illusion' at work in the therapeutic use of double-binds whatsoever. Instead, I see a genuine and sincere offer of alternatives. After all, the client and I have already agreed upon the outcome they are there for. Returning to the earlier shopping example, when the cashier asks me, "Cash or card?" it is not as if I snap out of my trance and object, "Hey, I know what you're doing! You're presenting me

55 Using 'double-bind' as an umbrella term is what usually takes place, especially in NLP circles. Erickson and his most pure devotees use the terms more specifically than we have here, (even admitting, 'we use the term in a very special and limited sense,') but now is not the time to unpack the distinctions.

with two options, but they both result in me paying something! I'm not fooling for this!"

No, the reality is that I went to the shop with the prior intention of paying for my goods. In fact, having previously bound myself to the general rules of society as I know it, we could even say that I went in to the shop *wanting* to pay. I simply needed someone to provide me with a means of doing so that was meaningful and accessible to me.

So, if double-binds do not provide an illusion of choice, what is their purpose? As I think of them, double-binds offer our clients extra possibilities that they may not have been aware they could make use of. On top of this, the way we word things presupposes that the desired outcome will take place. This, as we have seen above, can have a great impact on our client's expectations and their psychological flexibility.

I am presenting my clients with a win-win situation, whereas before they walked into my clinic, all they could envision was a continual cycle of loss after loss.

As Erickson wrote, I am providing, 'tactful presentations of the possible alternate forms of constructive behaviour that are available to the patient in a given situation. The patient is given a free, voluntary choice between them; the patient usually feels bound, however, to accept one alternative [due to their commitment to the outcome].'[56]

Additionally, simply speaking as if the destination is assured, but a number of roads to reach that goal are possible, is an incredibly empowering and freeing experience for our clients. They are being explicitly included in the therapeutic journey, not as a passive passenger, but as a co-pilot.

56 Erickson, *Hypnotic Realities*, p. 62. Parenthesis added.

Transderivational Search

We have already encountered Transderivational Searches (TDS) a number of times in this book. In fact, when handled skilfully, they can crop-up all over the place.

A TDS takes place when vague suggestions are used that the client must process internally, in order to to establish their own meanings.

Effectively, when a person is asked to 'go inside and think of a time when …' they will often do a TDS and search their memories, beliefs, desires, associations, etc. for an event that matches the meaning of that phrase.

For example, if I say to someone, 'mothers often act as if…' the client might have to consider their own mother to assess the validity of what I am saying.

More natural examples could include lines like:

> "You know, when you're watching a scary film..."
>
> "Those times when you hear a piece of music that moves you..."
>
> "I wonder what it's like to really recall your first classroom..."

Many people – often those from an NLP background – have a tendency to make TDS more complicated than they need to be. In effect, you are simply saying something. In effect, you are simply asking a question – or making a statement that is so vague – that your client has to 'go inside' to answer, or make sense of what you're saying.

Something that I have found useful – that I picked-up somewhere along the way – is to note when my client makes a TDS and to ask my client, "Where did you go, just now?"

EXERCISE

Why do you think that the idea of transderivational searches have cropped-up so often in this book?

What might be a more natural or accessible way to describe a TDS?

Can you think of times that you have inadvertently caused someone to go on a TDS? Perhaps you used a metaphor they didn't understand, or referenced a song lyric they were unfamiliar with?

What are the advantages – or goals – of a TDS? After all, we have introduced them without making a particularly strong case for them.

How would you describe the benefits of a TDS?

Can you think of direct as well as indirect ways of making use of TDS in a therapeutic context?

Analogies, Metaphors and Stories

If you think back to the 'mesmerising movies' analogy we gave at the beginning of the book, I'm sure you would agree that viewers would be less inclined to engage with (or get lost in) a lecture on Economics than a film about dragons.

There are no doubt a number of factors involved. However, chief amongst them may simply be the aspect of conditioning. If I look at the screen and it looks like I'm about to hear a lecture by an academic or politician, that I need to analyse and assess, that is completely different to seeing a scene that almost explicitly invites me to engage with it and get lost within.

In short, something about the nature of stories seems to lower our guard, invites engagement and carries the assumption that the rules are not set in stone; thus, who knows what is possible?

Utilising Analogies

A common way for hypnotists to employ the power of story is through the use of analogies and metaphors. Milton Erickson is probably the hypnotist most associated with this practice.[57] Erickson would use stories for everything from insomnia, to enuresis and even sexual dysfunction.

One famous example involves a twelve-year-old boy who was brought to see Erickson about his bed-wetting. Erickson dismissed his

57 *My Voice will Go With You: The Teaching Tales of Milton Erickson*, Sidney Rosen.

parents and began talking to the boy about other topics, avoiding a direct discussion about bed-wetting altogether. Upon learning that the boy played baseball and his brother football, Erickson elaborated on the fine muscle coordination it takes to play baseball, compared to the uncoordinated muscle skills used in football.

The boy listened raptly as Erickson described in fine detail all the muscle adjustments his body automatically makes in order to position him underneath the ball and catch it: the glove has to be opened at just the right moment and clamped down again at just the right moment. When transferring the ball to another hand, the same kind of fine muscle control is needed. Then, when throwing the ball to the infield, if one lets go too soon, it doesn't go where one wants it to go. Likewise letting go too late leads to an undesired outcome and consequently to frustration. Erickson explained that letting go just at the right time gets it to go where one wants it to go, and that constitutes success in baseball.

Therapy with this young man consisted of four sessions that included talks about other sports, boy scouts, and muscles. But bed-wetting was not discussed, and "formal hypnosis" was not conducted. The boy's bed-wetting disappeared soon thereafter.

There are a couple of benefits to this approach. One is the principle of being 'one step removed.' Sometimes people might struggle to talk about a particular issue, but can do so if there is some distance created between them and the actual issue. (Think of the common stereotype of a Police Officer using a doll to enable a child to speak about abuse they may have suffered.)

When I used to work in Social Care, my most productive sessions with troubled teenagers took place during the drive to and from the venue where we would do the official 'work' together. Alternatively, it was during the card games we played whilst waiting for another member of staff to arrive. Far more talk took place when the pressure was off.

With sensitive issues, taking a step back and talking about

something else may prove far more successful than addressing the issue head-on, whilst also giving you the opportunity to hint at some relevant themes.

Regarding this last point, analogies, metaphors and stories can allow us to 'seed' ideas. This refers to laying the foundation for ideas or experiences that will be more fully explored later on. If we tell a story that appears to have secondary and unnecessary references to words like comfort, rest, or safety, then when we later explore those themes, our client has potentially been thinking about such ideas already, even if only briefly and in passing.

Here is another example from Erickson:

> Erickson was asked if he could do anything for Joe, a florist who was suffering from a particularly malignant form of cancer and had been given a month to live. Joe was, not surprisingly, unhappy and depressed at this news, and in addition was experiencing severe pain and found it hard to rest.
>
> A relative begged Erickson to give him hypnosis for pain relief; Erickson agreed, somewhat reluctantly as he doubted he could do much for the man, especially as Joe was known to be sceptical of and even hostile to the idea of hypnosis.
>
> However, Erickson reasoned that if he conveyed by his presence that he was genuinely interested in Joe, and genuinely wanted to help him, that should at least provide some comfort.[58]
>
> As Joe loved growing things, Erickson decided to talk about a tomato plant: about how it grows, how the rains bring it peace and comfort, and how it can feel comfortable growing.
>
> He talked about how it took just one day at a time, how it could know the feeling of comfort each day, and how the

58 I honestly feel as if that paragraph alone is worth the price of this book.

> tomato plant knew what it was doing, and how thinking of the luscious tomatoes beginning to form could give you the desire to eat.
>
> In the course of the long story about how the tomato plant grows, Erickson interspersed many times, in many different ways, suggestions of comfort, ease, peace, all feeling well, taking it one day at a time, resting, and even increasing appetite – all sounding natural in the context of the story.
>
> The hypnosis-skeptical Joe went into a trance listening to the story, and afterwards was most appreciative. During his remaining time he was more content, his physical condition improved (although the malignancy continued to progress), and the pain was much reduced, so he could come off his pain relief medication.

The danger of using metaphors, analogies or stories is that if the connection is too obvious – when it seems that you are trying to be obscure or inconspicuous – then your client may feel patronised.

This can potentially feel almost insulting, as if you thought your client was not smart enough to pick-up on what you were doing.

There is an extremely simple way of employing what we might call *shallow metaphors*, or incorporating well-known stories and analogies. A simple example would be to use an analogy to reframe things and provide another perspective. For example, "Remember when Simba...."

Vague Stories

Another approach is to offer a story that provides some general themes. The specific application of those themes may rely on an internal search for meaning. This will be unique to each client and are my favourite way to use analogies, metaphors and stories.

I have a dozen or so stories that I employ on a regular basis. Here is one that I utilise, or riff-off in a myriad of scenarios. And each time I've used it, clients have responded as if it was composed just for them.

Even now, I couldn't tell you what it 'really' means:

> In the mid-1990s, I was around 19 years old and I was fortunate enough to join a group of people travelling to what was then known as Calcutta, India for 8 weeks. For the first 7 weeks, we worked and immersed ourselves in the culture and the all encompassing sights and sounds.
>
> Then, the final week, we got to go on holiday. And we travelled to what I think was the nearest coast, in the State of Bihar. And we spent day after day sat on that beach, just entranced by the sights and the sounds, and the waves that came in and then gently flowed back out again.
>
> One day, someone in our group suggested that it would be a good idea to go to the beach and watch the sunrise. Even now, some two decades later, that idea strikes me as sublimely romantic. It gives me chills!
>
> So, we all woke up wearily, about 3 or 4 am and made our way down to the beach. I remember clearly now that one of the things that most surprised me - and it might surprise you - is how many people were already there before us.
>
> I mean, fishermen, tourists, families, children, all kinds of people... looking up at the bright sky, before the sun had even risen...
>
> And I remember this scene - as clearly as if it was happening to me now - of a young boy running to the water's edge, golden from the dawning sunrise.
>
> And he dropped down to his knees and he looked - or tried to look - at his reflection in the water. He repeated this a number of times, until the Sun had fully risen, and each

time that he knelt down, it propelled a burst of sand up into the water, making his reflection murky at best.

I had become intrigued by what the boy was trying to achieve, so I watched as he walked dejected back to his grandfather.

"Papa, papa," he said, "I keep trying to see my reflection in the pure sea water. Yet, every time I drop down, it just shows me a pool of cloudy water. I don't look *anything* like I do in the photos at home."

The man held his grandson close and kissed his head. "My boy, he said. "Those photos are merely a snapshot, a brief capture of what you may have looked like for a split-second of time."

The reality, the *real* you, you're more like... *BAM!* You cannot be captured in a single snapshot. You are are bubbling cloudy ball of energy, ever changing from one moment to the next. The splash, the explosion of sand, the cloudy water - that's the glorious living boy I see before me..."

Nominalisations

Alfred Korzybski noted back in the 1930s that people often talked about processes e.g. thinking happily, wondering curiously, experiencing depressive feelings, as if they were static nouns – happiness, curiosity, depression, etc. In some situations, this can be unhelpful.

For example, although nominalisations might be thought to clarify and stream-line communication, they can lead to confusion and presumption and can therefore cause miscommunication. Some people make the mistake of presuming that they know what a client means when they use words like 'stress', 'depression' or even 'happiness'. Yet, there is no guarantee that someone is using a word in the same way you or I would to express their experience of the world.

Additionally, in a therapeutic context, when clients are over-focused on their own nominalisations it can create a sense of 'stuckness,' or being locked in their current condition. After all, they have taken a fluid experiential process – feeling stress, or being overwhelmed with depressive thoughts and feelings – and expressed it as a concrete and rigid noun.

Nevertheless, for our current purposes, it is worth remembering that a nominalisation is yet another thing that can be utilised. In fact, nominalisations can be extremely useful in the right hands as they provide us with the means to communicate complex experiences in simple and non-specific ways.

For example, you might frequently come across words like

"freedom," "happiness," "peace," "escape" and so on. Yet, there is no such thing as "freedom" - it is a noun description of the condition or experience of being free. We can therefore use this in two ways.

Firstly, we can choose to ask questions to unpack a nominalisation, transforming it from a static description to a living experience. This can be seen in the transcript where we also see the principles of revivification and utilisation being employed:

> Hypnotist: "So, what do you enjoy doing...?"
>
> Client: "Swimming. I'd swim all day long if I could."
>
> H: "All day long."
>
> C: "Yeah. I love it."
>
> H: "What is it that you love about swimming?"
>
> C: "Oh, so much! The freedom. Time to myself, to escape into my own little world..."

As already stated, 'Freedom' is a clear nominalisation, suitable for further unpacking. I could have asked what that freedom looks like, or what it feels like. That would have lead the client to consider and describe exactly what it was like when they 'escaped.'

The second way we can utilise nominalisations is by doing all of this in reverse. Once the client has begun to re-experience their previous trance, we now know that the simple phrase 'freedom' sums-up and evokes an experience that they find enjoyable. So, I don't need to struggle to come up with words to describe or elicit this experience for them.

If you are unsure on the nature of nominalisations, the classic test for determining whether or not something is a nominalisation is to ask the question, "Could I put this in a wheelbarrow?" If the answer is "No", then you may well be dealing with a nominalisation.

It can be helpful to think of nominalisations as words which allow people to add their own meaning. Or you might want to think of them as processes or verbs expressed as things or nouns.

For example, Communication is a nominalisation. Communication is not a 'thing' – you cannot put it in a wheelbarrow, after all. However, there is such an event as people taking part in *communication.*

The following list of nominalisations may help elucidate this point, as well as proving useful material for your practice of a number of inductions:

Learnings
Clarity
Curiosity
Development
Integration
Discovery
Awareness
Freedom
Relaxation
Serenity
Fascination
Decision
Leadership
Relationship
Confusion
Maintenance
Motivation
Openness
Fairness
Creativity
Enthusiasm
Honesty
Flexibility
Loyalty
Recognition
Satisfaction
Understandings
Knowledge
Nominalisation
Hope
Happiness
Contentment
Communication
Trance
Investigation
Courage
Continuation
Change
Desire
Resource

Transformation
Possibilities
Fulfilment
Realisation

Delight
Potential
Sensations
Exploration

HYPNOTIC SKILLS & TOOLS

The following section was originally entitled, 'Hypnotic skills.' However, that failed to clarify whether these were innate skills that good hypnotists are born with, or skills that could be taught and/or learned.

Additionally, some of what follows might be considered tools that are frequently employed by skilled hypnotists.

These are not best thought of as techniques to be used on clients, as much as practices that you will notice most effective therapeutic hypnotists utilising, consciously or otherwise.

Observation

Observation

For a few years, I have said that if I could imprint only two words on the minds of every newly qualified hypnotist, those words would be 'Observation' and 'Utilisation.'

When I first began my career in hypnosis, I trained with two of the giants in contemporary Hypnosis: Jonathan Chase and Stephen Brooks. From Chase, I learned the importance of my own personal presence and belief in myself and the art and power of hypnosis. From Brooks, I learned about the importance of *Observation* and *Utilisation*. From beginning to end, through stories, case-studies and demonstrations, Brooks emphasised and demonstrated their importance. I, for one, am glad he did.

It may seem strange for training in a practical skill to focus on such conceptual matters. However, the focus that Brooks placed on Observation and Utilisation was enough to completely change my approach and redirect my therapeutic practice.

That may seem like a grand claim for what is essentially quite a simple point, yet it remains true. This fresh focus challenged my ideas about what it is that I am seeking to do in therapy, as well as how I would proceed to do it.

In fact, I now tell my own students that there is literally nothing I have to teach them that is more important than this suggestion from Sigmund Freud:

> 'Suspend judgement and give impartial attention to

everything there is to observe.'[59]

Observation is a particularly important skill when it comes to the induction, as you need to be ready to pace and lead, based on what the client does, not just what they say. As you pay attention to your client's external responses, you can often paint a good picture of how they are responding internally.

One of the things you will want to look out for are the small physical changes that tell you your client is responding. From an Ericksonian perspective, these observable signs are what we have come to refer to as the "minimal cues" of trance. Whether or not that is an accurate description of what is taking place is beyond the scope of this book to argue. However, what such signs *do* seem to reveal is when the subject is having an internal experience that in some ways matches their external descriptions, and/or your verbal suggestions. That is, they are no longer just discussing something, or hearing what you say; they are, in fact, experiencing it there and then.

You may be surprised at how obvious some of these signs are. You may even be surprised that you didn't notice them before. Regardless, keep your eyes open and you will be unlikely to miss them again.

The great thing about these signs is that they can be a highly reliable barometer of how someone is responding internally. So, they can increase your confidence that things are proceeding as hoped, as well as informing your client that they are responding appropriately.

Here are some of the signs you will want to look out for. Maybe just one, or maybe more:

- Glazed eyes
- Pupils dilating
- Deeper breathing

59 Freud, S. (1909). *Analysis of a phobia in a five-year old boy*. Standard Edition, 10, 3-152. London: Hogarth Press, 1955.

- Flushed cheeks
- Flattening of the facial muscles
- Changes in skin colour
- Eye watering
- Twitching hands, arms or legs
- Slow response and speech
- Fixed gaze
- Non-responsiveness
- Frozenness / full body catalepsy
- Changes in blink rate
- Slowing of the swallow reflex

Once you see these, you can utilise them and – as with the Leisure Induction – feed them back to your client to go even 'deeper.'

Calibration

Within hypnosis and NLP, calibration can be thought of as making a record of default settings. For example, if someone talks about a phobia and their eyes widen, we cannot automatically presume that such an action means they are having a phobic reaction there and then. After all, as we got to know them, we might discover that they have a natural habit of widening their eyes whenever they are giving more details about a scenario.

Unfortunately, some therapeutic approaches and techniques can encourage practitioners to make assumptions about their clients. For example, if someone looks in *this* direction, they are remembering something, whereas if they look *there* they are likely creating or imagining something. You may be sick of me saying this by now, but the research does not generally support such positions.

Nevertheless, as you get to know your client as an individual, you might learn some of their idiosyncrasies. For example, they might look down if they are using their imagination, or rub their chin as they are concentrating. If you fail to calibrate them accurately, you might conclude that such actions mean they are, e.g. thinking negatively, or conjuring up a lie. (After all, a self-published e-book on Body Language can hardly be wrong!)

I have a friend called Michael that I've known for a number of years. I think that one of the reasons Michael and I get on is because we are very similar and at the same time very different. Michael is naturally quite serious, but can also be intense (in both a positive and negative way). I am naturally very humour-oriented and yet also quite intense.

The reason I have introduced you to Michael is because he has a very interesting habit when you are talking to him. Michael will often – at seemingly specific and significant times – frown as he listens to you. When I first met him, I thought that Michael perhaps did not follow what I was saying, or disagreed with me, or sought further clarification. Yet, after knowing Michael for a number of years, I came to learn that if Michael frowned whilst he was listening to you, it meant that he was extremely interested in what you were saying, was concentrating and wanted to hear more!

Of course, perceptive readers or experienced hypnotists will see that this can also be used in reverse. Picking-up on our clients' tone of voice, their physical gestures, their turns of phrase and more allows us to express different states, or even anchor alternative states for them to access.

Notice What You Notice

Anyone interested in any kind of therapeutic work would benefit from paying attention to their skills of observation.

I remember hearing David Sedaris – the humourist and author – talking about taking a flight from one country to another. He described a woman sitting down next to him, who seemed like she would need some interaction. (Interpret that how you will!)

Sedaris was tired and drained and very much in need of an event-free flight. However, he was also someone who wrote about the humorous intricacies of every day life for a living. And he was well aware that the flight he was about to embark on, sat next to this particular individual, might provide him with page after page of very interesting content.

So, he made the decision to put on his best face and engage his co-passenger in a meandering (and, it turns out, highly entertaining) conversation for the duration of the flight.

Whether or not Sedaris would have been better served by having some much-needed time-off, the perspective here is valuable for us to consider. Noticing every event that is happening to you, being fully aware of all that your clients express and paying attention to all physical responses, emotional demonstrations and psychological manifestations, ensures that you are more readily placed to see what is happening with your client, with you and with the general interaction between the two of you. And only then are you in the place to utilise what they give you and respond accordingly.

Calibration is not a technique, or a thing we do to my clients. It is simply taking an actual, effective and active interest in my clients.

Regardless of any other benefit that may be gained from such an approach, is this not the way that you want to work with your clients? Is this not the kind of therapist you wish to be?

EXERCISE

I quoted Freud above as stating, 'Suspend judgement and give impartial attention to everything there is to observe.'

How do you feel about that statement?

Would it not be overwhelming for a hypnotist to attempt to observe everything that takes place in a session?

Do you think observation incorporates more than we can see? Would listening, or picking up on a new perfume, constitute observation?

If so, do you think these might be as important as Freud implies?

Is calibration something you do naturally or intentionally?

What do you think of the David Sedaris story? Would he have been better served by simply sleeping on the plane, like he clearly needed to?

What about his readers?

Rapport

You do not need to spend a great deal of time around hypnotists or therapists before you hear talk of the importance of rapport. Some hypnotists would say it increases the chances of your hypnosis being effective. Others would say it is absolutely essential.

In the context of therapeutic hypnosis, Rubin Battino writes:

> 'Before you can effectively work with someone, rapport has to be established.'[60]

Personally, I am in complete agreement with Battino. In fact, I would say that rapport is needed for *any* hypnosis, not just for those in therapy. There are those who would argue that whilst desirable, rapport is not essential for Stage or Street hypnosis. However, I have found that in many cases, such people have a different understanding of rapport than mine.

What is Rapport?

Most formal definitions of rapport agree as to its nature:

> 'A close and harmonious relationship in which the people or groups concerned are "in sync" with each other, understand each other's feelings or ideas, and communicate smoothly.' (Wikipedia)

> 'A friendly, harmonious relationship; characterized by

60 Battino, Rubin. *Ericksonian Approaches*, p. 35

> agreement, mutual understanding, or empathy that makes communication possible or easy' (Merriam-Webster)
>
> 'A good understanding of someone and an ability to communicate well with them.' (Cambridge Dictionary)

Whilst we may say that they all refer to the same sort of interpersonal connection, there is a significant difference between the first two definitions and that offered by the Cambridge Dictionary.

Wikipedia and the Merriam-Webster Dictionary speak of a relationship with a certain level of intimacy. It is 'harmonious' and 'friendly,' or even 'close.' These two definitions are referring to relationships characterised by mutual affection and deep knowledge of one another. (However, I would note that Wikipedia's description of being 'in sync' with each other does not necessarily require the 'close and harmonious relationship' that it also describes.)

Interestingly, the Cambridge Dictionary does not necessarily require the elements of intimacy and mutual affection. It would seem to fit more with the notion of being 'in sync,' without requiring a close, friendly or harmonious relationship.

My understanding and use of the term would match the Cambridge definition more than the previous two. I simply think of being in rapport as *having a connection with someone*. This can be of an emotional kind – where we might speak of "clicking" or having "good chemistry" with someone – or a more distant sense of being on the same page as someone – where being "in sync" would be an adequate description.

In my experience, the sort of rapport that is required for hypnosis (therapeutic or otherwise) does not necessarily require a close or friendly relationship. I do not even think it requires my clients to like me![61] However, I do think we need to be in sync on some level and on the same page regarding what is taking place.

61 To be clear, it may be *preferable* for my clients to like me. It certainly makes for a more enjoyable session for all involved! I am just not convinced it is necessary, or an essential element of rapport.

My definition would include someone trusting me, but would not necessarily need them to think of me in an especially friendly manner. The reason why I view things this way is because from time to time I will use elements of provocative therapy in my sessions. I will normally have pre-warned my client, by saying something like, "I should warn you that a previous client once referred to me as being 'playfully provocative.' I think what they meant by that is that I like to play Devil's advocate and sometimes it might seem like I'm splashing a metaphorical cup of water in your face, or pushing you to answer a question more thoroughly."

I then add the all important line: "So, if it ever seems to you like I am being a bit of a jerk, just presume it's all part of the therapy and we'll get along just fine!" (All of this is said with a light-hearted glint in my eye and is usually met with an understanding smile.)

There is an example I use in my Stop Smoking book that I refer to frequently. I worked with a woman who had tried to quit numerous times. When I asked her how much she smoked, she laughed and said, "It's silly really… I only smoke ten a day." Throughout the rest of the session, I used the word "silly" at different times, often with a slight chuckle.

At one point, she slammed her hand down on the desk and said, "It's not silly! This could kill me!" I stopped what I was doing and acted shocked before saying, "You are absolutely right. Let's take this seriously."

I do not think anyone would say that I had developed a friendly or harmonious relationship with that client. In fact, I don't think they particularly liked me at that point! Yet, personally, I look back on that as a successful demonstration of rapport. We were on the same page in agreeing that 1) I was being a jerk and 2) this was no laughing matter. There was the kernel of a connection that we could utilise to get in sync and agree that smoking was not "silly" at all, despite what she has previously said.

Why do we need rapport?

So, if we are not looking to build close and harmonious relationships, why do we need rapport?

When we have rapport, there is a sense that we are going in the same direction. Our client trusts us. Given that some people seem to have a slight fear of hypnosis, their trust in us is invaluable.

With rapport, clients drop their guard more easily and follow our lead, or accept our suggestions, almost effortlessly. The look on my client's face after I said, "You are absolutely right. Let's take this seriously," was wonderful. I knew there and then that she was confident I had her back, that she trusted me to help her and would engage positively with the session.

Rapport helps communication progress more smoothly. There is less talking at cross purposes and more shared mutual commitment to the same goals.

Rapport removes any sense of you versus your client. Instead, it becomes you and your client versus their problem. (I don't actually think of my client's issues as being our enemy, but I'm sure you get the point.) Or, it becomes you and your client working towards the same end.

One benefit of all of this is that pacing and leading seems to take place far more organically and effectively.

Techniques to Build Rapport

There are a number of techniques hypnotists use to build rapport.

Instant Unconditional Positive Regard

Carl Rogers promoted the idea of 'Unconditional Positive Regard.' This means acting and speaking in such a way that our clients know we are there for them, with a warm concern for their well-being.

One way to express this is to listen to your client as if they were your best friend about to tell you a secret, or were telling you something incredibly interesting. The idea is not to pretend you are interested, but to step into that role, recreating your internal state as it would be if you were with your friend.

This should be easy enough for most hypnotists to achieve, but the following example from Igor Ledochowski unpacks this idea into a number of steps.[62]

1. Think of a person that you are close to – someone that you have those good feelings with. Recall the sensation in your body of really liking someone.
2. When you have the feeling, focus on it to make it grow. Let it spread over your chest, shoulders, arms, etc.
3. If you can associate a colour to that feeling, imagine that colour intensifying and spreading along your body until your whole body seems to pulse with the sensation.
4. Allow that feeling to project out of you, surrounding you in a ball of rapport-energy.
5. Send a beam of this colour/feeling out towards the person you want to have rapport with. Wrap it around them and inside them until you feel that connection inside you. You might get a sensation of empathy – a kind of knowing what the other person is feeling. Perhaps you'll get a sense of what it would feel like to be standing the way they do, or wearing the clothes they are wearing.
6. When the feeling of being connected settles in, you can let it drift to the back of your mind whilst you put your full awareness on the interaction.
7. If appropriate, remember to reduce/end the exercise when you are finished.

62 Ledochowski, *Deep Trance Training Manual,* p. 25.

One of the useful things about this technique is how flexible it is. For example, rather than thinking of someone you are close to, you might think of someone you find incredibly interesting, or someone that you find extremely funny, and so on.

Representational Systems (VAKOG)

Some people believe that we all have a *preferred representational system*. That is, we tend to perceive and record our experiences through a primary sense. That could be visual, auditory, kinaesthetic, olfactory (smell) or gustatory (taste).[63]

Furthermore, it is often claimed that the way we tend to express ourselves verbally can reveal our preferred representational system. So, the following sentences may mean the same thing, but they are expressed according to different senses:

"It looks a bit dodgy to me" (V)
"That doesn't sound right" (A)
"Something feels off" (K)
"It smells fishy to me" (O)
"This leaves a bad taste in my mouth" (G)

Whether or not there is much truth to the idea of preferred representational systems – and the research, as you would expect by now, is by no means conclusive – when it comes to dialogue with our clients, it may be good practice to adopt the same sense that they express themselves with.

So, if your client says, "it looks a bit dodgy to me," you would not generally reply with, "yeah, it smells fishy to me too." This potentially

63 In the NLP world, these representations are often referred to as modalities.

damages rapport, if your client feels that you are not listening to them or fully understanding what they are saying.

Instead, you might ask, "And what does that 'dodgy' look like?"

Matching Non-verbal Shifts

Human beings seem to naturally match some of the behaviours of people they are in rapport with. Examples could include a group of children, all speaking at the same pace and volume, or two adults adopting similarly relaxed seating postures.

As a sort of short-cut to rapport, you might act as if you are already in rapport, by matching your client's non-verbal shifts. Non-verbal shifts can take many forms: changes in posture, scratching the head, gestures, breathing patterns, etc. So, if they cross their legs, cross your legs. If they raise their eyebrows, raise your eyebrows and so on.

The key here is not to be too obvious. If your client realises what you are doing, they might conclude that you are mimicking them, or worse. Instead, they should not be aware of what you are doing, but may subconsciously sense that you are both in sync.

[Here's a valuable tip: You will know your matching is going well if it allows you to pace and lead. So, for example, you might cross your legs each time your client does. Then, after a while, you might just find that if you cross your legs, they will follow you.]

Mirroring and Cross Matching

Mirroring simply means that you match your client's behaviour, but as if in a mirror image. So, if they scratched the left side of their face, you might scratch the right side of yours.

An example of cross-matching would be tapping your leg each time they blinked. In my experience, cross-matching is a powerful and underrated technique.

Facial Listening

One of the techniques that I occasionally teach for rapport-building is what I call 'facial listening.' This is simply a case of using facial expressions to reflect that you are interested and listening intently.

One of the most common ways to do this is to lean forward as your client is talking. Then, after a while you lean your head to one side and frown slightly as they are speaking. Then after a second or two, you nod your head in response to what they are saying.

Finally, your frown turns to a smile, as you nod definitely a while longer.

You might want to try this first with friends and family. As long as you are genuinely interested, you will find that this little technique reflects your interest quite clearly.

Speaking of being genuine, let's finish by considering a different approach to building and expressing rapport.

An Alternative Perspective

The sort of techniques shared above intend to make the client feel there is a connection between the two of you. You are in sync, on the same team, singing from the same song-sheet and so on.

Yet, here's the thing – instead of perfecting techniques that give the impression of unconditional positive regard, why not actually have it? Rather than working to make your clients think you are listening, why not actually listen to them?

The sort of rapport building exercises we've looked at are used because of the well-known phenomena whereby friends and lovers mirror each other unconsciously. Yet, if we genuinely felt that way, would we not find ourselves acting in such a way without forcing ourselves to?

Instead of using the beam of rapport described earlier to give the *impression* of being in rapport, why not view it as a technique to help you actually get in rapport with someone? You could then use it before you even see your client, somewhat like a meditation technique to build and express positive regard for someone else.

It is rare to meet someone who is not interesting in some way. So, perhaps we can focus on listening to them, to find the point of interest. It would be difficult to find someone that we did not have at least one thing in common with. So, why not look for that thing in common, by listening intently and genuinely to what they have to say?

It seems to me that we could benefit from working on our own external focus and attention, rather than spending too long finding clever techniques to conjure up rapport. That means that a loving-kindness meditation might be a better use of our time, than practising "rapport-building techniques."[64]

Such an approach involves acknowledging that we are still a work in progress, not a perfected finished product operating on a higher plane than our clients. So, ironically, in order to be the kind of person who has a genuine interest and focus on other people, we need to start with ourselves.

64 Cf. *Lovingkindness: The Revolutionary Art of Happiness*, by Sharon Salzberg.

EXERCISE

Rapport is considered an important concept by many therapists. However, would you agree that it is *essential* for effective therapeutic hypnosis?

What do you currently do to establish rapport with your clients?

Practice with any of the methods described in this chapter than you may not already by aware of. How did it effect how (or what) you felt about your clients?

How did it effect how (or what) your clients felt about you?

What do you think of the 'alternative perspective' provided at the end of this chapter? Is it helpful, or not? If it is, how might you put it into practice?

Expectation

'Expectancy is an essential aspect of hypnosis, perhaps its most essential aspect.' (Irving Kirsch)

Expectancy

The field of medicine has long recognised the power of the "placebo effect." This is a situation where a patient's belief that they are getting an active drug when they are only receiving a sugar pill can generate the same level of positive effect as if they had been given an actual drug.

Practically all approaches to psychotherapy emphasise the role of positive expectations in enhancing results. A commonly used term is 'self-fulfilling prophecies' - the recognition that our behaviour can adjust to match our expectations, thereby increasing the likelihood of their fulfilment.

If you think of many of the practices of a typical "Hypnotherapist," creating expectancy is the desired goal of almost all of them. It might start with dressing smartly, to convey professionalism. Next comes hanging Certificates on the wall to announce your credibility. Similarly, you might have business cards with C.Ht. after your name. There's a good chance that your office would be connected in some way with a medical or health centre, to demonstrate the respectability and validity of hypnosis.

Then, think of some of the hypnotic rituals aimed at building positive expectations in the client. Most of what I would call 'response routines' are not solely to provide the hypnotist with information regarding a client's susceptibility to hypnosis. Instead, they are intended to convince the client that they are hypnotisable, that the hypnotist knows what they are doing and that something of substance is happening.

Hypnotic phenomena may also be used throughout a hypnosis session, both to maintain the expectancy, but also to increase it. So, if a client becomes aware that their arm is floating up into the air, whilst they sit there like an innocent observer, they will receive compelling evidence that they are in hypnosis. They will also have their expectations of the hypnotist confirmed and continue to believe that they can and will respond to his or her suggestions.

It is within the context of discussing how hypnotherapists aim to create expectancy, that Michael Yapko writes, 'Suffice it to say here that helping clients co-create a compelling vision of what's possible in their lives is one of the most important things that can happen in therapy.'[65] It seems fair to suggest that such a vision starts with what is possible in and through the hypnosis session itself.

The Response-Expectancy Model

Irving Kirsch has described a model of hypnosis that he calls response-expectancy theory. As you know but now, I do not adhere to any one particular model of hypnosis, preferring a more experiential approach.

Nevertheless, as Kirsch's model heavily emphasises the role of expectancy in hypnosis, it may be beneficial for us to explore it further at this point.

Building upon the idea of the placebo effect, Kirsch provides significant evidence to demonstrate that much of the effect of

65 Yapko, *Trancework: An Introduction to the Practice of Clinical Hypnosis (5th ed.)*, p. 143.

hypnosis is due to positive expectations on the part of the client. He even goes so far as to describe hypnosis as 'non-deceptive placebo.' Isn't that a great phrase?

According to response-expectancy theory, 'when we expect a particular outcome we sometimes unwittingly behave so as to produce that outcome.' Kirsch proposes that subjects in a hypnotic situation generally have the belief (that is, the 'response expectancy') that they will follow the hypnotist's instructions and will likely carry out behaviours that could be experienced as automatic or involuntary. The result is that these subjects attribute hypnotic responses to external causes (in this case, the hypnotist) and experience them as involuntary.

Hypnotic responses, according to this model, are carried out in precisely the same way as voluntary responses. The only difference is in how the behaviours are experienced and interpreted.

(I would politely suggest reading that last sentence again... And then the whole paragraph.)

If we return to the idea of an arm levitation being used in hypnosis, either as a response routine, or hypnotic phenomena during a session, it is easy to see the type of experience that Kirsch is referring to. Yet, whether you agree with Kirsch's model or not, it is difficult to dismiss it completely. It seems beyond doubt that expectancy is a core component in the hypnotic experience.

Expect More

John Cleesattel has a model of hypnosis which is markedly different to Kirsch's. Nevertheless, expectancy plays a key part in his model too, as the following quote demonstrates:

> 'When we expect something to happen, when we anticipate an outcome, our Imagination automatically reacts to it and prepares us for the expected event... Our Imagination treats it as an impending reality, then starts adapting our body to

> cope with the reality of it, and then just waits for the start of the anticipated event.'

Cleesattel is making the significant point that not only does our imagination consider that something is about to happen, but it actually prepares for it. If this is the case, we can see why Kirsch would argue that expectancy may even cause someone to 'unwittingly' produce the very outcome they expect.

This may be why many hypnotists begin a session with 'easier' phenomena, before working their way up to something considered more difficult. The idea is that it is perhaps a simple task for a client to expect their eyes to close, as they feel more relaxed. Once this is achieved, it is easy for them to expect that their eyes will stay shut when you make that suggestion, and so on. For some people, this type of staggered approach is completely unnecessary. They are comfortable with the expectation that they will do whatever you tell them to do. However, for many people, it does appear to be helpful.

An extension of this, which is widely used, but not often admitted, is to start with naturally occurring phenomena. As we have discussed previously, some hypnotists start their sessions or routines with something like magnetic fingers. Yet, that phenomena has absolutely nothing to do with hypnosis, *unless you say it has*! It works on purely physiological grounds, which is what makes it perfect as an opening gambit. It requires no level of expectation from your client and will work unless there is intentional 'resistance' or a physical difficulty of some kind. Once the phenomenon has been achieved, your client will usually then have at least some expectancy that they will experience what you tell them they will next.

Similarly, if I ask you to sit in my comfortable chair and speak to you with a soft and soothing voice, asking you to "rest" your eyes on a fixed spot above your eye-line, when I make the suggestion that your eyes will get heavy, it is a simple thing for you to expect that to happen. That is a very good place to start building a 'compelling vision' of how things could be.

Starting with You

Finally, an important element in building client expectations is the expectation of the hypnotist themselves. When I am working with a client, I do so from the position that I am confident that what we do can benefit them.

That does not mean hypnotists should make false promises, or even guarantee outcomes that are by no means certain. Neither does it mean that we should never say to our clients, "I'm not sure... let's see." However, what it does mean is that through the P3 approach, I am conveying confidence that they have within them the resources to achieve their desired future and that hypnosis is a powerful way to discover those resources.

So, although I may not know for certain that a particular technique or idea is exactly what will achieve success for my client there and then, I express – through my words, body language and general demeanour – a high degree of expectation that this will be a powerful and positive experience for their good.

Imagine you were going for your first ever vaccination. If you asked the nurse if it would hurt, which response would have the more positive effect on you:

1. "Hardly at all. Trust me, I've done this 1000 times. You won't feel any more than the slightest scratch."

2. "It could do?"

All things being equal, not only would the expectation in the first statement increase your own expectation, it would most likely also result in a more comfortable and pain-free experience.

EXERCISE

Can the role of expectation in hypnosis be *over*-stated?

What ways to do you currently work to build expectation in your sessions?

What small changes could you make to potentially increase your client's expectations during hypnosis?

What more significant changes could you make?

How do you currently convey *your* expectations to your clients?

What changes could you make to potentially increase *your* expectations during a hypnosis session?

Insertive Eye-Contact

I introduced the idea of 'analogue marking' whilst discussing my preference for *embedded ideas*. As a reminder, this NLP term refers to using a verbal or non-verbal cue to mark out words in a sentence. When this is practised in the form of "embedded commands" it is often simply a case of changing your tone of voice or tempo as certain words are picked out.

Within the world of NLP, analogue marking has something of a magical reputation, as examples provided by trainers often make the technique appear irresistible and undetectable. Examples abound such as, "I saw a *scratch* on what I think was *your* car. Who *knows*?" This is supposed to lead someone to scratch their nose. Feel free to try it out.

The trouble with the philosophy of analogue marking and embedded commands is appreciating their nature. All the practitioner is doing is disguising a command that will apparently be picked-up by the so-called subconscious mind. Yet, we know that the subconscious does not respond to every suggestion that comes its way. It still requires a meaningful reason to act, even if we believe that it is less rational or critical than the conscious mind. So even if the example above manages to bypass the conscious mind, there is no reason that its reception by the subconscious mind means it will be responded to.

As we have already seen, personally, I find it more meaningful to think of embedded *ideas*, rather than embedded *commands*. So, I am less concerned with making one-off commands. However, if during a conversation, I can drop in various suggestions and ideas related to e.g. relaxation, I may do so and then wait and see if these are picked up on by the client.

My book on the *My Friend John* induction includes a transcript where specific words are emphasised. The emphasised words are italicised, to demonstrate that they were singled-out by a technique that Stephen Brooks refers to as "insertive eye-contact." This simply involves looking in a different eye (often the left eye) when you want to highlight certain words.

In that transcript, words like the following are selected:

- go into trance
- notice your breathing
- relax more
- effortlessly
- shoulders relax
- get comfortable
- breathing starts to change
- notice the spreading relaxation
- wonder what that means
- go inside
- take some time for yourself

As you practice with this, you might find that you like to keep highlighting the 'trance' words through your tone of voice or tempo, just to reinforce what the client is experiencing.

I recommend insertive eye-contact as a technique to practice and get familiar with. At first, it will most likely feel extremely unnatural and you may fear that you are being blatantly obvious. However, I have found this to be amongst the most effective means of analogue-marking, as many people naturally look from one eye to the other during a conversation, so there's no reason that this one would be any different.

EXERCISE

Practice using insertive eye-contact during a normal conversation. Start by high-lighting related (though non-hypnotic) themes and ideas, e.g. food, during an otherwise wide-ranging conversation.

It helps if you are not always looking in the other eye at the same time (e.g. at the end of a sentence).

Ask your practice-partner afterwards if they noticed anything unusual about the conversation.

You get top marks if they say they are suddenly hungry!

Continue to practice the technique every opportunity you get, until it becomes second nature.

Utilisation

Utilisation

Utilisation is one of the fundamental principles of Ericksonian hypnosis. In fact, Erickson considered it to be one of his two original contributions to the field of psychotherapy, encouraging therapists to radically accept and use whatever the client may bring, however difficult or troublesome it may seem at first glance.[66]

It is no surprise then that Stephen Gilligan writes:

> 'Appreciating and utilizing the "realities" of the client [is] the basis for all hypnotic and therapeutic developments.'[67]

There is really no limit to how this can be applied. If your client comes in angry, use that anger. If they are tired, utilise their tiredness. If they complain of a neck-ache part way through your session, use that neck-ache to your (and their) advantage.

My clinic is based within a Complementary Health Centre and it is not unusual to hear a telephone ringing from another office, or even to hear a door opening in the distance. When this happens, I often employ these potential distractions in making statements like:

> And you may find that as your mind opens to new possibilities, you can allow the door to gently close on that past. The past is called 'passed' for good reason. And once

66 The other contribution was Confusion, which I will make an argument *against* in the next book in this series.

67 Gilligan, Stephen, *Therapeutic Trances: The Cooperation Principle in Ericksonian Hypnotherapy*, p. 98.

> we learn a lesson, we don't need to keep going back...

Or:

> And part of you may continue to be aware of sounds around you, in the back of your mind, reminding you what a natural every day experience this is...

A simple way to explain utilisation, is just to say, use whatever your client gives you. After all, why go through the trouble of forcing your ideas and experiences into someone else's mind, when you can simply use the ones that are already there?

When they give you a verbal response, feed it back to them. This may function as an 'embedded command,' but it is more than that. It is also a reassurance and an encouragement. Importantly, it functions as an acceptance of your client's experience. Thus, it assists rapport-building and reinforces the level of connection that you have with your client.

Additionally, when you receive a non-verbal response – the minimal cues spoken of previously – you can utilise this also. Again, this reassures the client that something is happening, but has the added effect of inviting them to go 'inside' to investigate.

If your client shuffles in their seat, or seems to struggle to go into hypnosis, or there is a loud clock in the background, or there is a thunderous storm outside: use it all to your and your client's advantage.

It is actually difficult to teach this principle adequately in a book. That may be because the notion of utilisation is both incredibly simple and extremely complex. This may be unhelpful, but this is literally about using *everything* that is offered to you. In one sense, we are allowing our client's to co-create the hypnotic journey they are having, by including their experience in the here and now, not merely relying upon a pre-written script.

Your client's experience is precisely that – so why not honour that and utilise it for their benefit?

If they shuffle in their seat, talk about moving around to get more comfortable. Then you can move on to using words like freedom, shifting, making changes and so on.

If they are physically strong, mention how a hard exterior can serve us well, whilst also allowing for a gentler inner way of being.

If they might hear the clock-ticking in the background, mention how time passes differently depending on how we are experiencing life.

If I can hear road-works and labourers in the distance, this might encourage me to speak of how my client's mind is working to find the perfect solution for them at this very moment.

There is nothing more important that I have to teach my students, or clients, than being fully aware of the experience they are going through and utilising that to their good.

The most effective therapeutic hypnotists are always observing and utilising. With practice, this will simply become a part of how you interact with people. And in time, this may even become as aspect of the kind of person you are becoming.

EXERCISE

Has the importance of utilisation been over-stated in this chapter?

Is it something you actively think about, or more of a 'subconscious' response?

Can you think of specific examples of how you can employ utilisation in your sessions, that you do not currently do?

Is utilisation something that we should make explicit to our clients, or more of a subtle unspoken tool?

Pattern–interrupts

Pattern Interrupts

We have already seen that inductions such as the Bandler Handshake fall under the category of so-called "pattern interrupts." To repeat myself, that description is based on the idea that there are specific patterns of behaviour that our minds run outside of our conscious awareness as programs or strategies.

If you interrupt one of these patterns, for example a handshake, with unexpected stimuli then your partner in the pattern may become temporarily confused. They then have to briefly pause to consider which course to take. Think of it in this way: you explain the rules of a game to someone and then you begin to play the game. Five minutes in, you – as the more knowledgeable player – do something that appears to break the rules. For a split-second, your partner will look to you for an explanation.

I am not talking about those times when they say, "Hey, you can't do that!" I am referring to the split-second before they even consciously object. For a brief moment, you have paused their understanding of how things operate and they will be searching around for an explanation, or new direction.

We could describe this brief moment as expectant waiting. If you can justify why you played an apparently illegal or innovative move, you may just be able to carry on with the game smoothly and without objection. They are looking to you for an explanation, even if they are not aware of it.

However, if you take too long, they will come to their own conclusion, evaluate the previously offered rules and conclude that you are cheating.

Obviously, all of this happens in the blink of an eye and eventually the "conscious mind" takes control again. However, for a split second, you have an opening, an opportunity to hi-jack the confusion and provide the direction for which they are subconsciously looking.

Simply put, for a brief second, they are looking at you and saying, "Hey, what gives?!" before that thought even consciously enters their mind.

This concept of pattern-interrupts is even more useful than it may seem.

Re-direction, Not Obstruction

In 1980, Donald Saposnek wrote an article entitled, *Aikido: A Model for Brief Strategic Therapy*. He was building on the work of Watzlawick, who had noted some similarities between Judo and Brief Strategic Therapy. Saposnek suggests that Aikido may be a more accurate model with which to make comparisons. As a practitioner of both Aikido and Brief Therapy, I am inclined to agree. Aikido is a predominantly non-attacking Japanese martial art, based on the principles of harmony and the peaceful resolution of conflict. Similar to Judo (with which it shares a common root), a practitioner of aikido relies upon their attacker's energy to perform their defence. However, Saposnek notes that whilst Judo might be described by the adage, "Push when pulled, pull when pushed," aikido is more properly expressed as "Turn when pushed, and enter when pulled." The movement is a circular one, as the aikidoist blends with his partner's energy.

In fact, watching an experienced aikidoist at work, echoes the title of Terry Dobson's book on the subject: *It's a Lot Like Dancing*. The blending of forces makes it almost impossible at times to see who is leading and who is following. The aikidoist does not confront or clash with their challenger. Instead, they accept and join the flow of their attacker's energy. In this way, the attacker has little opportunity for resistance, as nothing is offered to resist.

Once the aikidoist has blended with their partner's energy, they follow the movement to its natural end. Only at that point, do they extend the end point of the manoeuvre slightly further than it would naturally reach, causing their partner to be easily redirected. As someone who has studied aikido for a number of years, I can vouch that it is not an uncommon experience to step forward to attack your partner, only seconds later to find yourself on the floor, perhaps in an arm-lock, thinking, "How on earth did I get here?!"

Some of the parallels between aikido and hypnosis or therapy will no doubt be obvious. However, I am particularly interested in offering it as an example for performing pattern interrupts. If our partner experiences them as too direct, like a clash of different intentions, then we will most likely face objections. Yet, if we can blend with our partner's energy (that is, the momentum behind the beginning of their pattern), we can more successfully redirect it, creating a whole new movement.

Pattern-Interrupts Beyond the Induction

A simple example of pattern interrupts in a therapeutic setting could involve your very demeanour. If people are expecting you to be overly serious, yet you project a sense of light-heartedness, it can create all sorts of confusion. You might invite someone to sit in a chair, yet as their knees are bending, you could then say, "Oh, not that one. That's for when you go into hypnosis in a bit." Then invite them to sit in an alternate chair and say something like, "Let's decide how we are going to work together first." Obviously, you have given a suggestion that they will go into hypnosis later. Yet, also, by interrupting them mid-bend, you created a moment of anticipation whereby you can indirectly suggest how well the first part of your session might go.

One way that I like to interrupt patterns is by playing Devil's advocate. I always do this with a twinkle in my eye and most of the time, I forewarn people beforehand.

We have already encountered the smoker who objected when I used her word, "silly" to describe her smoking habit. She had fully accepted my prior warning about being 'rude or idiotic,' yet it was not long before she was objecting strongly to my behaviour. Thankfully, the strength of her objection simply made the pattern-interrupt all the more effective.

In fact, there were a number of pattern interrupts taking place for this woman, from me changing my style completely, interrupting her expectations, to literally interrupting her as she spoke. Working in this way can be somewhat like splashing a cup of cold water in someone's face if they are being hysterical. It creates a sudden shift in their awareness.

Pattern interrupts can help free people from Pavlovian responses. Yet, a pattern-interrupt is not always just stopping the behaviour. It can be seen as redirecting it, like aikido. In fact, when approached in this way it can face zero opposition, as your partner to some degree will still feel as if they are working on auto-pilot. It's just that you've reprogrammed that auto pilot!

If it is felt helpful, all patterns can be finished as they usually would be. So, you might do a handshake induction with someone, interrupting the handshake at the appropriate point. You then do your therapy or phenomena in the middle. And you can finish by completing the handshake. Interestingly, this can have the effect of eliciting automatic amnesia for what happens right at the deepest centre of the experience.

We can have already seen this principle at work when we looked at Nested Loops above.

Temporal Presupposition

At best, temporal presuppositions are an example of pacing and leading. They are used to talk to your client as if the past or future were somehow different to the here and now.

The following terms might be involved in the use temporal presupposition:

> Before, During, After, Since, While, As, Yet, Now, Again, When, Sooner or Later, Once again, Already, Once, As soon as...

When I am working with clients, I might use a phrase, such as, "That old smoking habit..."

Alternatively:

> "When you've blushed in the past..." becomes, "When you used to blush, " or even, "Back when you were a blusher."

To make this clearer, and to demonstrate how I might progress with presuppositions during a session, I might say something like:

> "Your spider phobia... your fear of spiders... that fear... that old fear..."

You will have noticed that I started with their "presenting problem/description." They spoke in terms of identity, as clients are prone to do, and permanence. Typically, they do not describe a temporary current issue, e.g. "I'm currently not keen on spiders." Instead, they describe themselves as someone who suffers from a specific phobia.

I then demote this phobia to a simple fear. Next, I refer to 'that fear,' dissociating from it and effectively normalising it. Only after using such statements and having done some therapy, I may *then* say, "that old fear..."

In reality, temporal presupposition assumes your client's time-based actions:

> You don't need to X before/until you Y.

Or:

> When you notice how good your nails look, you'll (i.e. you will then) remember the strongest motivation that made you stop biting them.

However, I should make it clear that temporal presupposition is not the same thing as temporal *presumption.*

Therefore, when I first started working with a client, who would get anxious during Zoom calls, I did not begin our sessions with, "When you used to get anxious," or, "that old anxiety." That would be disastrous for rapport, presumptuous and possibly cause my client to think I was not listening to – or fully appreciating – their situation.

Yet, after we had worked on the issue for a while, I would say something like, "that old thing that used to bother you," or, "the way you used to respond..."

Fractionation

By this point in the book, we have already encountered the idea and practice of fractionation a number of times. We have employed it as a tool for both induction and deepening.

As we have stated, fractionation was a principle discovered by Bernheim, later refined and developed by Elman. Both men believed that when you take a person 'in' and 'out' of Hypnosis, they tend to go more deeply into trance each time they return.

Richard Nongard offers, as an everyday example of fractionation, those times when your alarm clock goes off and you hit the snooze button. Do that just two or three times and when you eventually get up you are likely to be more tired than when the alarm initially went off. Can you imagine how deeply you would sleep if someone crept-in and turned the alarm off after you'd hit snooze for the third time?

Fractionation functions as another example of utilisation. Even if Bernheim's insight is not literally correct, it often feels like a more intense experience to the client when they re-enter hypnosis, so why not pace-and-lead this by suggesting they will go deeper?

At times, fractionation also makes use of what Stephen Brooks refers to as "frustrating the trance," or simply delayed gratification. The client is either just about to enter into hypnosis, or is presently enjoying it, when you pull them out of it. This means that when they next sense the opportunity to go back 'in,' they do so quickly, eagerly and usually to a greater depth.

Fractionation is a useful principle for the hypnotist, making our task easier and often adding a sense of ease and flow for the client.

EXERCISE

I have referred to the phenomenon of fractionation a number of times throughout this book.

Then I moved on to another topic… returned to the subject of fractionation… and the cycle continues.

What possible reason could there be to drip-feed this topic in such a way?

Is fractionation really as significant as I have argued?

Can you think of as many covert ways to utilise fractionation, as overt? Can modalities and even sub-modalities be incorporated into fractionation?[68]

Test the effectiveness of stretching the technique in this way.

68 Each modality can have specific distinctions. I could describe something I *see* as being black and white or colour; or it could also be bright or dim. *Sounds* could be loud or soft. *Feelings* could vary, or have different temperatures. *Smells* might be pleasant or over-powering, strong or faint. *Taste* could be sweet or bitter, strong or mild. Within NLP, these distinctions are called submodalities and are believed to define the qualities of our internal representations.

Revivification

To revivify means to restore to life, revive or reanimate. We have seen it a number of times already in this book, most explicitly with the Leisure Induction.

In a hypnotic context, revivification is more than simply recalling something, though that is often how it begins. Although we may start by, for example, simply asking someone about their favourite leisure activity, in reality we are getting them to recall a previous experience of trance, *in order to go on to relive it.*

Part of the reason that we feed back what the client is saying during e.g. the Leisure induction, is to situate them in their retelling of their experience. After all, we do not want them to simply say, "I like to play Golf." Instead, what we want for them is to undergo the experience of playing golf *in the here and now* (i.e. begin to re-live the trance they experience whilst playing golf). The responses they provide, following an internal search to answer our questions, flesh out the details and make their recollection more real.

Additionally, the feeding back of those answers also acts as something of an embedded command, as if you were saying, "...and do that now" to each answer that is given.

> Client: "And I feel my mind slowing down, as my body relaxes."
>
> Hypnotist: "Your your mind slowing down..."

Each question that is asked invites your client to relive some small part of the answer. For example, if I were to ask you, "what did it feel like when you were scared watching that movie?" you would have to feel at least *some* of that fear again to be able to answer the question with any degree of accuracy.

This is an essential element in hypnotic revivification. In order to properly recall a previous experience of trance (or relaxation, or confidence, or unwinding, or fear, or any state), the client has to begin to relive certain aspects of it. The more they are encouraged to do this - via different senses and in different modalities - the more likelihood there is that you will have a hypnotic revivification.

A very simple way to use revivification to your advantage is to start by asking about any previous experiences with hypnosis. This carries the wonderfully subtle presumption that they are about to enter into hypnosis again. Yet, it also implies the kind of things that the client should look out for (and thus expect), as well as the aspects of experience that they should prepare for as the conversation progresses.

This is, in essence, one more example of utilisation, taking your clients experience with trance (or something like it) and employing it to assist you in leading them into hypnosis.

However, revivification takes place outside of the induction as well. You might reference how your client first learned to walk – with the therapeutic implication that we have to be willing to fall down and get back up again if we want to make progress – and then move on to other early lessons.

Soon, you will be describing (and implicitly inviting them to recall) them learning something for the first time in class. Handled skilfully, this can be a natural way to lead someone into a state of receptivity, curiosity or readiness to learn something new.

Anchoring

Conditioned Connections

The simplest way to think of Anchoring may be to view it as the process of conditioning connections between a stimulus and a desired response. This can happen unintentionally or intentionally (naturally or artificially), so it might be helpful to give an example of each.

Natural Anchoring

I visited Kolkata, India in 1992. It was a life-changing experience; eight weeks of bombardment on my senses and emotions. As a red-head, I spent every day caked in sunscreen, desperately darting for the cover of shade whenever I could find it!

Later that year, I visited my home-town on the South Coast of England and was surprised to be greeted by an unexpected day of Sunshine. Fortunately, my hosts had plenty of sunscreen and as I began to apply it, a remarkable thing happened. Instantly, I was transported back to the busy, noisy chaotic streets of that city I had grown to love. Please don't underestimate the reality of this experience. I am not saying that the smell of sunscreen merely reminded me of India. It was far more than that.

I could smell the food stalls I used to walk past on the way to catch the Bus to Mother Theresa's *Prem Dan.* I could hear children laughing and the mercilessly incessant beeping of taxi horns. I had an emotional response of longing and yet contentment, like the yearning for a long-lost love that you were happy to let go. I had a memory, so clear that it bordered on visual hallucination, of the streets we used to walk down to get to the bustling marketplace.

All of this seemed to be experienced instantly and actually took me by surprise. In fact, it was a while before I actually realised the link between the smell of the Sunscreen and the revivification of eight weeks in that wonderful land of contradiction.

It seems that my time in India was such an emotionally and sensually powerfully one that it created a connection between the unique smell of sunscreen and all that I had experienced there. That connection, I was to learn, had been 'anchored' in my mind.

However, anchors can also be artificially created.

Artificial Anchoring

A common example used by some hypnotists is that of having someone squeeze their hand into a fist whilst they are in a happy or resourceful state. If this is done at the right time, when the 'state' is at or approaching its height of intensity, it is a relatively straightforward thing to anchor the state to the squeezing of the hand. Later, this anchor can be triggered by squeezing the fist, causing the client to re-experience the previously anchored state.

The Steps to Good Anchoring

During my time in India, I was not aware that I was creating an association between the smell of sunscreen and the memory of my time there. Yet, it just so happens that the sense of smell is the one most closely connected to memory. That, plus the intensity of everything I experienced - tastes, sights, sounds, heat, emotion - meant that I went through eight weeks of connecting the two.

Now, when anchoring in the context of hypnosis we do not typically have eight weeks. At times, we might not even have eight minutes. Yet, even with such limitations, it is possible to condition a connection so powerful that it releases a flood of positive emotions and well-being.

In fact, the process of anchoring a state is remarkably simple when you know how. Take a look at what are often taught as the keys to good anchoring and see how closely they match my 'accidental anchoring' in India:

1) Intensity

The intensity of the experience affects how easily, quickly and strongly you can anchor the connection. Think of how a phobic response can be learned (or, anchored) after just one emotionally intense experience. Conversely, if an experience is less intense, it can take longer – or more repetitions – to create a strong association.

2) Timing

There are debates as to the most effective time to anchor an association. Many NLP trainers and practitioners will say that it is important to do so at the peak of the experience. However, I am with Robert Dilts in suggesting that the most effective time to anchor is just before the peak is reached.

As the intensity of the experience lessens, so does the association. If you can maintain this intensity for a longer period of time it is more likely the anchor will be established.

3) Uniqueness

Anchoring is most effective when it involves an anchor that is uniquely associated to the experience. This saves confusion or watering-down the connection. As I suggested above, I also prefer to find a trigger that is particularly appropriate to the desired response, e.g. making a diver's "OK" sign with my finger and thumb if I am anchoring a state of confidence, a clenched fist for strength and so on.

4) Repetition

The more you repeat the process of anchoring a response to a stimuli, the more likely you are to be successful. Additionally, it naturally follows that the anchor needs to be something that can be replicated at a later time. So, don't anchor sitting in the chair in your treatment room with a state of focus, if you want your client to be able to replicate that out in the real world.

Break State

After you have established an anchor, it is good practice to 'break state' before continuing. This is simply a temporary distraction or separation to move your client out of the state you have just anchored. The reasoning is that unless you break state between establishing an anchor and testing it, you will have no real way of knowing if it has actually worked. You would effectively have them test the anchor to revisit a state that they have not yet fully left.

To break state, you can simply ask an irrelevant question, make an illogical statement, or have them carry out an action such as jumping up and down, shaking their body or getting up to get a glass of water.

We say far more about anchoring and even breaking state in our book on the PHRIT induction, *Revisiting Hypnosis.* Talking of which, as you have already encountered PHRIT, you may not be surprised to learn that you have already discovered a useful and complete tool for anchoring.[69]

How to Use PHRIT for Anchoring

As you will recall, PHRIT involves taking a client through a 4-stage process: Active >> Permissive >> Passive (Observer) >>

69 In fact, I often refer to PHRIT as 'Rapid State Training' nowadays, precisely because it functions as far more than an induction or re-induction tool.

Automatic.

Here is a transcript of a time the PHRIT process was used to help a client anchor in a feeling of being "Unstoppable."

> So, we've got those 3 memories that give you that "UNSTOPPABLE" feeling you are after: i) winning the Netball award, ii) your daughter's speech, iii) painting the back room... And you've managed to recreate those feelings... fairly easily... as we've talked about them here right now.
>
> Next, I would like you to imagine that when you slowly squeeze your first, in a moment, you are drawing-in that "UNSTOPPABLE" feeling from each experience, one after the other, like they're being stacked on top of each other. And as you clench your fist tight you are locking-in that feeling from all 3 experiences. Then, as you release your fist, you are releasing that feeling up your arm and out to fill your body.
>
> [Stage 1: They recreate the experience.]
>
> Go ahead now and clench your fist slowly and recall and recreate those feelings... That's it.
>
> [Client clenches fist]
>
> And when that UNSTOPPABLE feeling is at its peak, when you've locked it in, you can release your fist and send that feeling out to fill your body.
>
> [Client unclenches their fist, smiling as they do so]
>
> That's right... sending that feeling throughout your entire body.
>
> [Stage 2: They allow themselves to experience it.]

Now, this time, as you clench your fist, you can allow those feelings to return. All three experiences, rolled into one... UNSTOPPABLE feeling… just clench your fist and allow it to return.

[Client clenches fist, inhaling deeply]

That's it, locking it in.

And now, as you release your fist, let that feeling out, to flow through your whole body, filling you up with that UNSTOPPABLE feeling.

[Client unclenches their fist, smiling as they do so]

That's right…

[Stage 3: They notice what they experience.]

You're a natural at this.

So, this time, I am going to invite you to clench your fist and *notice* as those feelings return. All three experiences packed together into one super UNSTOPPABLE feeling.

Just go ahead and clench your fist, noticing as that feeling returns.

[Client clenches fist]

Yep, noticing as that feeling *really* returns now. Locking it in.

And now, you know what to do… simply unclench your fist and feel what it's like as that UNSTOPPABLE feeling *flows through you.*

[Stage 4: It happens automatically.]

We are going to do this once more. And this time, as you clench your fist, that super feeling – that UNSTOPPABLE feeling – will *automatically* return.

So, just clench your fist and that feeling will automatically return.

[Client clenches fist, inhaling deeply, then smiles]

Locking it in there... That's it... There it is.

Now, just release that fist and it will spread throughout your body.

[Client unclenches their fist, their smile widening as they do so]

Now you can go ahead and close your eyes... as that feeling fills you and envelopes you... you can learn to enjoy that now...

[Break State]

Okay, you can open your eyes... [Client opens their eyes] And tell me, how did you get here today? Did you walk? Drive? Bus?

– "Er, I drove."

Perfect. So, what you can do now is clench that fist and see what happens.

[Client clenches fist tightly, then laughs]

– "Oh, my god! Ha! That's... That's like, whoosh!"

EXERCISE

Why would you use PHRIT for anchoring, when it can be much simpler?

Anchor a state for yourself, using basic anchoring.

Next, anchor another state, using PHRIT.

Compare the difference.

Anchor a state for a practice partner, using basic anchoring.

Next, anchor another state for them, using PHRIT.

Ask them to compare the difference.

HYPNOTIC PHENOMENA

We will turn now to consider hypnotic phenomena. In what ways, if any, are they different to everyday 'normal' events?

Some practitioners strongly feel that hypnotic phenomena should be limited to the entertainment or impromptu scene.

As you will see, we take a fundamentally different perspective.

Therapeutic Phenomena

In therapeutic hypnosis, everything that we do is for the benefit of our clients. However, as we have stated earlier, this can include even relatively playful phenomena, such as sticking someone's hand to their leg, a table, or their drink. The point is that we do not do such things just because it is amusing, or because it makes us look good.

Ultimately, hypnotic phenomena is a vital element in altering our client's experience, both through promoting mental and emotional flexibility during hypnosis and in assisting them to make lasting positive changes in their lives.

Therapeutic Hypnosis is Phenomenal!

> 'Hypnosis is fundamentally an experiential method.' (Jeffrey K. Zeig)

An essential aspect of therapeutic hypnosis is the fact that it aims to assist clients to have a phenomenal experience. Phenomena is not an optional extra. In fact, it is key.

'Hypnotherapy' is not fundamentally psychotherapy.[70] Neither is it talk therapy. That may be the opposite of what some schools teach, but it might be the one essential element that differentiates my approach from some others.

This may sound like a strange assertion to be making. After all, even if phenomena is key, it is often through discussion or the use of

70 The second book in this series will discuss why we believe that the term 'hypnotherapy' can be misleading.

hypnotic language that such phenomena is achieved. Nevertheless, I firmly believe that it is not words that truly change clients in hypnosis. It is the experience(s) they have.

This is one of the reasons that I usually begin a session with response routines. I want the client to feel that something unusual is happening; that the normal boundaries of reality might not currently apply.

This is also why at least half of the inductions I have included incorporate hypnotic phenomena as a core component. In fact, handled skilfully, even something as 'normal' as a PMR can feel as if something extraordinary is happening. It is not uncommon for people to comment that they did not realise they could relax so quickly, never imagined they would ever lose that tension and so on. (In our experience, such comments are particularly likely with the Tension Observation variation.) I don't want my clients to be reflecting on it later and saying, "Well, he just kinda relaxed me a bit and then started talking..." Instead I aim for responses a bit more like:

> "It was actually really weird. I was sitting there and it was like he was pointing out all of the bits of tension in my body. And I was thinking, "Yeah, I know I'm tense. That's why I'm here!" And then they just... melted away. Completely. Like, instantly. And my whole body became this mass of relaxation. It was *so* weird!"

During hypnosis – and usually by the end of the induction – I hope to have clients who are wondering what else is possible in this new pliable version of reality they are inhabiting. Perhaps they were wrong in thinking they would never be happy again. Maybe they could find themselves flying without fear one day. Is it possible that they really could learn to live pain-free? Who knows?

Hypnotic Phenomena is Purposeful

I also use hypnotic phenomena after the induction. (In reality, there often is no 'after the induction' with my approach. However, you can think of this as that space often perceived to be the place where the real 'therapy' takes place.) Whenever or wherever hypnotic phenomena is elicited, it serves a number of functions, besides opening wide the door of possibilities.[71]

Firstly, it may serve a metaphorical role. If you have a client who speaks in terms of "constantly feeling down," an arm levitation gives them a physiological feeling of rising up, as well as providing you with an excuse to utilise language, metaphors and stories of elevation.

Of course, this is not to suggest that an arm levitation in and of itself will lift someone out of depression. Saying that, it is also not to suggest that it can not!

Similarly, I have had clients who periodically spoke of themselves as being "stuck" in their current undesirable situation. With some of them, I used the experience of their hand being stuck to their leg, or my desk. I should perhaps add that if they had only used that description, I might not have used such phenomena, as it may have come across as too predictable, tacky, or even somewhat mocking.

However, it is the experience of release, freedom and becoming "unstuck" that we are seeking (from the solution-focused approach we discussed with inductions). So, the phenomenon of a hand-stick is not the actual focus. Instead, it is the experience of un-sticking that we utilise.

We can see that this is more than simply a metaphorical role. The phenomena-as-metaphor can serve to unlock resources that the client did not know they had, as well as teach them lessons they may have missed. Perhaps they could never imagine feeling free. Yet, after they experience their hand being stuck (which softly questions their limited perception of what is possible), they then experience it breaking-free (which had momentarily seemed impossible). Now

71 We will say more about the *elicitation* of phenomena in a later chapter.

their experience is able to be utilised to talk more about becoming unstuck, or introducing further phenomena and trance-experiences based around the idea of freedom and breaking free.

The second role of hypnotic phenomena is of course clinical. After all, if a client has come to see you for pain management, it would be slightly poor practice not to allow them to experience analgesia or anaesthesia.

Some of the phenomena we will explore in this section include:

- Arm Levitation
- Anaesthesia
- Amnesia
- Hand stick
- Time–distortion
- Hallucination

There is a variety here (e.g. hand stick as well as anaesthesia), as we aim to demonstrate the different principles at work. So, some phenomena may seem more suited to metaphor, whereas others are more directly clinical. Before we turn to any specific phenomena, we will begin by looking at some wider perspectives that could be useful to consider.

EXERCISE

Do you agree with the statement that 'Phenomena is not an optional extra. In fact, it is key'?

Can hypnosis be helpful or successful without phenomena? If 'hypnotherapy' is not psychotherapy or talk therapy, what is it?

The Suggestion Pyramid

Pyramiding Suggestions

When it comes to suggestions for hypnotic phenomena, whether that is a hand stuck to a leg, or a needle inserted painlessly into an arm, a useful idea that some people subscribe to is the notion of the hypnotic ladder, or 'pyramiding suggestions.' The idea is that someone may easily experience something like magnetic hands, so you start there. When they have achieved that – which it is fairly difficult not to do – you then build on it by sticking their hands together. Once you have that, you could stick their hand to their head and so on. Or you might start with an unbendable arm and gradually build on up to analgesia in the arm and so on.

It is a simple idea and not without merit. In one sense, this is an example of experiential pacing and leading. You take what you and the client know they can experience and lead from there on to the next. At no point are you taking yourself too far out of your comfort zone, or pushing them beyond what they might perceive to be possible. As what they experience increases, the notion of what is or is not possible also grows. You then build up and up until you reach the point you are aiming for.

This is a useful concept, which is easily grasped. However, I prefer to take a slightly different approach.

Cascading Suggestions

Personally, I find it more beneficial to think of moving *down* the pyramid, not up. This is true not just in the case of phenomena, but with the hypnotic process itself.

Think of the first brick at the very top of the pyramid as your first suggestion. "You might want to just go ahead and close your eyes," for example. This suggestion is easily followed and that action in itself makes your client more likely to follow the next. As your suggestions increase – as you move 'deeper' down the pyramid – the number of bricks increases also. As I envisage the model, this refers to the number of potential suggestions – with an increasing number of connections and associations – that can be made.

It is not necessary to conclude from this idea that I am suggesting that a certain 'depth' of hypnosis needs to be reached before some phenomena can be achieved. Although that is a popular notion, research does not currently appear to support it. A good number of people seem able to achieve all manner of hypnotic phenomena – including anaesthesia or visual/auditory hallucinations – at any of the supposed 'levels' of hypnosis.[72]

However, what this model does demonstrate is that some clients may benefit by being eased into the experience. As they proceed, their belief in what is possible – and therefore the credibility they will perceive and engagement they demonstrate – increases. The number of suggestions that will be accepted (and by implication the variety of effects that will be achievable) increases as the process continues.

For some people, this might be experienced as moving from 'easier' to 'harder' phenomena, the deeper they go into their experience. However, in essence it is simply the fact that each suggestion that is accepted increases the likelihood of the next suggestion being taken on board. Viewed in this way, the whole

72 Cf. Wood & Barnier. 2008. Hypnosis Scales for the twenty-first century: what do we need and how should we use them? In: Nash & Barnier ed. *The Oxford Handbook of Hypnosis*. Oxford: OUP, pp. 3-15.

hypnotic process – from the induction onwards – is an opportunity to take someone on a journey where they experience a progressive flexibility in their perception of reality.

Natural Suggestions

One of the fundamental principles of hypnotic phenomena, at least from an Ericksonian perspective, is recognising that nothing happens within hypnosis that cannot take place outside of hypnosis. If that is true, then it would mean that all hypnotic phenomena can be discovered – to one degree or another – in everyday life.

Which of us has not had the experience of forgetting where we parked our car, or why we walked into a room? When I was in College, I was talking to a close friend that I had known for a number of years, yet I momentarily forget their name! This means that the human mind has the ability to forget something relatively easily. And that means, we can make use of that ability during hypnosis, eliciting the phenomena from the client's experiences.

Similarly, many of us have seen someone accidentally cut themselves, but apparently not feel the pain until they noticed they were bleeding. So, we would seem to possess the natural ability to ignore, block-out or otherwise not feel pain. This then becomes an ability we can utilise during hypnosis.

One thing that distinguishes hypnotic phenomena from such natural events – aside from the fact that they might be experienced as taking place in response to suggestion, rather than as an accidental occurrence – is the focus we place on them. We tend not to notice when these things take place naturally. Yet, in hypnosis, we dive into them, explore them and make good use of them.

EXERCISE

Is the notion of 'cascading suggestions' a useful one for you and your practice?

Does it not contradict what has previously been written about not needing deeper states to achieve more 'difficult' phenomena?

How does the idea of cascading suggestions fit with the theory that all hypnotic phenomena are naturally occurring events, simply elicited during hypnosis?

Chain of Command

In my book, *The Elman Induction*, I originally referred to this idea as 'Priority of Thought.' I was never completely satisfied with the label, so now refer to it as 'Chain of Command.'

Ironically, I hardly ever think of myself as giving *commands* to my clients. However, I think the newer description conveys the familiar idea of authority flowing from the top down. As we will see, the authority I speak of here is not from the hypnotist down to the client. It is from the first 'command' (i.e. suggestion) to those that follow.

This idea was initially explored as a way of explaining the process at work in the eye lock seen at the beginning of the Elman induction. Elman actually employs it in other places too, however it is most conspicuous at the beginning with the catalepsy of the eyelids.

I cannot speak for anyone else, but when I first learned of the Elman induction, this 'catalepsy of a small group of muscles' seemed too simple to be true. However, after years of using the induction – and then exploring the most effective way to teach it to others – I came to believe that it relies upon an idea that I would now call the Chain of Command.

In its most basic form, you invite your client to hold two opposing ideas, or carry out two opposing actions, at the same time. Then, you imply – or even state explicitly – that one of those ideas takes prominence.

A Basic Example

You can road-test this for yourself, right now! All you need to do is simply follow these basic instructions:

1) Place your hand on your thigh and DO NOT MOVE THAT HAND.
2) Now, whilst adhering to the first instruction, go ahead and try as hard as you can to lift your hand up.

If you followed the instructions correctly – and accepted the priority to be given to the first one – then you would have had the interesting experience of trying with all of your might to lift your hand off of your leg, but it just would not budge.

Easy, right?

This might be a good time to jump back to the Elman Induction seen in a previous section, look-it up online, or pick-up your copy of my book on the subject, which you obviously have, right?[73] It might now be clear that what we see at the early stage of the Elman Induction is a linguistic trick. If that trick is too obvious then it will not function to sufficiently bypass the critical faculty (considered an essential aspect of Elman's model of hypnosis). It will just seem as if the hypnotist is asking you to do something that he's just told you to ensure that you do not do. Yet, if you can frame it as a game, or as a consequence of e.g. relaxing well, then it provides you with an effective bypass of the critical faculty and a wedge into hypnosis.

Here is the technique used on a young girl, by a Dentist that Elman had trained. I have highlighted the basic two-stage Chain of Command that you have already experienced yourself:

> Dentist: "Jean, I guess you play a lot with your dolls when you're home. And you probably pretend a lot with them,

73 Or see https://howtodoinductions.com/inductions/elman

> isn't that right? Well, we have a little game of pretend too. And if you can learn to play this little game of pretend, nothing that happens in this dentist's office will bother or disturb you. You won't feel anything that we're doing if you learn to play this little game. Would you like to learn it?"
>
> Patient: "Yes."
>
> Dentist: "All right, open your eyes wide. I'm going to show you this little game. I'm going to pull your eyes shut with my forefinger and my thumb, like this. [Gently places thumb and finger on eyelids and draws them down.] **Now you pretend with your whole heart and soul that you can't open your eyes**. That's all you have to do. Just pretend that. Now, I will take me hand away [removes hand] and you pretend so hard that when you try to open your eyes they just won't work. **Now try to make them work *while you're pretending***. Try hard. They just won't work, see. Now just because you're pretending like that, anything we do in this office won't bother or disturb you at all. In your mind you can be home playing with your dolls and you won't feel anything I have to do."[74]

When that bypass of the critical faculty is effective enough then it may automatically lead to 'selective thinking.' Looking at the game played above, you will likely have noticed that the dentist piggy-backs another suggestion onto the previous successful ones. That is, he suggests that if the girl continues to follow the inherent priority of the first suggestion – pretend that you can't open your eyes – then, not only will she not be able to open them (which she experiences herself), but also 'anything we do in this office won't bother or disturb you at all… you won't feel anything I have to do.'

---

74 Elman, Dave, *Hypnotherapy*, pp.41-42. (Emphasis added.)

Accepting Alternate Realities

If describing Elman's technique as 'a linguistic trick' seems a little dismissive, we could say that it relies upon an alternate 'reality lens' or a shifting 'reality frame.'

However you describe it, it works in exactly the same way with adults – as you have already experienced for yourself – as it did with the young girl and the dentist. Sticking with Elman's use of the technique, essentially, the simple catalepsy of a group of small muscles – by virtue of the chain of command – is used to bypass their critical faculty. They now perceive that the process is working and that you are successfully engaging them to experience a shift in their reality. This prepares them to accept your further suggestions and gradually builds up to selective thinking, which for Elman was when hypnosis was reached.

(Of course, you can also see the idea of Cascading Suggestions at work here. In fact, is there really any substantial difference between this chapter and the previous one?)

You essentially ask someone to consider two different versions of reality at the same time:

- In one, you tell them that their hand CANNOT move.
- In another, you tell them that they can lift their hand off of their leg.

You then say, whilst giving priority to the first reality they should go ahead and test the latter (which is usually their normal expected reality).

They do so and see that reality is not as they had expected. Reality is changed (albeit, perhaps temporarily).

We can see how useful the chain of command concept is for establishing an altered experience of pliable reality (i.e. 'hypnosis'). It certainly works very well for eliciting the sort of phenomena that we might associate with Street Hypnosis, which often rely on binary tests, with a pass or fail element to them. Yet, is it sophisticated enough to work with things like pain control, or hallucinations?

I would suggest that it is and that this idea of shifting their lens or frame of reality is key.

So, we ask ourselves, what are the two opposing ideas – or versions of reality – involved here? And what is the chain of command? If someone is in pain, the two realities you will be working with are their natural ability to not notice pain and the fact that they are currently focused on their pain. We need to change which reality is prominent in that case.

Using pain as the example, the desired chain of command might look like this:

1. Elicit your innate ability to achieve pain control
2. (Whilst doing that) Try to feel pain

It really can be as simple as that. However, often we might dress it up a little. For example, you might hypnotise someone and lead them to their special place. And one of the rules that the two of you might establish for that location – their current experience of reality – is that they are completely relaxed, safe and filled with confidence. Then, whilst embracing the rules of that reality, they might be invited to try to experience their previous phobia, only to find that they cannot.

To present this in a less binary or oppositional manner, the chain of command can be seen as a progressive experience. In the chapters that follow, you might notice places where it takes this form:

1. Elicit naturalistic examples of phenomena
2. Experience them automatically in this context

I would invite you to look closely at the various phenomena discussed. Pay attention to the places where the client is invited to allow an alternate lens on reality to take precedence over their current experience. If my suspicion is correct, it may be that you find the chain of command principle at the heart of a number of them.

A less direct or "command-focused" way to describe all of this would be to say that we utilise phenomena to increase a client's range of possible responses. However, if I had written that, some readers might have skimmed over it and possibly dismissed it as too simplistic. Therefore, we now have the same idea expressed in a neat little 'technique,' that can be easily verified and shared with others.

Whichever version you use – oppositional, progressive, or simple recognition of possibilities – I trust you will enjoy experimenting with it and employing it for the benefit of your clients.

Catalepsy

When we consider the *Chain of Command* notion, it should be easy to think of a number of ways that catalepsy might be achieved.

After all, you could simply set it up as a direct challenge.

Or you could share a number of stories, metaphors or analogies where catalepsy plays a part – it's not difficult to think of natural every day examples – and then say something like:

> "And whilst learning everything you can from that, you might find it more and more difficult to bend your arm now... In fact, as you continue to think of that, the harder you try to bend it, the harder, more determined and more solid it becomes."

As with arm or hand levitation, the only difference between experiencing this as a simple response routine or an effect of hypnosis, is how automatic it feels. Sarbin spoke of hypnotic phenomena – and, in fact, hypnosis itself – as a case of "believed-in-imaginings."

When we experience something like catalepsy during a response routine, it simply feels like a response to what we have imagined. However, when it is experienced later during hypnosis, it feels like we have moved from *doings* to *happenings*. It just seems to happen – as a result of what the hypnotist says – and not something the client is doing themselves. That massively increases the odds of future engagement and success.

Arm Levitation

We have already seen how easy it can be to achieve arm levitation as a response routine.

The only real difference between its occurrence then and as a hypnotic phenomena is how it feels. This is often described as the difference between doings and happenings.

A hypnotic 'doing' feels like something I am doing, even if in response to the scenario the hypnotist is describing to me. I might feel like I am correctly engaging with what they say and – as a result – I am experiencing what they describe.

By contrast, a hypnotic happening is something that feels as if it merely happens to me, as if I have no active part in it. In effect, it feels more automatic.

One way to achieve this phenomenon directly would be by explicit use of the *Chain of Command* idea. However, this can either be overt, or covert. The latter is likely to feel more like an automatic happening.

There are all sorts of natural examples of phenomena. Someone at school throws a tennis-ball towards your head and *without thinking* you raise a hand and catch it. You feel an itch on your head and even though you are not aware of choosing to do it, your hand lifts up to scratch it.

You might then say something as simple as, "And whilst you think about what those experiences feel like, you can begin to notice your hand rising up, of its own accord."

Anaesthesia

> [I would hope it goes without saying, but if you are working with someone in pain, it is advisable for them to have seen a doctor first and – depending on where in the world you practice – to have received a release to work with you.]

Many parents will be familiar with the occurrence of natural everyday anaesthesia and analgesia.[75] In fact, it is something I would predict we have all experienced, it is simply more noticeable to parents.

Personally, I can recall numerous occasions when one of my children were playing in the garden, or running round the park and they may have tripped and fallen, or caught their leg on a protruding branch or stray thorn. Yet, frequently, they would jump-up and carry on playing as if nothing had happened. Until…

Maybe a few minutes later, perhaps even some time later in the day, my child would look down and see some blood, or an unexpected bruise. Then, almost instantly, it was as if their body was filled with pain and they cried out in apparent agony.

There are a number of ways to make sense of this phenomenon, particularly from the child's perspective. They may have been so thoroughly engaged in what they were doing that they genuinely did not register any pain until they saw the blood or bruising.

They may have briefly noted a *slight* discomfort, but again have

75 Analgesia is localised pain relief, whereas anaesthesia is a complete loss of physical pain or sensation through the whole body. For sake of space, we will use the more general term *anaesthesia* to refer to both in this chapter.

been busy enjoying themselves, so they did not fully realise the extent of the pain until they had cause to focus on it.

Alternatively, they may have felt the pain, but been aware that their friends were watching them, or they were an integral part of the game taking place. Therefore, in order to save face, or keep the fun going for their friends, they pretended they could not feel the pain until it felt more 'acceptable' to do so.

Finally – and related to the last explanation – it is possible that the pain genuinely did not seem too bad when it was first experienced. However, when the child realised there was an opportunity for some attention or sympathy, along with undeniable visible proof of the pain, that may have provided motivation to either imagine the pain, or focus on it so well that they could access it for the first time. Some more uncharitable descriptions of this explanation might describe it as 'faking it.' A fairer description might be playing a role, perhaps reminding us of actors who get so caught-up in their role that they actually do experience the very things they are only 'pretending' to go through.

The reality is, we could not say with any real certainty which explanation makes sense of the experience of my children and many like them. After all, it may well be that different explanations apply to different people on different occasions. The thing that is of particular interest to me is that each of the ideas discussed above are also provided as descriptions of hypnotic anaesthesia, by both researchers and their subjects (along with participants in Stage Hypnosis shows and therapeutic clients).

Eliciting Anaesthesia

This rather long explanation has been a means of making a point we have covered multiple times already. Hypnotic phenomena is not a case of installing previously unknown abilities. It is instead simply the elicitation of natural human capabilities.

So, the experience that we might call 'hypnotic anaesthesia,' may better be demystified and understood as nothing more than not noticing unwanted pain.[76] As well as the possible explanations we provided for natural childhood anaesthesia (including absorption in a pleasant experience, focusing on something more important than the pain, or peer-pressure (and other sociological reasons)), there are a host of other natural means of ignoring pain, whether we intend to or not:

Temperature – I can recall playing in the snow as a child. It was such a good experience that we didn't want it to stop, even after we have begun to lose feeling in our hands and feet!

Distraction – Similar, to the absorption spoken of above, merely focusing on something else can have a surprising effect on our ability to ignore pain.

Boredom – I had a client who was experiencing painful cramps in his leg, every single night. He told me that he managed to feel less of the pain – which would often last well into the next day – when he simply got bored and "thoroughly fed-up" with it.

(To briefly move aside from an experiential description, did you know that many tattoo artists now recommend that new clients, who tend to be the most nervous, are now often encouraged to *not* use pain-numbing creams? The reasoning is that if you use the cream, it will eventually wear off and you will be left with an experience of pain that your body has not prepared for. However, if you go with the pain, you will find that body eventually begins to release dopamine as a natural pain-relief, usually within twenty minutes.)

Relocation – An old friend of mind discovered, purely by accident, that if they felt pain in one part of their body, it would help to focus on another part of their body and imagine the pain there. (As this was now purely imagined pain, it was then easier to dial-it-down.) I know

76 As you will be familiar with by now, I am primarily interested in experiential descriptions of my clients' experiences. So, I am more likely to speak of being absorbed in a pleasant experience than 'dissociating' from an unpleasant one.

other people who incorporate this technique, without really thinking about it. If they stump their toe, they might dig their nails into their thigh. If they bang their knee, they might bite their tongue or hit their other leg.

Focus – This has come up in a number of the other methods, but it should not surprise us how useful it can be. The very phenomenon we are seeking to elicit is ignorance of pain. It therefore makes sense to place less focus on it.

A previous client of mine had tremendous tooth-pain, had taken all of the medication they could, but would still have to wait a number of hours until they would be able to see a dentist. I asked them where the pain was and asked them to describe it to me. They said, "excruciating."

I asked them to "really notice it" so they could "really describe it." They said it was "throbbing." I asked if it felt like it was moving and they said, "A bit. It's staying in one place, but it's like it's pulsating too." I thanked them and asked if there was anything else about it, like a particular colour, weight, or anything else that came to mind. They said it felt red, solid and heavy.

I then asked them what parts of their mouth did *not* feel like that; they pointed to the back of their teeth on the other side. I asked what they felt there and they said, "nothing." I smiled and said, "Come on, I now know you can do better than that. What does that 'nothing' feel like? Give me a real description of what 'nothing' feels like." They paused for a long time before saying, "It's still. Quiet. Soft and almost cosy."

I asked them where else they could feel that still, quiet, soft and almost cosy nothingness. They mentioned a few other places and I asked them how it felt when they focused on the nothingness. They said, "It's good. A relief. It's almost like it's spreading."

Various Pain Control Methods

Before I describe a popular and effective means of utilising the ideas above, I will share some brief pain control methods that you are welcome to explore further as you desire.

Dial-it-Down

I have already alluded to this when I spoke of relocating the pain from one part of the body to another. Regardless of the element of relocation (which we will return to again in a moment), if your client is able to feel their pain in a very specific part of their body, this method is more likely to prove effective.

Invite your client to focus on that pain and then to become aware of a control panel in the control room of their mind. (I have not yet had a client reject, or fail to understand, this metaphor.) I then say to them:

> "Now, I'm going to ask you to do something a bit strange, but it is just for a second or so. Okay?"
>
> [Client nods]
>
> "I would like you to see that control panel in your mind and tell me what number your pain is at. Like, 10 is the worst that any pain could ever possibly be and zero is non-existent."
>
> – I think, about a 7.
>
> "Okay, so, just for a second I want you to turn that up to a 7.5, even an 8, if you can."
>
> – Okay. I think that's about an 8?
>
> "That's brilliant. So, now just bring it back down to a 7."

– Okay.

"Easy, right?"

– [Laughs] Yeah.

"So, now bring it down to a 6, maybe even a 5, or a 4.5... And tell me where you are when you get there."

– That's about a 5.

"Do you want to keep it at this 5, or go back to the old 7?"

– Oh, I'll stick with the 5, I think! [Laughs]

"Well, you go ahead and lock that in place then. I don't know how you do that in your control room, but just lock it in there..."[77]

Pain to Hand

A variation of the relocation method is one that I believe I first heard described by Jonathan Chase. In my experience, this works particularly well for headaches that have a throbbing sensation, or e.g. the beginning of a migraine.

The method involves having the client imagine the throbbing or pulsating pain right at the front of their forehead. They are then instructed to place a hand horizontally across their forehead and to focus on the feeling of contact between their forehead and their hand.

When your client is able to feel as if their hand and their forehead and one object, they are invited to begin feeling the pulsating in their hand, each time it pulsates in their forehead. Once that is achieved, it

77 You may have noticed that both the Control Panel and the previous example of focus limit the number of times they reference 'pain.' Some hypnotists can seem almost superstitious about using the word 'pain,' fearing that it will remind the clients of what they are hoping to avoid. Nevertheless, as a matter of practice, I do prefer to move on a gradient where I speak less of pain and more of comfort.

is an easy enough step for most clients to shift the pulsating completely from their head to their hand. (However, I would not word it as such, as it may sound too obvious. I would simply say, "Now, you can go ahead and feel that pulsating *completely* in your hand." It's not necessary to say it is no longer in your head.)

Next I would invite my client to bring their hand away from their head, making it into a fist, the pulsating going with it. They can then a) crumble it up and let the discomfort sprinkle like dust from their hand, b) release it out into the air to go off and find somewhere else to be at peace, c) put it into a box and send that box out of the room they were in, so it is out of sight and "out of mind," d) dial it down, e) fold it up – or any other creative disposal you can think of.

Fold it up

This method is a similar to the above. You begin by asking your client to 'locate' their pain. When someone is overly focused on their pain, this is often the last thing they do. Instead, the may feel an overwhelming presence of pain throughout their body. However, if they are able to, it helps to hone-in on the pain, even if this is only an imaginary location (e.g. imagine it in one part of your body).

As your client may be used to trying to avoid the pain, they may require some encouragement to access their pain, to really pay it some attention. I may then ask them to symbolise how big the pain is, along with its colour, weight, solidity, translucence and so on.

Once the client has effectively symbolised their pain in this way, we have something objective we can work with. The client can then be invited to fold "it" in half. I then ask them to notice the effect it has as they fold it in half again, and again and then once again.

You may then want to invite them to take it out of their body to fold it in half again, notice the difference, then fold it again. You can then proceed as you would have with the *Pain to Hand* method above.

Glove Anaesthesia

The previous brief methods are offered as examples of the various ways we can utilise the natural human ability to ignore pain. The following method is a more well-known technique that further demonstrates some of the principles at work.

If I am using this method, I will almost always start with a phenomenal rapid induction that leaves one of the client's hands elevated, or at least distinguished from the other hand in some way. So, the rehearsal induction, modified wicks, or the auto wrist-lift are common choices. Alternatively, if I had more time, I might use the Elman induction, or add-on the Super Suggestion.

> I wonder if you'd be happy for me to take your hand by the wrist, like so… this hand that almost seems to have a mind of its own. And I'm curious whether you have already begun to notice how that hand is feeling slightly different to the other hand there?
>
> And I'm sure you can feel that gentle amount of pressure, barely noticeable, but you can feel it, right? Perhaps imagining or already experiencing the blood flow to that hand slowing down… maybe aware that your hand can begin to feel numb. That's right. You can feel and focus on that, maybe wondering what it means.
>
> [Hypnotist begins to stroke the back of the client's hand, having previously obtained permission to do so, of course!]
>
> As I stroke the back of that hand here, you might feel a tingling sensation, perhaps the numbness spreading… maybe already spreading into your fingertips, perhaps beginning to continue spreading… like pins and needles. And you can keep feeling those sensations… spreading… noticing them… until that entire hand is becoming more and more numb.

[Hypnotist stops stroking the back of the client's hand, having done so 3 or 4 times.]

You can go ahead and keep feeling those spreading sensations until there is no more feeling in that hand.

I remember as a child, playing in the snow... Can you remember that? Or perhaps you can imagine your hand in a bucket of ice, becoming completely numb now... all on its own... I remember playing in that snow for so long, it was as if my hand *was* a block of ice... but I didn't even notice. I wasn't aware of what was happening, as all sensation left my hand, just as your hand becomes more and more cold now, more and more numb.

[The Hypnotist may notice changes in the colour or temperature of their client's hand. If you are working with a client who has never felt snow, you might ask if they've ever received medical anaesthesia and use that example instead. Alternatively, you can speak of someone's hand become comfortably warm, so warm that it is relaxed and goes to sleep. This then allows you to refer to the common experience of e.g. lying on an arm and finding that it goes numb as a result.]

What is really interesting here is that as I release your wrist, that hand will continue growing more and more numb and your hand will begin to feel completely anaesthetised.

[Therapist releases the wrist, which remains cataleptic.]

That's right...

Now, notice what happens when I pinch the back of your hand here... doesn't bother you in the slightest... the feeling's all gone.

And now that whole entire numb hand can become like a glove, an anaesthetised glove.

> [Hypnotist strokes the back of the hand again, and the fingers, as if placing a glove on the client's hand.]
>
> And any part of your body that you stroke 3 or 4 times with that anaesthetised glove will immediately become numb.
>
> Just go ahead and experience this for yourself, by stroking your right hand, just as I stroked your left... And notice that numbness spreading... due to that anaesthetic glove and your powerful creative mind...

It is not necessary to have the client touch the part of the body that they want to anaesthetise. You might instead simply allow them to have the feeling spread through their body until it reaches the desired point.

This is not a technique that I use all that often, however it is useful for demonstrating a number of points, not least of which is the idea that hypnotic analgesia is not a goal only ever reached by the most powerful and experienced hypnotists amongst us. It is a natural human ability. Additionally, this transcript highlights a number of metaphors and everyday occurrences that you can utilise.

Finally, if you are dealing with chronic pain, it is useful to have a means of identifying if the pain is serving any particular purpose, or if the client will miss it when it is gone. This could involve ideo-motor signals, parts work or simply inviting the client to consider their situation whilst in trance.

Amnesia

Hypnotic amnesia sounds far more complex and impressive than the actual experience we are talking about: forgetting something, or choosing not to recall it (during, or as a result of hypnosis). After all, we all forget things all of the time. None of us are immune to it.

Ever walked into a room and forgotten what you were doing in there? Or watched a film with an actor you knew very well, but you just could not place their name? Maybe you momentarily forgot where you parked your car? You might not be able to recall the name of a teacher from school, or perhaps you forget *once again* to carry out the task you specifically went into town to perform.

The only difference between these everyday experiences and hypnotic amnesia is that the latter is explicitly labelled 'hypnotic.' Of course, hypnotic amnesia may *seem* to be different because it is often sought intentionally, whereas everyday amnesia appears accidental and unpredictable.

Yet, in effect, we are talking about the exact same experience: an inability (or unwillingness) to remember something. In fact, we can narrow it down even further. Amnesia, in essence, is nothing more than the natural human ability to forget things.

Eliciting Natural Amnesia

One way to begin utilising this natural human ability within hypnosis us by employing metaphors and experiential examples of forgetting something.

I often use the example of seeing someone – perhaps an actor in a movie – and their name is "on the tip of your tongue," (note that I've changed the focus from my experience to theirs) but you just can't get it. In fact, I'm sure you've had this, somehow the harder you try to recall their name, the more and more it slips out of your reach. I am yet to meet someone who cannot relate to this example, along with the added experience of it being even harder to recall something, the more you try. (I may also reference a fading dream, that we can remember snippets of when we first awaken, but the harder we try to recall specific details, the more the dream evaporates.)

To apply this in a rather basic – and temporary way – I may then say to a client:

> "You can experience this right now. You know the numbers 1-10. You know that you know them well. Now, I would like you to imagine the number between 3 and 5 just fading away. We'll get it back later, but for now, it's like that item of clothing that falls down the back of the radiator. And you just can't quite get it. Like that name? The harder you try – you can feel it on the tip of your tongue – the further it slips away. That number is just beyond your reach, on the tip of your tongue, but you just can't get it. And the harder you try, the further it slips and fades away. Now, when you can feel it beyond your reach, when you know that you just can't get it, go ahead and count your fingers for me."

As well as employing the familiar Elmanian 'Chain of Command' [e.g. 'when (and whilst) you know you can't do this, go ahead and try to do it…'], this simple example uses a familiar example of amnesia to allow a client to achieve so-called hypnotic amnesia.

Alternatively, if you desire to be less direct, it is possible to make mention of various ways we can experience forgetting something, at different points during a session, seeding the idea that your client has the ability to do this. In my own clinical practice, if I aim to utilise amnesia for therapeutic purposes, I generally offer it as a choice, as something the client *can* do, if they would find it useful or desirable.

A line you will frequently hear me use in my clinic is, "And you can feel free to forget anything you would like to forget, or perhaps even remember those parts that you feel it would be useful for you to remember."

Wording things in this way, in this order, emphasises that the amnesia is a natural and expected occurrence, whereas remembering is the secondary optional outcome. Or, you may choose to opt for the more natural sounding, "And you can remember to forget anything that is not needed, or forget to remember everything that your conscious mind is happy to let go of now."

Experiences That Encourage Amnesia

There are some experiences which often seem to elicit amnesia, even when it is not explicitly sought. A common example would be boredom. Can you remember (temporarily, of course!), ever hearing someone talk about an event that you had absolutely no interest in? It is highly likely that if you were later asked to recall the finest details of the event that you would miss large segments of it.

As well as boredom, overload is a common experience that seems to naturally produce amnesia. If someone is concentrating on too many things at once, it is not rare for them to lose track of some of the details, as they seek to discern which information to prioritise.

Dreams and daydreams are a common example of amnesia. Discussing an event, as if it were a dream, it a useful way to invite clients to forget it as non-essential information.

Similarly, distraction, or changing contexts – often dramatically – is a useful way to encourage amnesia with our clients. I might use a metaphor of amnesia, talk about something my client wants to forget, use another metaphor and then swiftly change contexts to talk about something else altogether. In effect, you are reminding your client of their ability to forget things, along with providing them an example of something they could forget there and then, if they so choose.

Finally, and not unrelated to the previous point, nested loops – as we have previously discussed – often naturally result in amnesia for the details in the middle of the story.

Additional Amnesia Techniques

The following techniques may potentially appear rather gimmicky. However, I assure you that they are not limited to a Street Hypnosis or performance scenario. Instead, take these brief notes as inspirations and conversation-starters for you to consider amnesia from a number of different angles.

The Blank Card

A routine I used to use with people some time ago was to show them a playing card from a normal deck and to then turn the card face-down. I then had them blank the card in their mind. I would encourage this via a number of modalities – for example, *see* the card going blank, imagine the ink dripping off of the card, *hearing* the letters be scratched-off like chalk on a black board, and so on. I asked them to let me know when they knew that the other side of the card was blank.

Most people would, eventually, agree that the card was blank. I might then state that we have waxed (or e.g. laminated) the card and could not put fresh ink on it if we wanted to. I would then ask, "So, that card is blank? You know that it is blank?" And they would say, "Yes."

I might then say – and I would have seeded some everyday experiences of amnesia throughout – "So, seeing that blank card, knowing that it is blank, focusing on that, tell me what the card you saw was..."

And, if the client had engaged well, they would be unable to recall the card. Of course, in many ways this is another example of the Chain of Command – 'When you can't recall it, try to recall it...' – however, it also simply teaches a client that they can just as easily focus on the forgetting of something, as on its recall.

Screw-up the Paper

Similar to the above, I might ask a client to write a word down on a piece of paper. I would fold the paper up and ask them where the word was. They would of course point to the paper.

I would then invite them to focus all of their "cognitive attention" (without defining what that actually means) on the word on that piece of paper. And I might repeat that the word is on that paper and (add the implication that) that is how they know what the word is.

At times, I would play with this and say something like, "So, if this piece of paper just vanished now, evaporated in front of us, the word would go with it, yeah?" And they would agree.

Once I had that agreement, I would point at the folded-up piece of paper and say, "Focus on this word, here, for now. That's where the word is. Right?" Again, they would agree.

Then, I would screw the piece of paper up and – without moving my hand very far – I would throw the paper out of sight. I would then ask, "What is left here?" And they would say, "Nothing?"

I would ask, "So, that word is gone?" And they would say, "Yes." If I then asked, "And whilst focusing on this empty hand here, can you tell me what the word is?" the answer would frequently be, "No."

In effect, we are training clients that if they look or focus somewhere, then they can remember something easily. If we can convince them that that is because the memory resides in that place, we then invite them to not-recall it if they look elsewhere, or if the object of their focus is removed.

An explicit example may demonstrate what is happening here. If I asked you to recall an old friend's name, I might ask you *where* you recalled that. You might say it was at the front of your head, or the back, or in your chest. Then I could ask you to think of a child from school that you can remember very little about. I might ask where that non-memory resides and you might suggest it is somewhere else, for example the back of your head, or your belly. Then, I could say something like:

> "What I would like you to do is focus on that area of non-memory, where you cannot access those earlier memories. And whilst you focus there – *don't move from there* – try and recall the old friend's name."

Effectively, I am inviting my client to access the experience of not-remembering something and then *whilst staying in that experience*, trying to remember something. We could again see this as an example of Chain of Command, though there may be more at work.

This may demonstrate that all hypnotic amnesia is, in reality, nothing more than an unwillingness to recall, or express the recall, of a memory. Yet, if my clients describe it as amnesia, or being unable to remember something, I am more than happy to accept that label.

Why Use Amnesia?

Some therapists like to use amnesia to deter clients from overly analysing what has come up in a session. Whether or not this is required is a debate for another time.

Or you might choose to utilise temporary amnesia, to allow you and your client to explore a particular point, without getting too focused on an issue they are ruminating over.

As I have already alluded to, I prefer to give my clients the choice as to whether or not they remember or forget specific details of a session.

Hand Stick

The "hand stick" – which has become a common staple of Street Hypnosis – is really nothing more than an *unwillingness* to lift the hand, experienced as an *inability* to do so.

If you wish to appear sophisticated in your achievement of a hand-stick, you might employ metaphors and experiential examples. Perhaps talking about how if we are watching a film, we can be holding the remote control in a certain position for hours, without even being aware of it. Or, although it is a completely different phenomenon, I might talk about waking-up in the night and calling-out, but no words come forth.

I give a number of examples where our bodies just do not respond in the usual way, almost as if they are paralysed, or (and this is a useful phrase) as if they have a mind of their own.

Then, I simply proceed with the *Chain of Command* notion we have previously seen. However, it is possible to be less overt now. I might say something like:

> 1) For example, as you place that hand on your thigh that you know will not move – it's already made up its mind about that – when that unmovable hand is on your thigh...
>
> 2) Go ahead and try as hard as you can to lift up that hand that won't move.

I once co-lead a weekend training on the *Therapeutic Inductions* approach. I should add that during one of the demonstrations – on how to develop impromptu solution-focused inductions – the course participant who volunteered later announced that we had just saved her marriage. And yet, all everyone was talking about after the event was a quick hand-stick that I had performed during a Coffee break. Seeing someone's hand stuck to their leg in less then 30 seconds was mind-blowing to this select group of counsellors, new hypnotists and highly experienced hypnotherapists.

It turns out that discovering that we can change our experience of reality in a split-second is as paradigm-shifting for practitioners as it is for clients.

EXERCISE

What place do things like a hand stick have in therapeutic hypnosis?

Is there a risk that they come across as entertainment, self-aggrandising, or mere gimmicks?

Would it be possible to find a way to incorporate such routines more organically within a specifically therapeutic context?

Time Travel

This group of phenomena could quite easily have been placed at a number of sections in this book. We might have discussed it as a Skill, Language pattern, or hypnotic phenomena. We may have described it as 'time distortion,' 'future pacing,' 'pseudo-orientation in time,' or 'life-progression.'

In reality, there may be slight differences between each of these tools, but they are – at heart – very similar, if not the same thing incognito.[78] So, let's start with the most common, natural and often inconspicuous: Time Distortion.

Time Distortion

Time distortion – the experience of time moving more slowly or quickly that it actually is – is a common natural phenomenon. Ask any child who is engaging in an activity they love, compared to sitting in a lesson that bores them senseless. The experience perceived there is perfectly captured in the phrase, *time flies when you're having fun*.

However, it is also frequently experienced in hypnosis, whether it is intentionally pursued or not. If this is news to you, you might want to begin asking your clients after they come 'out' of hypnosis, "So, how long do you think you were in hypnosis for then?" You may be surprised to hear how many say, "Um, five to ten minutes," when it was closer to an hour, or vice-versa.

78 The one aspect of "time travel" we will not be discussing – for reasons made abundantly clear in the next book – is age-regression.

This can also be intentionally implied by the hypnotist. I often use the phrase, "Now, but not yet..." which begins creating a doubt in the client's mind that they have a full grasp on what is happening when. Or, I may suggest that they hear a clock ticking in time with their breathing, noticing as it slows down, as their breathing slows... "now entering that time-less space-less place of freedom."

Of course, the words are fairly meaningless, but you might be surprised by how often they match your client's experience. This can then be used therapeutically – along with other metaphors – to teach your client the skill of slowing time down, or even speeding it up.

I remember working with a teenage boy who loved to read. He would invariably be reading when his parents called him to say that dinner would be in 10 minutes. He said that it always felt like just a few seconds before they were calling him again to say that dinner was ready. This was a useful experience to utilise, because when he ever felt like he wanted time to go quickly, e.g. at the Dentist's office, he would simply imagine reading and time would zip past.

Pseudo-Orientation in Time

We have already seen some examples of *pseudo-orientation in time* in this book. Remember the *Perspective Induction*? That provided a perfect example, along with the same technique presented in a less obvious way.

Milton Erickson was well-known for using what was referred to as 'the Crystal ball technique.'[79] This involved having a client looking into an imagined crystal ball and seeing themselves in the future, when the problem was resolved. Erickson would then take this in a number of directions. He might ask the client to describe exactly what it was that he had done to help them resolve the issue. He then

79 In 1954, Erickson wrote a paper entitled, *Pseudo-Orientation in Time as a Hypnotic Procedure.* Some years later, Steve de Shazer would build heavily on Erickson's paper in writing, *Brief Hypnotherapy of Two Sexual Dysfunctions: The Crystal Ball Technique.*

gave them amnesia for that portion of the session, and simply did what they told him he would do.

Alternatively, he would have a client work 'backwards' from their resolved future, getting closer and closer to the present, noting each step that they took towards resolution. The clients literally wrote their own treatment plan.

This one technique eventually (and explicitly) became the basis for a whole approach to therapy – Solution-Focused Brief Therapy.[80] Over time, SFBT developed what the early practitioners referred to as "the miracle question." In the early days, it would take forms such as:

> "I have a rather strange question to ask you... Suppose tonight, while you slept, a miracle occurred. And the miracle was that the problem that brought you here today is resolved. But you're asleep, so you don't know that a miracle has happened. So, when you wake-up, what would you notice that would tell you a miracle has happened?"

To really equate this with pseudo-orientation in time, you might want to move the question – or following conversation – into the present-tense. Thankfully, there is a natural way to introduce the present tense as your post-question conversation continues. This relies on the use of feedback:

> Therapist: "Suppose a miracle happened whilst you were asleep tonight and the problem that brought you here was resolved. Yet, because you were asleep, you didn't know the miracle had occurred. When you wake up in the morning, what will be the first thing you will notice that will tell you things are now different?"
>
> Client: "I would wake up in a good mood and not have a headache immediately."

80 More on SFBT in the next book in this series.

> T: "So, you wake up in a good mood. You don't have a headache. What else?"
>
> C: "I'd smile at the children and give them a kiss, instead of grunting."
>
> T: "You smile at the children. Give them a kiss. What next?"

If you are trained in NLP, you might want to see this as related to embedded commands. However, we have said enough about that already.

Over here in the UK, we tend to ask a much more simplified version of the miracle question, that naturally connects it with the future-pacing we will turn to shortly. A British-trained SFB Therapist is more likely to ask something like:

> "If you woke up tomorrow and your hopes for coming here had been realised what's the first thing you might notice yourself doing?
>
> ...
>
> "And what's that like?"

There are numerous different ways to practice *pseudo-orientation in time*, not all of which are time-focused. We can talk about time-travel and portals and parallel universes and more. You could have your client imagine opening a family photo album in 40 years and describing all of the things they might find. You might speak of stepping into the TARDIS.

The only real limitations are your imagination – and your client's ability to engage with what you are saying.

Future Pacing

In one sense, future-pacing is what we have been doing all along. Effectively, it is simply inviting your client to imagine themselves in a future devoid of their problem. And we have already done that.

Yet, particularly within the world of NLP. The term and practice of 'future-pacing' has a rather specific meaning and usage. And it is a helpful one.

In this more narrow sense, future-pacing is what takes place after a therapist has taken a client through the required change-work. The intention is to then have the client imagine a future scenario – outside of any hypnotic or formal trance-work – and (without specific reference to the work you have been doing) consider how they would respond. They would do this from an associated position. That is, not merely watching themselves, but seeing through their own eyes, as if they have stepped into their future self. An obvious example would be removing someone's spider phobia and then having them imagine encountering a spider on their path to work. How do they feel? How do they respond? And so on?

One reason for such future-pacing is to ensure that all changes that have been established are *ecological.* This refers to checking that the desired changes fit comfortably within the client's everyday life and the numerous contexts they encounter. This is an effective way to test that the changes you have achieved are applicable to the client's day-to-day life and – more importantly – appropriate.

This also allows your client to rehearse and consider future road-blocks and the steps their new resourceful self takes to overcome them.

Additionally, this is an opportunity for you as a therapist to see if you missed anything. Your client might find that they're okay with spiders, as long as they're not moving. Or, they may discover that they are no longer scared of spiders, as long as they are not on their body and so on. This new information allows you to polish and complete your previous change-work, if that proves necessary.

Finally, future-pacing is a great way to increase expectation. Your client will leave your office *knowing* that the work has been effective, because they have just experienced it as such in the future.

EXERCISE

Consider the three Time-travel techniques discussed in this chapter.

Which do you already use? Are there any changes you would make to your current practice, based on the ideas presented here?

Are they any techniques that have been discussed in this chapter that you do not use at the moment?

In what other ways could *pseudo-orientation in time* be disguised as a non time-travel technique, other than by means of a portal? Are there any benefits to such duplicity?

Hallucination

As unlikely as it sounds, the truth is that we all hallucinate – visually and aurally – numerous times without any need for hypnosis. After all, there's a reason that the idea of someone hearing their name in the wind is a tired cliché.

Many people have experienced something like catching a glimpse of a ball of thread on their living-room floor and 'seeing' a spider crawling across the room.

A number of years ago, I briefly rented an apartment, only later to be informed that there had previously been an infestation of cockroaches. For the first few weeks, whenever the sunlight shifted and cast a new shadow in the room, I was convinced I was seeing a cockroach scuttling across the floor.

So, we can all hallucinate and, it turns out, do so quite easily. The issue with so-called hypnotic hallucination is the idea that it is difficult. After all, if I said to you, "Imagine there's a black dog over there," it might seem like an unreasonable and unrealistic request. Yet, when you realise that hallucination is not quite the impossible task it is presumed to be, it might already seem more achievable.

Another hindrance to phenomena like hallucination is clients overestimating what it is that others are experiencing. After all, it would be easy to imagine that, for example, a volunteer during a Stage Hypnosis show might seem as if they are literally seeing a solid and 100% real black poodle. Yet, in many cases, they are simply imagining well enough and engaging with their imagination to such a degree that they react to it as if it were real.

This observation provides us with a useful way to proceed:

Train someone to hallucinate

People can actually improve their ability at hypnotic hallucination. The first step in this is adjusting their expectations. So, when you react to the ball of thread on your floor, you do not actually clearly focus on the perfect representation or illusion of a spider. Instead, you see enough of something that provokes the 'that is a spider' reaction inside you.

Some people who are new to hypnosis or hallucination might be surprised to learn that those subjects on stage dancing with a broom that they believe to be George Clooney, are unlikely to be seeing a solid and irrefutable hologram of George Clooney in front of them. (After all, very few scream in terror at the unusual prospect of Mr. Clooney suddenly appearing before them, or faint like a star-studded fan.) In reality, they are most likely to be imagining George Clooney so well that they can emotionally engage as if it were really taking place.

What can we learn from this? Well, for starters, it tells us that the line between seeing something and *not* seeing it may not be as solid as it seems. Instead, we might think of hallucination as something we can improve on by degrees. Here as an exercise you might want to practise a number of times, to experience the possibility of increasing your ability to hallucinate.

1. Stare intently at the corner of your room. Take it all in.
2. Close your eyes, but keep the image of the corner of the room clearly in mind.
3. Now imagine a black Labrador sat, panting, in the corner. Take it all in.
4. Next, open your eyes and continue to 'see' the black dog.

This exercise can be repeated numerous times, in a number of ways, to work towards improving your – or your client's – ability to hallucinate.

When we consider that a hallucination can seem more or less real, it increases the number of ways that we can access and utilise the phenomenon. For example, if we use the sort of "chair therapy" often associated with Gestalt therapy, there is a world of difference between saying to someone:

"Imagine your mum sitting in the chair opposite you..."

And:

"See your mum over there... what's she wearing?"

The second question *assumes* that your client is going to hallucinate, without actually placing any pressure on them as to the quality or realism of that hallucination.

Alternatively, I might work with a client and gradually increase the level of realism, starting with simple imagination and building-up to a more full-blown hallucination. When working in this way, it can be helpful to seed the idea by discussing the natural everyday ways that we all hallucinate at different times.

"So, we can imagine your mum sat opposite you. And I'm not sure what sort of emotions that brings up for you… Perhaps she's wearing particular clothing that she was fond of, or an outfit that you always think of her in. Maybe she looks exactly the way you imagined she would.[81]

"I wonder how she smiles at you… What is that like? As you see her now, perhaps smiling back, you can be aware of the fullness of what you are feeling…"

81 This line can be quite useful, subtly drawing a distinction between what you imagined and what you are actually now seeing.

EXERCISE

What is your experience with natural (i.e. non-hypnotic) hallucination?

Does the description of Gestalt chair exercises seem like it belongs in a discussion on hallucination?

What do you think of the idea that hallucinations can vary in how 'real' they are?

Do you think that the Stage Hypnosis presentation of hallucinations contributes to the notion that all hypnotic hallucinations are 100% real, solid, etc.?

Experiment with the hallucination training exercise for yourself and evaluate the results.

Once you have done the above, find a practice partner to go through the exercise with.

Repeat the last two steps on separate occasions, noting your progress.

EXITING THE EXPERIENCE

So, we appear to have reached the end.

I will leave aside, for now, questions like, *Do we, in fact, ever really end hypnosis?*

Instead, the question I will be focusing on is:

Is there any way to bring a hypnotic experience to a close, in a such a way as to sustain the hypnotic element of the experience?

In other words, how do we bring Alice back from Wonderland, without leaving all of the wonder behind?

Post-Hypnotic Suggestions

If it is my intention to set-up a post-hypnotic suggestion (that is, a suggestion that will take effect after the session is over), I now almost always start-off by teaching my clients PHRIT as a re-induction.

Not only does this demonstrate to me that my client is responding well to my approach, it also gives them the confidence that they can do what is expected of them.

Post-hypnotic Suggestions (PHS) are simply suggestions which are given during hypnosis for an action or response to take place after the hypnotic experience. This could be a suggestion to trigger an anchor (e.g. "when you see the podium, you will re-experience that state of confidence"), or it may simply be a suggestion that a particular thing will happen at a particular time, or that from now on a particular action will or will not take place.

Let me try to explain my approach from the perspective of a client experiencing such procedures. I may give the suggestion that when someone emerges from hypnosis, they will no longer be able to remember the number between 3 and 5. I bring them up and ask them to count the fingers on my hands and they count to 11, because they jumped to the number 5 when they reached my 4th finger.

Similarly, I might suggest that someone laughs when they see a red Pen or feels calm curiosity when they see a Spider.

It may seem that when such actions are later carried out they happen automatically, completely outside of the agency of the client. Yet, there is a host of research to suggest precisely the opposite. It would seem that when someone, for example, misses out the number

4, there is invariably part of them that is intentionally restraining the information from being recalled. They may or may not be aware of it, but both anecdotal evidence and scientific research appear to demonstrate that the seemingly 'automatic' behaviour happens because the client intends to do it.[82]

I would actually argue that this is not simply the case with hypnotic phenomena, but is also true with something like a spider phobia. If that does not yet sound particularly plausible, just think of the old phobic response as an anchored behaviour which through hypnosis is replaced with a new and alternative outcome. The client may not feel like they are intentionally choosing the new behaviour, yet they are actively doing different things to that which they did when they 'did' their phobia. They are simply doing so outside of their conscious awareness or attention.

In all of these cases, the client has learned *how* to respond, regardless of how automatic it now feels. This is precisely why effective post-hypnotic suggestions are always couched in terms that the client can understand. They need to be able to do what they are asked to do and that requires them knowing what is expected of them.

Not only does the client learn how to respond, but through things like future pacing, they can learn *when* to respond. The only difference between these responses feeling hypnotic and them feeling intentional is whether or not the client is aware of deliberately intending to do them.

So there are actions we carry out without being consciously aware that we are the ones doing so (e.g. driving whilst experiencing the frequently mentioned 'highway hypnosis.') This may be for any number of reasons. It could be that such actions do not require conscious thought because they are perceived to be simple and make use of natural processes. It might be because trauma or overwhelming emotional reactions have taught us not to consciously dwell on them.

82 Cf. http://www.mheap.com/nature%20of%20hypnosis.html, as well as sources cited in the bibliography.

Or it may be that they have been learned to such a degree that they are second nature.

Post-hypnotic suggestions, I would argue, rely on this very phenomenon. Instead of giving instructions that are automatically carried out, we as hypnotists make suggestions that the client understands, agrees to accept and intends to carry out. They may just not be aware of that.

You can learn everything you need to know about my approach to PHS, by looking at the previous discussions of PHRIT, compounding suggestions and future-pacing earlier in this book. It is an incredibly versatile process.

EXERCISE

The preceding chapter has been intentionally vague about how the hypnotist might make post-hypnotic suggestions.

The intention behind this omission has been to be evocative and entice the reader into finding their own way to implement PHS based on the principles so far discussed in this book.

Does this approach seem helpful, or lacking?

Does PHRIT seem like a beneficial means of setting-up post-hypnotic suggestions?

Is there anything you would add to the PHRIT process to make it a more effective means of making PHS?

The So-Called Wake-up

When it comes to 'waking-up' our clients, it will be obvious by now that such language is not meant literally. You do not wake someone up at the end of a film (at least, not one with which they have been highly engaged). At the most, you might let them know that the film is over and it is time to leave the Cinema.

However, with therapeutic hypnosis, although we want our clients to return to 'normal life,' we do not necessarily want them to return to 'live as you knew it.' That could imply that all of the changes they have achieved are only reality within the clinic.

There are no hard and fast rules here, but I will share a few ways that I re-orient clients to life outside of hypnosis.

Count Them Out

If I have used any kind of count to lead a client 'into' hypnosis, whether that is a staircase or the Old Finger Lift, I will usually count them back up. More often then not, that involves terminology like the following (assuming I counted *down* from 10 to 1 initially):

1 – Preparing to return to life as you know it

2 – Bringing with you all of those changes you have made

3 – And employing all of the resources you have discovered

4 – Ready when we reach 10 to implement this into your life now

5 – Embracing all of the lessons you have learned

6 – Energy beginning to fill your body, as it has your mind

7 – Every muscle, fibre and inch of your body returning to normal

8 – A rush of energy filling you now, ready and raring to go

9 – As you prepare to open your eyes and live your new life on...

10 – And... open your eyes, there, you are, welcome back!

I usually say, "Welcome back" with the intonation of a question. It is as if I am implying, "How the hell was that?!"

The key with a count-up is to increase the level of energy with each additional step. So, number 1 may involve my usual relaxed 'hypnotic voice,' whereas number 10 will be quite up-beat and involve a fair amount of energy.

Gradual Integration

If I have not counted down, I would not tend to count back up again. Instead, I prefer to model an approach that I believe I first learned from Stephen Brooks. (That usually means that it originated with Milton Erickson!)

In this approach, I am likely to use fairly naturalistic terminology, such as:

> "And when your conscious and subconscious are ready to begin working together to start implementing some of the changes that we have already begun to see at work today, you can – in your own time – open your eyes..."

One thing to be aware of, if you adopt this approach, is that some clients will rush to come back to normality. This is sometimes due to a time-distortion, but often because they simply are not aware of how or when to open their eyes. One risk of returning too quickly under this method is that your client might rarely be left with a slight headache. This may particularly be the case if a fair amount of fractionation has been involved, or the client has otherwise gone quite 'deep.'

It is possible to retain some control over how quickly your client returns, depending on the words you use:

> "And in a moment, not now but in a moment, when your conscious and subconscious are ready to *begin* working together to start *gradually* implementing some of the changes that we have already *begun* to see at work today, you can – slowly and in your own time, when you are ready, there's no rush – eventually prepare to open your eyes... Take your tine... Enjoy that experience... There's no rush."

Staggered Return

When I have used an induction like Deeper Sleep, I might have the client return in the exact way they entered hypnosis.

> "And when you are ready, you can float effortlessly from deepest hypnosis to deeper hypnosis... That's it... Taking your time... Enjoying the journey back...
>
> And you might then naturally find yourself easily moving from deeper hypnosis back up to deep hypnosis... And notice how good that feels... knowing you have this skill within you... You had it all this time.
>
> Now may be the time to move from deep hypnosis up to hypnosis. That's it... a very natural state for you...
>
> And, now, whenever you are ready, you can, in your own time, in your own way, take your time... and open your eyes.

On Being Hypnotic

In my opinion, practitioners of therapeutic hypnosis would be well served to aim at progressing from *doing* hypnosis to *being* hypnotic. It would therefore be a fair question to ask why that has not been my focus.

I would argue that I have, in one sense, done precisely that. For example, one of the first principles I taught was P3. That is all about your presence and the atmosphere that you create with your clients. The fact it was taught as something of a technique does not mean it is a gimmick or something that we *do* to a client.

I have presented things as I have to hopefully take the reader on an experiential journey, in some ways comparable to the one your clients will go through. Rather than jumping in at the deep end, I have sought to provide the skills and tools to enable you to at least get your feet wet.

If I had focused solely and directly on the ideas and principles of being hypnotic, that would be akin to sitting in a classroom to learn a long list of the physical elements at work when someone is swimming. You might even learn about being a swimmer – not just going swimming – and discover some of the mindset and deeper aspects involved. Yet, would this effectively equip you to swim at all?

So, I have sought to teach a variety of principles and techniques in an accessible and evolving way. It might help to think of this book as an example of pacing and leading. I taught a technique, idea or skill that you would most likely have been able to put into practice there and then. Next, we took another step forward and so on. Step by step.

If this approach has worked, then the engaged reader will hopefully have reached this point in the book and found that, without even really thinking about it, they are swimming! That's a rather long-winded way to stretch a metaphor and say that I have been intentionally, if indirectly, teaching you to be hypnotic precisely by teaching you to skilfully do hypnosis.

There is one final stage in this educational tactic. This may seem like a strange suggestion, but I believe that it will be hugely rewarding. I would now invite you to read the book in reverse order. Read the last chapter and digest it. Then read the chapter before and so on, all the way back to Chapter 1.

By doing this, not only will you find some remaining pieces falling into place, but you will discover things you had learned without realising it, as well as reinforcing those lessons that you found most valuable.

In short, by practising this final step you will find yourself both swimming and being a swimmer. You will have learned how to do hypnosis hypnotically.

Where Next?

This book has predominantly focused on the approach, skills and general tools of the therapeutic hypnotist. You might think of this volume as focusing on creating and enhancing hypnotic experiences. This has very much been about laying the foundations for what is to come, which is a unique perspective on the utilisation of therapeutic hypnosis.

The next volume in this series will unpack some of the models, therapeutic schools and techniques that most effectively fit with the way hypnosis has been presented here, whereby the whole encounter is considered one of creating fresh possibilities, new experiences and alternate realities.

EXERCISE

Consider for a moment, the distinction between *doing* hypnosis and *being* hypnotic. Are these really two different things, or is it simply a matter of style and/or focus?

If you accept the distinction, what do you make of the assertion in this chapter that I have sought to show you how to *be hypnotic*, by first teaching you how to *do hypnosis*?

This book has primarily laid the foundations for what is to come. One aspect of those foundations has been the importance given to the notion of possibilities. I have also repeatedly alluded to the ideas of emotional agility and psychological flexibility. Keen readers will have noted that I even suggested that trance may be an example of the latter.

The next book in this series will introduce a host of therapeutic models and methods that take these ideas even further. I will also discuss Hypnotic and NLP techniques which utilise these ideas to good effect.

How do you feel now that you have read – and engaged with – an entire book that is an introduction for what is to come next? Prepared? Frustrated? Excited?

Bibliography

Allen, R., (2000). *Scripts and Strategies in Hypnotherapy: The Complete Works.* Carmarthen: Crown House Publishing.

Bandler, R. and Grinder, J., (1975). *Patterns of the Hypnotic Techniques of Milton H. Erickson, M.D, Vol. 1.* Cupertino, Calif: Meta Publications.

Bandler, R., Grinder, J. and DeLozier, J., (1977). *Patterns of the Hypnotic Techniques of Milton H. Erickson, M.D, Vol. 2.* Cupertino, Calif: Meta Publications.

Bandler, R. and Grinder, J., (1989). *The Structure of Magic, Vol. 1.* Palo Alto, CA: Science and Behavior Books.

Bandler, R. and Grinder, J., (1989). *The Structure of Magic, Vol. 2.* Palo Alto, CA: Science and Behavior Books.

Banyan, C. and Kein, G., (2001). *Hypnosis and Hypnotherapy: Basic to Advanced Techniques for the Professional.* St. Paul, Minn.: Abbot Pub. House.

Barrios, A. (2009). *Understanding Hypnosis: Theory, Scope and Potential.* New York: Nova Science Publishers, Inc.

Battino, R & South, T. (2005). *Ericksonian Approaches: A Comprehensive Manual.* Carmarthen: Crown House Publishing.

Benson, S. and Gafner, G. (2000). *Handbook of Hypnotic Inductions.* New York: Norton.

Bertolino, B. and O'Hanlon, S. eds., (1999). *Evolving Possibilities: Selected Papers of Bill O'Hanlon.* New York: Routledge.

Chase, J. (2005). *Deeper and Deeper.* Devon: Academy of Hypnotic Arts.

Edgette, J. and Edgette, J., (1995). *Handbook Of Hypnotic Phenomena In Psychotherapy.* New York: Routledge.

Brann, L., Owens, J. and Williamson, A., eds. (2015). *The Handbook of Contemporary Clinical Hypnosis: Theory and Practice.* West Sussex: Wiley-Blackwell.

Elman, D. (1964). *Hypnotherapy.* Glendale, CA: Westwood Publishing Co.

Elman, L. (2010). *Blueprint of the Dave Elman Induction.* Henderson, NC: Dave Elman Hypnosis Institute.

Erickson, M., Rossi, E. and Ryan, M. (1998). *Creative Choice in Hypnosis.* London: Free Association Books.

Erickson, M. H. (1976). *Hypnotic Realities: The Induction of Clinical Hypnosis and Forms of Indirect Suggestion.* New York: Irvington Publishers.

Erickson, M. and Rossi, E., 1975. Varieties of Double Bind. *American Journal of Clinical Hypnosis,* 17(3), pp.143-157.

Gibbons, D. & Woods K. (1917), *Virtual Reality Hypnosis: Adventures in the Multiverse.* Gibbons & Woods.

Gilligan, S., (2019). *Therapeutic Trances: The Co–*

Operation Principle In Ericksonian Hypnotherapy. Routledge Mental Health Classic Edition. New York: Routledge.

Haley, J. (1993). *Uncommon therapy: The Psychiatric Techniques of Milton H. Erickson, M.D.* New York: W.W. Norton & Company.

Havens, R., & Walters, C. (2015). *Hypnotherapy Scripts: A Neo-Ericksonian Approach to Persuasive Healing.* New York: Routledge.

Heller, S & Steele, T. (1987). *Monsters and Magical Sticks: Or, There's No Such Thing as Hypnosis.* Carmarthen, Wales: Crown House Publishing.

Hunter, R., (2010) *The Art of Hypnosis: Mastering Basic Techniques.* Carmarthen, Wales: Crown House Publishing.

Jacquin, Anthony (2004). *Reality is Plastic: The Art of Impromptu Hypnosis.* Derby: Anthony Jacquin.

Jacquin, Freddy (2018). *Hypnotherapy: Methods, Techniques & Philosophies.* England: Freddy Jacquin.

James, Tad. (1999). *Hypnosis: A Comprehensive Guide.* Carmarthen: Crown House Publishing.

Jensen, Mark. P. ed. (2017). *The Art and Practice of Hypnotic Induction: Favorite Methods of Master Clinicians (Voices of Experience Book 1).* Kirkland, WA: Denny Creek Press.

Korzybski, A. (1994). *Science and Sanity: An Introduction to Non-Aristotelian Systems and General Semantics.* New Jersey: Institute of General Semantics.

Kumar, V. K. ed., (2019). *Hypnotic Induction: Perspectives, Strategies and Concerns.* New York:

Routledge.

Nash, M. & Barnier, A., eds., (2008). *The Oxford Handbook of Hypnosis: Theory, Research, and Practice.* Oxford: OUP.

Nongard, R. (2007). *Inductions and Deepeners: Styles and Approaches for Effective Hypnosis.* Andover, KS: Peach Tree Professional Education.

Nongard, R. (2018). *Reframing Hypnotherapy.* Andover, KS: Peach Tree Professional Education.

Lynn, Steven J., and Irving Kirsch. (2006). *Essentials of Clinical Hypnosis: An Evidence–based Approach.* Washington, DC: American Psychological Association.

Lynn, S. & Rhue, J., eds. (1991) *Theories of Hypnosis: Current Models and Perspectives.* New York: Guilford Press.

O'Hanlon, B. (1999). *Invitation to Possibility Land.* New York: Routledge.

O'Hanlon, W.H. (1992). *Solution-Oriented Hypnosis.* New York: Norton.

O'Hanlon, W. H. (1987). *Taproots: Underlying Principles of Milton Erickson's Therapy and Hypnosis.* New York: Norton.

Old, G. (2017). *The Anxiety Guide: Self-help for the rest of us, Vol. 1.* Milton Keynes: Plastic Spoon.

Old, G. (2016). *The Elman Induction.* Milton Keynes: Plastic Spoon.

Old, G. (2018). *Hypnosis with the Hard to Hypnotise.* Milton Keynes: Plastic Spoon.

Old, G. (2018). *The Hypnotic Handshakes.* Milton Keynes: Plastic Spoon.

Old, G. (2014). *Mastering the Leisure Induction.* Milton Keynes: Plastic Spoon.

Old, G. (2018). *My Friend John.* Milton Keynes: Plastic Spoon.

Old, G. (2016). *Revisiting Hypnosis.* Milton Keynes: Plastic Spoon.

Old, G. (2018). *Therapeutic Inductions.* Milton Keynes: Plastic Spoon.

Overdurf, J & Silverthorn, J. (1995). *Training Trances.* Portland, OR: Metamorphouos.

Tiers, M. (2010). *Integrative Hypnosis.* USA: Melissa Tiers.

Van Boxtel, J. (2020). *Stephen Brooks and the Art of Compassionate Ericksonian Hypnotherapy: An Ericksonian Guide. Volume I: Phobias.* Utrecht: Mindspring Publishing.

Yager, E. (2008). *Foundations of Clinical Hypnosis: From Theory to Practice.* Carmarthen: Crown House Publishing.

Yapko, M. (2021). *Process-Oriented Hypnosis: Focusing on the Forest, Not the Trees.* New York: WW Norton & Co.

Yapko, M. (2019). *Trancework: An Introduction to the Practice of Clinical Hypnosis (5th ed.).* New York: Routledge.

Zeig, J., (2014). *The Induction of Hypnosis: An Ericksonian Elicitation Approach.* Phoenix, AZ: Milton H. Erickson Foundation Press.

Zeig (2017). *The Anatomy of Experiential Impact Through Ericksonian Psychotherapy: Seeing, Doing, Being*. Phoenix, AZ: Milton H. Erickson Foundation Press.

About the Author

Graham Old is a Solution–focused Hypnotist from the United Kingdom. A Graduate of the University of Wales, Graham is a former University Chaplain and Community Pastor. He has experience as a Father's Worker and Assistant Social Worker, as well as working in private clinical practice and running the most popular inductions site on the web.

Graham is a popular conference speaker, writer and trainer, with over two decades experience teaching meditation and self–hypnosis. He is an insightful presence in contemporary hypnosis and developer of the popular *Therapeutic Inductions* approach.

As an internationally recognised expert on *Brief Acceptance Therapies*, Graham is often consulted on the subject of mindfulness and acceptance-based therapies.

Made in United States
North Haven, CT
08 April 2023

35196714R00264